ALSO BY GEORGE F. KENNAN

American Diplomacy, 1900–1950

Realities of American Foreign Policy

Soviet-American Relations 1917–1920
Vol. I: Russia Leaves the War
Vol. II: The Decision to Intervene

Russia, the Atom, and the West

Soviet Foreign Policy, 1917–1941

Russia and the West Under Lenin and Stalin

On Dealing with the Communist World

Memoirs 1925–1950

From Prague After Munich: Diplomatic
Papers 1938–1940

Democracy and the Student Left

The Marquis de Custine and His "Russia in 1839"

Memoirs 1950–1963

The Cloud of Danger: Current Realities
of American Foreign Policy

Decline of Bismarck's European Order

The Nuclear Delusion: Soviet-American
Relations in the Atomic Age

The Fateful Alliance: France, Russia,
and the Coming of the First World War

SKETCHES
F·R·O·M A
L·I·F·E

SKETCHES
FROM A
L · I · F · E

George F. Kennan

PANTHEON BOOKS   NEW YORK

All rights reserved under International and Pan-American Copyright Conventions. Published in the United States by Pantheon Books, a division of Random House, Inc., New York, and simultaneously in Canada by Random House of Canada Limited, Toronto. Originally published in hardcover by Pantheon Books, a division of Random House, Inc., in 1989.

LIBRARY OF CONGRESS CATALOGING-IN-PUBLICATION DATA
Kennan, George Frost, 1904–
Sketches from a life.

Includes index.
1. Kennan, George Frost, 1904–   —Diaries.
2. Ambassadors—United States—Biography.   3. Historians
—United States—Biography.   4. Europe—Politics and
government—1918–1945.   5. Europe—Politics and
government—1945–   .   6. Europe—Social conditions—
20th century.   I. Title.
E748.K374A3   1989   327.2'092'4 [B]   88-43282
ISBN 0-679-72877-5

Portions of this work originally appeared in *The New Yorker*, May 29, 1974, issue.

Grateful acknowledgment is made to the following for permission to reprint previously published material:

Little, Brown and Company: Excerpts from *Memoirs, 1925–1950*, vol. 1, by George F. Kennan. Copyright © 1967 by George F. Kennan. Excerpts from *Memoirs, 1950–1963*, vol. 2, by George F. Kennan. Copyright © 1972 by George F. Kennan. Reprinted by permission of Little, Brown and Company.

Princeton University Press: Excerpts from *From Prague After Munich: Diplomatic Papers 1938–1940*, by George F. Kennan. Copyright © 1968 by Princeton University Press. Reprinted by permission of Princeton University Press.

BOOK DESIGN BY ANNE SCATTO

Manufactured in the United States of America

First Paperback Edition

PREFACE

As the stage for any and all adventures there suffices a single human heart.

—ALFONS PAQUET

This book might be described as a collection of diary excerpts, illustrating one person's reactions, over a long span of time, to a variety of scenes, places, and landscapes. When the suggestion for their publication came, as it did, from a good friend, I confessed myself unable to form any judgment as to what impression such papers might make upon a wider public or whether this would be useful enough to warrant their publication. For this they were too close to me—too close to a life advancing age had taught me to view with neither excessive pride nor excessive remorse. It was too late now for such exercises in introspection. I had done what I could. I was aware of my faults and mistakes. They could not now be corrected. And I knew the pitfalls of self-satisfaction. I tried, therefore, to avoid judgments on myself, my doings, my attempts to understand the life of my time. All that would have to be left, I thought, to a deity held—if only by faith—to be benevolent. The reader would have to arrive at his own conclusions as to whether the reactions to certain aspects of the external environment, as assembled in this volume, could help them to understand, as the younger man who wrote these pieces had tried to do, the pageant of his time. But it occurred to me that if there were then no claims, no promises, no apologies I could advance on behalf of the bits of prose assembled here, there were at least a few explanations I might offer as to how and why they came to be written and for what they were intended.

There have been three kinds of reactions that I, like so many other people, have from time to time felt the impulse to put to paper. There were the intimate ones; there were the intellectual ones; and there was a third category, for which I can now find no brief generic designation, but into which the offerings contained in this book may be considered as falling.

The intimate reactions were those that concerned the more intense aspects of involvement with the self or with others. These I have always found it difficult to commit to paper—at least for the eyes of others. Perhaps I was too much of a coward: too conscious of the fragility of the individual's innermost identity; too respectful of that identity's need for, and right to, privacy; too accustomed to view this as a privileged inner chamber, cluttered with fragile objects, into which the clumsy finger of the outsider could not be thrust without creating breakage and havoc. I preferred, I thought, to leave all this to the novelist or the poet, whose greater brutality, in the one case, and more natural use of the allusive rather than the explicit, in the other, permitted a bolder penetration into these dangerous premises.

The intellectual reactions (thought, history, social and political analysis, scholarship in general) have been the ones that strove hardest for depersonalization and sought the greatest possible distance from subjectivity (from which, of course, there is never, and should not be, any total emancipation). Of this sort of literature I have written a great deal; and this, in a number of incarnations: as a "reporting officer" in the

American foreign service, as an historian, as a commentator on international problems. This writing has of course constituted the backbone of my professional life; and I have had much satisfaction from it. I view it (when honestly pursued) as a respectable, useful, relatively innocent and inoffensive employment, capable (with some luck) of earning for its devotee a living, but with possibilities for usefulness to others as well in the measure of its honesty, seriousness, and persuasiveness.

The third category of writing, as mentioned above, operates in the no-man's-land between these two others, borrowing a bit from both, contributing a bit to both. As purposed in this book, it might be described as the effort to depict isolated bits of reality, casually observed, in a manner that, while as faithful as possible to the features of the scene observed, also reveals something of its inner meaning. Something of this sort is, of course, essentially what takes place in the more naturalistic of the visual arts, where, again, the object is not one of the artist's own creation but is rather an existing external reality, in the depiction and critical interpretation of which the artist expresses things he could never have expressed in direct assertion.

The inspiration for this kind of writing came from a book I happened to stumble upon at a time when I was quite young and living in Europe—in 1928, I think it was. It was a volume of travelogues from the pen of the talented itinerant correspondent of the *Frankfurter Zeitung* of that day, Alfons Paquet, a highly cultured European cosmopolitan of his time, half-French, half-German (as I seem to recall), and a fine writer.* I was much impressed with this book and took it, as young people often do in such circumstances, as a model for my own writing. What I thought I learned from it was that there was nothing wholly meaningless in life, and that in all

---

*Alfons Paquet, *Städte, Landschaften, und Ewige Bewegung* (Hamburg-Grossborstel, 1927). In English, *Cities, Landscapes, and Never-ending Motion.*

scenes observed in remote places, and hence with the freshness of first impression, there was normally and quite literally
"more than met the eye"—a deeper reality seldom visible on
the surface but there to be sensed, if not seen, with the requisite intuition and effort.

In Paquet's sketches the writer was not the center of attention. He was there, of course. How could he not be? He
supplied the eye, the heart, the perspective. His perceptions
were the prism through which all things were apprehended
and understood. Without him the image could not have existed. But that was all he was. The further details of his person
were irrelevant. The reader was not normally told who he
was or even what he was doing at the place in question. The
great clutter of trivial involvements and concerns that everyone accumulates around his person and drags with him
through the struggles of life was superfluous to this particular
type of literary effort. All that had no place in the picture and
no interest for the reader.

It was this literary genre that the writer of the pieces collected in this volume tried initially to imitate, while develop-
ing it gradually into something that was more his own.
Whatever the success of this effort, the model was a good one.
The careful reader will perceive its beneficent effects in the
comparison between the juvenile entries from Hamburg of
1927, full of romantic preoccupation with self, written before
Paquet's book was read, and the greater extroversion—the
greater turning of the gaze outward—in the pieces written
thereafter, in the Baltic countries and in Berlin.

The great majority of these pieces were not written with
any particular thought to publication. This assertion, of
course, does not deserve too sweeping an interpretation.
Every diarist has moments, I am sure, of a vague hope that
what he has just written, particularly if he himself is pleased
with it, will some day fall under at least a few eyes other than
his own. I cannot claim to have been totally immune to this
very human impulse. But my recollection is that most of the

pieces reproduced below were conceived at the time of writing in the mind of the man who wrote them primarily as reminders to himself of the particular experiences they described, lest he forget them, lest they cease to take their part in the richness of remembered experience and rot away, neglected and unused, in the attic of memory. But in some instances, too, these entries were conceived by him as benchmarks of intellectual and emotional growth by which he hoped to be able to measure in later years his progress, his false starts, his retrogressions.

The pieces were written, for the most part, only when traveling. For this there was good reason. At home, in the performance of daily professional and personal duties, there was normally no time for this sort of thing; beyond which, this sort of writing required, as mentioned above, the novelty and freshness of first impression. You would not write this way about things you saw or experienced every day. Familiarity deprived such scenes, as it did people, of their mystery and their magic.

So the sketches were, measured against the ordinary substance of life, a digression of sorts—a private luxury. And they were a digression not just from daily life in general but from other, and far more demanding, forms of writing. During the years from which these excerpts were drawn, their author produced some eighteen books, diplomatic reports and despatches in great number, as well as lectures, articles, and speeches running into the hundreds. Anton Chekhov, a doctor, said somewhere that medicine was his wife, literature his mistress. The situation of the writer of these pieces was analogous, except that the mistress was far less beautiful than Chekhov's and had to content herself with much smaller pickings. The pieces brought forward in this book constituted, in other words, only a fringe—a fringe reflecting impulses of another kind—on a far greater body of professional writing.

The reader will note that these efforts were widely and irregularly scattered over the decades they embrace. There were long lapses when next to nothing was produced. For this, too, there were reasons. One of those reasons, coming in at the outset of the 1930s, was marriage and parenthood. When impressions were shared, at the moment, with someone else, there was less incentive to commit them to paper. And travel with small children, instructive as it was in other ways, permitted only the most harried and distracted glances at the passing scene. More important still, large portions of the decades of the 1930s and 1940s were spent either in Stalin's purge-plagued, terrorized Moscow, or in Hitler's Berlin. In both places official service was strenuous, rigorous, and absorbing. Opportunities for travel were few. Urgent involvement with the problems of the day was the enemy of relaxed reflection. And in those politically hostile environments, security considerations created a disinclination to commit to paper anything more than was necessary.

The considerate reader will note, finally, that these sketches were spread out chronologically over a very long stretch of time. More than sixty years elapsed between the writing of the first of them and the last. During that period the environment to which they were addressed changed greatly—more, one would suppose, than life had ever changed in a similar span of time. When the first of them were written, Calvin Coolidge was president of the United States; the First World War was still of recent memory; Lindbergh was electrifying humanity by flying the ocean; Fitzgerald, Hemingway, and Thomas Mann were the writers of the day. The world with which the last of the sketches dealt was separated from that earlier one by a whole series of momentous and in part mind-shattering events: the Depression of the 1930s; the two great tyrannies of Stalin and Hitler; the Second World War; the gathering of the shadows of nuclear apocalypse and environmental disaster. The world of 1988 was not, in short, the same world as that of 1927. Even the sounds, as the reader may note, were not the same at the outset of this sixty-one-year period as they were at the beginning of it. And the change had not come all at once but had been spread, through these and other upheavals, over all of the intervening years.

But if, then, the external scene was a different one in 1988 from that to which the observations of 1927 were addressed, so were the eyes with which it was observed. The twenty-three-year-old vice-consul of 1927, full of uncertainty about himself and wonderment about everything else, was not the same man as the retired professor of 1988, aware that his own contribution to the life around him had been, for better or for worse, substantially completed, but still profoundly concerned for the imminent fate of his own country and of the European civilization of which he had always considered himself a part. Here, too, the change had not been abrupt. It had been in process over the entire span of intervening time. The glimpses of external reality presented in this book must therefore be seen as the interaction between two moving objects: the scene observed and the pair of eyes that observed it.

It will not be easy for the reader to bear that in mind. On the other hand, to do so may give to these glimpses the greater part of whatever value they may have for those who read them. For one of the keys to the understanding of the human predicament is the recognition that there is, for the human individual, no reality—no comprehensible and useful reality, at any rate—other than that of an object *as perceived* by the human eye and the human mind—no abstract reality, in other words, detached from the eye of the beholder. All that we see around us may be considered to some extent as a part of ourselves, the reflection of our own astigmatisms, our own individual perspectives, and—sometimes—our intuitions. Unless it is taken that way, we cannot recognize its reality, or even know it to be real.

The documents produced in this volume must, I fear, be seen in this dynamic perspective—as a progression in the development of both the viewed and the viewer—if they are to have any significant meaning. But it is the hope of the man who now looks back on them (rather than that of the man who wrote them) that they will, if viewed in this way, add their bit to the understanding of this troubled century, and help others to find their bearing at the pass to which the events of these sixty-one dramatic years have brought us.

THE
FOREIGN
SERVICE

My first regular foreign-service post (there had been a brief temporary assignment at Geneva that preceded it) was at Hamburg, where I served as vice-consul over the last half of 1927. There had been earlier attempts at literary excursions in my diaries, but they will be most charitably treated if disregarded here and this collection is allowed to begin with the slightly less immature entries from the months of service in Hamburg.

OCTOBER 30, 1927
HAMBURG

It is a strange thing about cities: there are some which are simply collections of buildings—inanimate, impersonal things; and there are others, like Hamburg, which reach out for you, when you live in them, and spread the tentacles of their beauty and their evil quietly around you. They establish a personal relationship, which you can never shake. And just so, here in Hamburg, the city talks with a thrilling breathless strength through the restless machinery of its harbor, and yet talks with the voice of unutterable horror, through the lurid, repulsive alleys of St. Pauli.

The Zillertal (great popular beer-hall for the petite bourgeoisie) was more crowded and more gloriously relaxed tonight than I have ever seen it. That is the one place in Hamburg where one can sit down and stretch his feet and forget the passage of time. There is a magnificent camaraderie about it.

We sat at a table with four or five other people. We all talked together when we felt like it; and when they played the toasting song, we all stood on the table together, with our hands on each other's shoulders, and swayed to the music and sang and shouted "Prosit" at the end. The man at the table next to us stood alone on his table and drank first out of one stein and then out of the other; and someone else was standing on another table and giving a speech which no one could hear but which everyone applauded, and a young man, in the sentimentality of his third beer, got up and hung gingerbread hearts around the necks of two quite strange young ladies, with much ceremony and complete self-assurance; and the band sat on each other's shoulders and played, while three young Bavarians hopped about on the stage and slapped each other in all the standard formalities of peasant dancing.

NOVEMBER 7, 1927

Yesterday was a rainy Sunday. I walked down to the post-office in the morning and ran into a huge Communist demonstration—thousands and thousands of people standing in the drizzling rain before the Dammtor Station, with their red flags and arm-bands, listening to soap-box orators, singing the *Internationale,* marching around behind sickly fife and drum organizations, buying propaganda literature and Sacco-Vanzetti post-cards.

I stood around and watched, listened to snatches from the speeches, looked at the people themselves. And the strange thing was that for all my contempt for the falseness and hatefulness and demagoguery of communism, I had a strange desire to cry when I first saw those ranks of people marching along the street—ill-dressed, slouching, brutalized people.

It was the first time in my life that I have ever caught a hint of the real truth upon which the little group of spiteful parasites in Moscow feeds, of the truth that these ignorant, unpleasant people were after all human beings; that they were, after centuries of mute despair, for the first time attempting to express and to assert themselves; that under the manifold hokus-pokus of the red flags and the revolutionary ritual they had found something they considered to be essentially their own, something that they believed in, and were proud of; that tomorrow, just as yesterday, these same people would again be mutely absorbed in the work of the world, with barges, railways, drays, factories, street-cars, and what not, while other people—the industrialists and journalists and politicians—gathered the fruits of their labors and held the center of the stage; but that today was *their* day, and they were marching under *their* banner, sullied and cheapened as that banner might be; that they were marching sullenly and defiantly, but with hope and a tremendous earnestness.

Here, it seemed to me, was certainly error and hatefulness and pathos; but here, also, was seriousness and idealism. And after all, in the present state of the world, I am inclined to regard any sort of idealism, be it ever so beclouded with bitterness and hate and bad leadership, as a refreshing phenomenon.

NOVEMBER 12, 1927

This afternoon there was a charity tea dance on the new *Cap Arcona*, the latest and largest liner for the Germany–South America service. She lay out in mid-stream, along the dolphins, and we went out to her on a tender.

It seemed strange, after we had gone on board, to be sitting so comfortably over tea and champagne in all the warmth and luxury of those beautiful new cabins, and yet to hear, outside, the hoarse voices of a thousand harbor craft, sturdily pushing their way through the rain and the smoke and the gloom of a raw autumn evening. And when, through the port-holes of the dance lounge, I saw the high mast lights of a black tramp freighter gliding silently past us, down the stream, I felt an irrepressible yearning to exchange, as though by some magic transformation, my cutaway for sailor's dungarees, and the brilliant comfort of that gay ballroom for the sooty forepeak of the tramp steamer—to ride into the darkness and the night rain, down the long black aisles of twinkling channel buoys on the river, past the clustered harbor lights of Cuxhaven at the mouth, on beyond, to where the channel buoys ceased and the revolving beams from the lighthouses cut great sweeping circles around the black line of the horizon, and farther on to where the wind, coming sharp and cold and salt-tanged from the North Sea, sung an ecstatic low song in the stays and the wireless aerial, and the bow of the freighter rose almost imperceptibly to the first long swell of the sea.

But the mast lights of the tramp glided inexorably past the vista of the port-hole; the orchestra struck up "Nizhni Novgorod"; we drank more champagne, and danced.

Perhaps it was just as well. . . .

NOVEMBER 28, 1927

Went this evening to hear the twenty-three-year-old Horowitz, whom the European critics acclaim as the greatest pianist since Artur Rubinstein. He is Jewish, from Russia, and evidently is rumored to be near to death with tuberculosis.

I was so keyed up, watching the player (we sat in the third row) that I got very little out of the music, except an impression of exquisite musical taste and incredible technique. I don't think I ever in my life saw anyone who seemed to be under a more excruciating nervous strain. He is a slight boy, with a long black pompadour, ashy gray complexion, handsome, other-worldly face, on which there is a drawn expression, as though he were in continual pain. His mouth and eyes were indescribably sensitive. When he played (it was a Tchaikovski concerto) it seemed as though he himself were being played upon by some unseen musician—as though every note were being wrung out of him. His nervous, spidery fingers trembled on the keys, his face worked as though he were in agony, perspiration dripped from his forehead, and he groaned with every chord of the crescendo passages. Whenever the accompanying symphony orchestra played a few measures of accompaniment without him, one could see his whole body, from head to foot, vibrating tensely to every note of the music.

DECEMBER 20, 1927

Reading *Buddenbrooks* (Thomas Mann), this *Forsyte Saga* of old Lübeck, I cannot help but regret that I did not live fifty or a hundred years sooner. Life is too full in these times to be comprehensible. We know too many cities to be able to grow into any of them, and our arrivals and departures are no longer matters for emotional debauches—they are too common. Similarly, we have too many friends to have any friendships, too many books to know any of them well; and the quality of our impressions gives way to the quantity, so that life begins to seem like a movie, with hundreds of kaleidoscopic scenes flashing on and off our field of perception—gone before we have time to consider them.

I should like to have lived in the days when a visit was a matter of months, when political and social problems were regarded from simple standpoints called "liberal" and "conservative," when foreign countries were still foreign, when a vast part of the world always bore the glamour of the great unknown, when there were still wars worth fighting and gods worth worshipping.

In the winter of 1928, persuaded by experiences at Hamburg that my education was incomplete, I returned to Washington with the idea of resigning from the Foreign Service. But then I was offered, in the State Department, appointment as the first officer to receive special training for service in Russia—this, under a program which envisaged a preliminary period of one and a half years of normal service in eastern Europe (the United States then had no official relations with Soviet Russia), to be followed by two or three years of study in language and other Russian subjects at a European university—in this case, Berlin. The posts selected for the preliminary service were Tallinn (then usually referred to by its German name of Reval), the capital of Estonia, and Riga, the capital of Latvia. This assignment I happily accepted. On March 26, 1928, I left Washington for Berlin, where I was given a brief temporary assignment before taking up my duties in the Baltic countries. The following excerpts date from this short period of service in Berlin in the spring of 1928.

A wet snow is falling throughout the Sunday afternoon. We turn up our coat collars and walk to the foot of Unter den Linden. In the gray fading of the old imperial buildings, in their weather-streaked, unpainted walls and their peeling facades, there lies revealed the insecurity of the era from which they have come.

By way of contrast, I go in the evening to the famous Communist theater on Nullendorfplatz. The same exaggerated dogma is being acted out with all the classic hoaxes. The capitalists appear, as ever, in high silk hats; brutal soldiers shoot down martyred members of the proletariat; the *Internationale* bursts forth at frequent intervals from the orchestra; and several unseen individuals hoot valiantly off-stage to represent the mighty voice of the oppressed masses. And yet, under all this boring repetition of doctrinaire tommy-rot one feels the heat of a brightly burning flame.

In this, as in all Berlin pensions, there are the unfulfilled pretensions of a bygone day. Vast rooms, rococo furniture, and colossal ovens; ornate frescoes of garlands and cherubs on the walls; all this is the dust of the glory of 1912. Now, in the high-ceilinged dining room, where Prussian officers once clicked polished heels on the polished floor, only a few dour foreigners eat their hurried meals in depressed silence.

Taxis and omnibuses stream between the pillars of the Brandenburger Tor. Between these same pillars there once marched the proud files of Napoleon's victorious army. I seek at times, in vain, for some bond of cause and effect between that day and this—for some connection between those fiery Frenchmen who stormed the world under the banner of an individual, and the sodden, tired beings who, in the late afternoon, hang on the back platforms of the swaying buses.

In the freshness of the morning, I walk on damp paths, along the sides of a quiet, tree-lined canal. Ripples murmur placidly against stone embankments. An occasional barge, with its cargo of yellow bricks, moves unhurriedly under the bridges, while the restless traffic pours overhead. Watching those slow-moving barges and the shimmering reflections of the trees in the water, I can almost feel again the spirit of the day when the world had time to dream and to consider. But then, I turn up into the roar of the Potsdamerstrasse; the mood is ruined, and the twentieth century is on me again.

APRIL 22, 1928

I walk along the Tiergartenstrasse on this bright Sunday morning.

The spring has appeared overnight. It now pours itself, as Heine once wrote, over the earth like a sea of life. The park has been born again. Yesterday the ponds lay stagnant. Today they have come to life; and they lend new purpose to the little rustic bridges which cross and recross them.

Across the street, before a beautiful old villa, a big red signboard announces that a new building will soon be erected on that spot. One feels a wrath at this crass, insistent memento of another world—a cold, hard, week-day world of business, which feels no more than would a vast automaton the imponderable distinction between winter and spring.

MAY 6, 1928

At a charity ball in the Künstlerhaus someone points out to me one of the celebrities of the Russian émigré society. Of all the aspects of émigré life, that pointing out of celebrities is the most pitiful.

Alive they still are, these "celebrities," but their world is dead. All around them lives a new world, which they do not understand—a world which no longer celebrates the illustriousness of their respective ancestors. The glory they once enjoyed in the bright salons of St. Petersburg has faded in the glare of a new day; and they move like lost phantoms in a world which is, and always will be, a distorted and gilded memory of the past.

◆ ◆ ◆

Cologne at Whitsuntide. The white columns of the great cathedral leap up, with calm, graceful audacity, to lose themselves in a world of transcendent, colored light. The crowds
stand thousands deep in the nave, and one cannot even approach the distant blaze of white and gold which is the altar.

There, in brocaded robes, the bishop of Mexico, having
been expelled from his own land, officiates in all his splendor,
surrounded by the high functionaries of the local church.
These are men whose career is religion. They are avowedly
holy men—men who do not even know women. They are
proud; they are adorned; they are the men of God; they are
set apart and above, through their holiness and their sexless-
ness: apart from and above the sinful mass of beings which
kneels and humiliates itself before them. I feel that the strong,
fearless men whose idealism these columns express must have
seen far beyond the dogma and the wax candles into the
hopeless breach between man's dreams and his environment.
But my feelings, on this bright Sunday morning, are very
superficial and indistinct.

We have moved, at this point, to Riga, the capital of what was in those years the independent country of Latvia. I am now third secretary of the American legation there, serving my trial period of preparation for training as a Russian specialist.

The "M." referred to in the first of these items was an older and somewhat legendary figure in the Riga American community of the time—a man who had served, adventurously, in Russia and the Baltic states at the time of the Russian Revolution and the end of the First World War, when the Riga legation was first founded, and had remained there ever since. I suspect that he was the last holdover from the American military intelligence effort of World War I. We younger officers, in any case, did not know him well, and his continued status at the legation was a mystery for us. A southern gentleman, himself not very old but of the old school, now ravaged by alcohol addiction, he was finally retiring and leaving that part of the world for good. Here: the account of his final send-off at the railway station.

JANUARY 20, 1929
RIGA

We stand in a little group under the dim lights of the station platform, collars up against the icy night air, stamping our feet on the cold brick pavement. Nothing is visible but the waiting trains on both sides of us: the streaks

12

of snow on the high sloping roofs of the wagons-lits, the dull glow of light through the heavily frosted windows.

We have come to bid M. farewell.

For six years he has lived in Riga, courageous and chivalrous, always dignified even in his weakness. And now we assemble on this winter night to bid him farewell.

Why this demonstration? Why should we inflict our presence on the last moments he spends in Riga? Has any of us ever shown him real affection during the course of these six years? Have we ever treated him with anything warmer than the mixture of distrust and hypocrisy and curiosity which passes off in foreign colonies for affability?

Poor M. This should be for him a group of loyal and staid companions, a group of those whom he knows and trusts, who understand him and wish him well. But it should not be any of us. Better have let him slip away alone in these small hours of the night, accompanied only by the ghosts of these few things and persons in Riga that have really held significance for him.

The good-byes are being said. One by one, we talk to M., talk volubly to conceal our uneasiness, shake his hand, and try, in momentary impulses of warm-heartedness, to make him feel that we like him, that we are sorry to see him go.

The minutes drag on. It becomes somewhat of a strain. We are not accustomed to playing the part of solemnity for more than a few moments at a time.

Suddenly, the train starts quietly to move. M. does not hear it. We are filled with a sudden reaction of relief. Like a group of hysterical children, we laugh, we shout "Hurry up, M., hurry up," and we push him to the door of the car.

Standing on the moving steps, waving his hand, smiling his sad, courteous smile, M. disappears into the night—disappears out of our lives—and leaves us there, a trifle embarrassed to find ourselves all together at this late hour, waving senselessly at the black emptiness of the Baltic night.

MARCH 29, 1929
GOOD FRIDAY
RIGA–DORPAT (NOW KNOWN AS TARTU), ESTONIA

The train pulls slowly out of the old railway station. For a time, tenement houses, cobble-stone streets, lumber yards, oil-tanks, sidings and factories slide past the window. Occasionally, the squat domes of a Russian church, rising above the roofs of the city, blink dully in the sunshine. It is a half an hour before we leave the last of the factories behind and enter the pine forests. Here the scattered streaks of snow are disappearing under the warm sunshine, but the lakes are still frozen fast, and peasants are fishing through the ice.

There is much activity at the little way-side stops. In front of the gray wooden stations, inherited from the Russians, the dirt platforms are lined with country people in ill-fitting holiday clothes, waiting for a train going in the other direction to take them to the city. Seedy-looking railway officials, in khaki overcoats, push officiously through the crowds. Peasant women carry milk cans between the baggage cars and their dingy carts. Railway station loafers lean against the railings, surveying the train and the crowd. These are always present in considerable numbers, such characters: wearing muddy Russian boots, dirty mackinaws, and the big Finnish fur caps with a leather covering, and ear-flaps across the top.

The morning wears on. The flat countryside of central Latvia has been left behind. Ravines, hills, and streams appear, interspersed with more open fields and peasant huts. The sky, however, has now clouded over. The west wind tears at the tops of the pine trees. The country again looks cold and wintry.

Occasionally, peasant farmsteads slide past the window. A couple of stone or log structures, in a clearing; usually a well nearby, worked by a primitive sweep-and-bucket; possibly an empty hay-rick, a stack of firewood, and a half-buried vegetable cellar. These, except for the land itself and the livestock, constitute the worldly goods of a Latvian peasant.

Valk, the border point, is reached about one o'clock. The border line divides the community into two parts, and each country maintains its own railway station. After much switching around on the Latvian side, one third-class carriage is hooked up with a string of Soviet freight cars, and in this conveyance two or three passengers, including myself, are hauled the few hundred yards across the border to the Estonian station.

An hour's stop-over here permits a stroll around the town. It is a sprawling village, with very little of the picturesque. The shops are all closed in observance of the holiday, the streets nearly deserted. In the marketplace, two muddy autos and a dejected droshky wait patiently, but with an air of being there more from force of habit than from the expectation of business.

There is a tinkling of bells from a little Russian church, situated on a knoll, under tall trees. The grass in the churchyard lies gray and dead, but there are fresh pussy-willows on a solitary, isolated grave. Inside, the rude wooden floor has been strewed with balsam twigs, and an odor of the Western Christmas mingles with the incense of the oriental church. The burnished metal of many icons reflects the flickering candle-light, and a long ray of sunshine drives down from a window in the little dome, over the heads of the gathering congregation. From the sight of these drab peasants, staring at the icons, crossing themselves, shuffling the balsam twigs under foot as they wait for the commencement of the service, one can sense the full necessity for their presence here. One can feel their need for the glittering things, for all the light and color which is so completely lacking in the smoky cabins and bleak fields, and which the Church, and the Church alone, is in a position to give them. They do not understand the service, but they see the gilt and the roses and the candles; they hear the chanting and the singing; and they go away with the comforting feeling of there being a world . . . somewhere and somehow . . . less ugly than their own.

◆ ◆ ◆

In the late afternoon, we walk up the Domberg, in Dorpat, to see the ruined cathedral. It is already dusk; the air has turned piercingly cold, and a full gale blows out of the west.

The dark columns of the cathedral grope up through the trees, with a grace which their decay has not yet obliterated. Even the hideous water-tanks on top of the crumbling towers, and the jarring effect of the library which later generations have seen fit to build into the apse, cannot detract from the power of the architecture. It stands there through the centuries with a scornful immobility. Even as a ruin, it puts to shame every other product of man's handiwork in the neighborhood, and becomes a towering reproach to the weakness of our own generation.

As we stand there on the hill, the storm approaches. A weird, dirty glow is all that remains of the wintry sunset in the west. Against this glow are silhouetted the crumbling buttresses and the skeleton arches of the ruin. Black cloud masses, growing out of the western horizon, take on the funnel shape of our American cyclones. They rise on the murky sky, against the yellow glow, and spread themselves menacingly over hill and city. As the first flurries of snow sweep across the valley, and the gale screams with doubled fury through the trees, we start back down the hill to the town.

Even the warmth and good cheer of the evening cannot shake the consciousness of that majestic ruin, standing unmoved in the driving snow and the deepening night.

APRIL 30, 1929
RIGA

The first thin rain of the spring season falls on a tired city— falls on thousands of house-tops, on cobble-stones, on flag-stones, on towers, on men and beasts and vehicles, on ships, on merchandise lying on the wharves, on the muddy gray waters of the river, on grass and trees and railway cars and bridges, falls gently and cleansingly and forgivingly from a relenting heaven.

MAY 26, 1929
RIGA

Summer has come to the Baltic, and with it the long white nights. Driving back from the shore at one in the morning, I see that the first drops of the dawn are diluting the darkness. The waters of the Düna have taken on a bluish tint from the lightening sky, and the lights from the distant quai throw down across the water their rugged yellow paths, against which the forms of masts and stacks and roofs and bridges are still colorless and distanceless.

At noon—Sunday noon—a summer sun bathes the city in golden, vibrating warmth. The Kaisergarten is a mass of bright foliage, and the dandelions float on a sea of high, thick grass. Crowds stroll along the gravel paths, sun themselves on the benches, listen to the soldiers' concert at the bandstand. There is a confusion of human voices, talking in Russian or German, a hum of invisible insects, a rush of warm breeze through the fresh foliage, a rumbling and honking of distant motor-cars, a crying of children, and a laughing of young people.

It is all too rich, too full, this summer day. It is more than one can stand. One would like to cry out to the gods to take it away again. We, on whom these gods have spat the venom of their snow and rain for so many months, how shall we receive this sudden surfeit of warmth and tenderness? We are not prepared for it. We would like to clutch it and hold it, but it is too immense, too illusive, to be grasped. We have no loves, no triumphs worthy of this day. We can only walk blinking and bewildered through the hot paths of the park, in the disturbing knowledge of a glory we cannot share, a glory in which the indomitable pettiness of our own lives prevents us from participating.

From the summer of 1929 to that of 1931, while still a foreign-service officer on active duty, I was in Berlin, studying Russian subjects at the Seminary for Oriental Languages and the University of Berlin proper. In the winter of 1931, during a break in the academic schedule, I went for a brief holiday to a skiing resort in the Swiss Alps.

MARCH 8, 1931
A WINTER RESORT IN SWITZERLAND

At a height of 6,000 feet, the high wall on one side of the gorge was broken by a large hollow, with one or two small lakes. In this hollow, like a jewel carried in the white palm of the mountains, lay the resort. From the prim little railway station a narrow street wound, slanting, up the hillside, to the more elevated mountain village from which the community derived its name. The narrow, climbing street was the main thoroughfare. It was lined on both sides by coffee-shops, apothecaries, sporting-goods stores, barber-shops, photographers' shops, travel bureaus, and newsstands that sported the daily papers of five capitals and bad selections of the Tauchnitz editions. On both sides of the main street, side-roads and paths led to the hotels and pensions and sanatoriums. Several feet of snow over everything; not an inch of ground to be seen anywhere.

A large hotel, clean, well run, utilitarian, somewhat cold. A severe and expressionless drawing room, with comfortable chairs and a table with the London papers. A bar, modernly decorated and obviously endowed with the best of intentions, but somehow strangely out of place in this respectable Swiss hostelry, its atmosphere spoiled by poor heating, over-cleanliness and a sedate, prim Swiss bar-maid. Fellow guests, scraped together from the bourgeoisie of four countries. Germans of all sorts, including a young sheik with wavy gray hair, fashionably sun-burnt face, and a weak, unpleasant mouth. Young British women, without their husbands; rather hard-boiled, and trying ineffectually to be gay. An American college boy, with a tremendous physique and no forehead, who maintained frankly, "I'd rather have a good body and be dumb than vice versa." A French family and one Dutch couple, who stood out clearly among the rest through their breeding and poise.

In the evenings one danced in the casino. There was a single listless table of roulette, where people sometimes risked as much as ten francs. On the dance-floor the usual European "Kurort" crowd, even to the professional dancer with the padded shoulders and shiny-glued hair, always with an eye to the young British women. And the evenings were long, as only such evenings can be when one feels one's youth sliding gently but firmly away without the compensations of either vice or virtue. "Have you been here very long? Have you done any shee-ing? Do you like to play bridge?"

In the music which droned across the dance floor, the notes of a Negro cornetist danced and played and ran circles around the conscientious rhythms of his less-imaginative European colleagues.

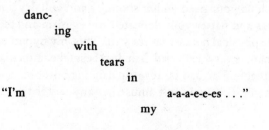

(Well, well, just think of that. You are dancing with tears in your eyes, are you? Dear me, that's quite serious, you know.)

"No, I haven't done any shee-ing. I came here for the skating, you see."

(And what might be wrong with you, my good fellow, that you in your young years should be dancing with tears in your eyes? Do you think that manly and proper?)

                            arms

"For the girl

                                    isn't yo-o-o-o-o-o-ou . . ."

                my

             in

"Yes, I can imagine it must be wonderful, if you know how."

(But after all, now, don't tell me that you, an upstanding American young man, as we must presume, would cry—*cry*, mind you, like a damn baby—because you had to dance with some girl other than the one you wanted to dance with.)

"No, I haven't played any bridge since they started contract; I've never had time."

(Don't you think, really, that there is something unnatural, something positively abnormal about a young man dancing around with tears in his eyes for such a reason? Don't you see that in this condition you scarcely present that bulwark of strength and self-assurance that a woman has a right to look for in a man? Don't you see that you really don't want a woman at all, as a woman, that you only want a mother, who will let you hold your head on her shoulder and will dry your dancing-tears and flatter your delicate little egotism and tend to your little physical necessities for you? This, my hypothetical young man, is very, very bad. You had best take immediate steps to correct it. You had better stop dancing with this poor unappreciated girl if you can't amuse her any better than by spoiling her make-up with your messy tears. And you had better go out into the open air and realize that Mother is far away and that no one is ever going to understand you and that it is not very important whether anyone ever does. You might even try to understand someone else for a change.)

"Now look here, you'd better let me pay for this; you paid last time. Let's see, you had what? One straight cognac, three cognac-sodas . . ."

The snow creaked underfoot as one came out of the casino and started down the hill in the clear, crisp cold of early morning. The moonlight was reflected on the snow; and the world, as a result, was bathed in a fragile semi-darkness, through which the snow-covered peaks leered preposterously out of the sky and the lights in the valley gleamed as unreally and artificially as though they were all part of the cheapest sort of scenic effect.

Upon completion of the two years of Russian studies in Berlin, in the summer of 1931, I went to Norway in September and married my present wife, Annelise Soerensen. We then served for two years at Riga, where our first child, Grace, was born.

In December 1933 I accompanied to Moscow our first ambassador to the Soviet Union, Mr. William C. Bullitt, when he went there to present his credentials. I was then assigned there as second secretary of the new embassy and served most of the time until mid-1937. This service was arduous, and there were few opportunities for travel. But I did make several trips to the countryside, primarily to visit places where the writer, Anton Chekhov, about whom I had thought to write a biography, had lived. And there was one trip to the Black Sea and the Caucasus.

What follow here are excerpts from the diary accounts of such travels.

MARCH 1936
TRIP TO BABKINO, A
VILLAGE NEAR MOSCOW

The sky was overcast. The road was full of half-melted snow and mud, with a pair of deep, slippery ruts in the middle.

Construction was proceeding on the Moscow-Volga Canal.

The whole district where the prisoners were working was a sea of mud out of which, like mountains out of the ocean, rose the embankments and piles of fresh dirt thrown up by the steam-shovels. Guards, sheepskin collars turned up against the wind and rifles silhouetted against the sky, leaned against the railings of the wooden towers that commanded the construction plot.

At Voskresensk we saw the domes of the New Jerusalem Monastery flaring up ahead of us, and went in to see the place. A moon-faced girl in overcoat and felt boots was commissioned to take us through the historical museum. The latter turned out to be an enormous establishment, strung out by means of connecting passageways and bridges through the walls and buildings of the erstwhile monastery. The exhibits seemed more extensive than even those in the Historical Museum in Moscow. Somewhere in the middle, a complete manor house was fitted in: study, salon, bedroom, dining room, and entrance hall—all complete with wax figures. In the study the figure of the old *pomyeshchik* himself (the landowner), attired in a gorgeous oriental dressing-gown, reclined in his arm-chair before the *écritoire* and smoked a long pipe. Similarly, a serf girl, ostensibly scrubbing the floor of a window-niche, presented a broad posterior to the room in general. We asked our escort where the furnishings had come from. She looked frightened and professed ignorance. Somewhat to our consternation, however, at this point, the posterior of the serf girl in the window-niche promptly came to life, and we were informed that the things had been collected from nearby estates.

Following on the manor house, there were a few more suites devoted to peasant uprisings and the revolutionary movement. Upon the completion of the civil war, one moved with relief into a long gallery which bade fair to constitute the exit. But no. One was not to be released thus prematurely from the stern realities of Soviet history. The gallery led to several enormous rooms where the achievements of the Soviet

Union were assembled, from the cultured, waxwork proletarian in his prosperous home to the tractors, combines, and airplanes that had given him his prosperity. These exhibits were capped by a fantasy in wood, faintly reminiscent of the baroque *Pestsäulen* of Austria. Here tractors, railways, airplanes, and factories were piled one upon the other in the glorious confusion of a young Communist's dream. A wooden Stalin, in great-coat and Red Army cap, embraced the blast-furnaces of Magnitogorsk. And on top of it all Lenin, smaller in stature than Stalin but still supreme, pointed characteristically with raised arm toward the promise of a distant world.

From Voskresensk we drove out a side-road toward Babkino. When we got within a mile or so of where we thought the village must lie, we left the car and continued on skis, in order not to attract too much attention. There was a firm crust on the snow. A strong south wind, heavy and moist with the tang of melting snow, swept us along, and it was easy going across the fields.

We passed through a woods. On the other side, a valley opened up, two or three miles in length. The village (now the kolkhoz) of Babkino lay in the meadows at the bottom.

With a little inquiry, we found the spot where the old manor house had been. A long, low wooden building of one story was still standing. It was deserted and neglected. Windows and doors were broken out. The wind howled through the empty caverns of the rooms. The floors were littered with human offal.

I went out to the road and asked a passing peasant woman if that was really the old manor house. She said it was. Had it ever been used since the war? Yes, they had done some construction down the road a piece, and the prisoners had lived in there. Prisoners? Yes, of course—prisoners.

Sure enough: a mile or so down the valley, a big round silo gleamed against the dark background, very new and out of place in the Russian landscape.

The old manor house had stood on the high banks of a bend

in the river. Some of the plot had apparently been dug away, for there was a deep cut extending to within a few yards of the remaining building, and in the cut an abandoned steam-shovel reclined disconsolately on its side.

We went over to the village. It lay not along the road, as most Russian villages do, but out by itself in a meadow, by the stream. Two rows of log cabins, one just like the other. Not a tree in the place; not a single attempt at improvement or beautification of the site; not a fence or even so much as an improved path. Just a dozen log cabins in a meadow.

I went into the house of the chairman of the collective farm. Like most Russian izbas, it was entered through the wood-shed. There were a number of people in the single heated room which served as bedroom, living room, and everything else. Some women had part of the floor taken up and were removing potatoes from a bin under the floor. A partition, running almost up to the ceiling, shut off one corner of the room, where the stove must have been. From over the top of the partition, a child's eyes surveyed the scene with unblink-ing curiosity. A young man in Red Army uniform, papyrossa dangling from his mouth, sprawled in a chair by a little table. On the table: an open book and two copies of the Moscow *Pravda*. Above the table, in a corner: a row of icons.

The chairman, who was sitting at the other side of the table, got up, offered me his hand, and asked me to sit down. He was a big, brown-bearded peasant with clear, serious blue eyes.

I told him what I had come for. He couldn't tell me much. He remembered having heard something about a writer once living there. The building we had seen was only a wing of the manor house; the main building had burned down. The estate had changed hands four times in the years between 1886 and the War. Everything had changed. In the next village there was an old man who remembered "the days of serfdom" and who might be able to tell me something about the previous owners of the estate.

On the way back we paused on the hill by the woods and looked back at the valley. Fifty years! What were the changes that had taken place over that time? The one really cultured spot in the district had been essentially obliterated: the only spot where life had been lived in a dignified way, and where there had been cleanliness and beauty and gaiety. The bells of the little church on the knoll at the end of the valley, which used to ring out so weirdly and dolefully in the darkness on the eves of the holy days, were now silent. The homes and conditions of life of the peasant had probably changed little, if at all, although the organization of their work was different. To replace the manor house and the church they had—what? A new silo, and a strong master in Moscow, who promised them great things for the future. Perhaps they had the hope—some of them—that some day things would really be better.

We stopped in Voskresensk on the way home to see another building where Chekhov had once lived. It was at that time the quarters of the village schoolmaster, a position occupied by Chekhov's brother. It was now a kindergarten. We entered through the kitchen. It was dark and smoky, and full of women who slopped around bare-footed on the dirty floor. The rooms inside were dingy and full of bad air. A row of little blue smocks hung along the wall, on hooks over which were marked the names: Olya, Nadya, Alesha, et cetera. A battered piano, little tables and chairs, constituted the furniture. In another room there were rows of little cots, where the children rested in the middle of the day.

The children were just leaving as we arrived. Charwomen were washing the floors with a reddish solution. A tired girl in a white kittel received us and apologized for the looks of the place. Yes, the children were all from town here; none of them came in from the country. She didn't know anything about Chekhov. We must come some other time when the superintendent was there. Sometime in summer . . .

The plane took off at dawn from an icy field. It was an old, single-motored plane, filled with freight. I was the only passenger.

As we took off, the sun appeared over the Moscow housetops and cast a cold beam over the jagged ice of the landing field.

We followed the railroad south toward Kharkov, for an hour or two. The snow on the fields gradually began to give way to a crust of dirty ice, with spots of bare soil showing through here and there. Where the steppe began, the snow stopped altogether, and there was nothing more below us but the muddy, treeless plain of the Ukraine, wrinkled with countless rivulets and ravines.

Along the edges of the ravines were strung the endless villages: hundreds—in some cases—of thatched houses with white plaster walls, side by side in one long straggling line. Rarely a tree or a garden wall to break the monotony.

I had brought with me, to read on the trip, a copy of Gogol's *Dead Souls*. It was difficult to believe that this could be the same country pictured by Gogol. Where were the estates, with their columned manor houses, their honeysuckle and lilac bushes, their birch groves, their *Allees* and lakes?

They had to be there somewhere, of course—most of them, at least; and they could not look so vastly different from a plane in the spring of 1936 than they would have looked from the same perspective a hundred years ago. Indeed, except for the disappearance of that modest admixture of culture which the nobility supported, conditions could not have changed so much as one thinks, in that vast prairie country. If Gogol were alive today, I asked myself, would he not continue to rant, as he did then, at the ignorance of the inhabitants? Would he not continue to cry out that Russia was in danger of being ruined not by "foreign influences" but by its own failings—by the fact that in addition to the legal administration, there has grown up an entirely different administration, much more powerful than anything legal. Peculiar conditions have been established; everything has been given its price, and the prices made public. And no ruler, even though he be the wisest of rulers and legislators, can remedy the evil, however much he may restrict the activities of bad officials by appointing other officials to check up on them. It will all be of no avail, until each of us feels that he must revolt against falsehood just as he revolted at the time of the uprising of the peoples. . . .

There was a wait of two hours at the Kharkov airport, while they sent up a special plane for me from Rostov. In normal circumstances there would have been no plane at all that day from Kharkov to Rostov; but they wanted to keep up appearances, for my sake. (One of the pilots complained to me that civil aviation was being neglected in the USSR. The military got everything.)

Boredom hung heavily over the little airport at mid-day. A chilly wind swept out of the north and made life uncomfortable outside the building. Only on the sheltered south side a crowd of loafers and three peasant women sat on the concrete steps and sunned themselves. The loafers kidded each other and gossiped. The women huddled in their shawls and observed the others in inscrutable silence.

Inside the building, in the waiting room, a few of the more privileged loafers slouched at the tables, drank tea, and smoked. The woman who tended the buffet dozed behind her dead fish and stale sandwiches, and a lone mouse disported himself with impunity on the counter before her. A radio loudspeaker rasped out Russian folk songs.

The wheels of time seemed almost to stand still, and provincial Russia to be enveloped in a pall of boredom as oppressively vast as the Russian territory itself.

At two o'clock my plane finally arrived from Rostov. It was an ancient affair; an open bi-plane with all the paint worn off the struts. They gave me a helmet and glasses which effectively blinded me for the duration of the journey and, in addition, a shaggy old shuba such as night watchmen might wear in Moscow, but with all the buttons missing, and with a gaping rent in the back. For more than two hours on the way to Rostov, I, being partly out in the wind, fought blindly with the wind for the shreds of that shuba. The odds were against me. I had only two arms; the wind had a hundred. In the end, the wind had most of the shuba. I had a magnificent cold.

The train left Rostov in the early evening. A fiery setting sun raced along the Kuban steppe, at the edge of the horizon.

In the morning we were in the mountains. The sun was shining, but the cold north wind was still blowing. There were wild flowers on the mountain slopes and fruit trees were in bloom in the valleys.

Tuapse, on the Black Sea, was reached in the middle of the morning, and from there the train followed the coast to Sochi. The right-of-way skirted the shore, at the base of the hills. The latter rose almost directly out of the sea. On one side there were only rocks and foliage; on the other—a very blue and very deserted body of water.

Sochi was sunny but cold. The biting north wind twisted the leaves of the palm trees, carried clouds of dust through the streets, drove the patient vacationists indoors, and stirred up a surf which knocked huge sections of the seawall to pieces and opened up a crack two feet wide in the concrete foundation of the dining room. Nobody seemed to care. Some fresh concrete was poured into the cavity, and the foundation wall was left leaning drunkenly toward the sea. The dining room continued to be used.

The guests appeared to be mostly workers, or at least officials, of proletarian origin. (The season for the intelligentsia had not yet set in.) The proletarians spent the bulk of their time eating, or waiting for their food, in the big glass-enclosed veranda out over the sea, which served as a dining room. Between meals, they wandered silently and gloomily, collars up against the wind, through the storm-torn paths of the garden, or played chess and miniature billiards in a wing of the building provided for that purpose.

I looked days on end—in vain—for a single fresh, vivacious face, for a single hint of health and youth and eagerness for life. Only once did I see any real signs of activity and interest. I got up at two in the morning to watch a "dance evening" at its height. The town itself was dark and quiet. The streets were utterly deserted. But in one big smoky room, in a newly constructed wing of the hotel, three or four hundred people were assembled at tables, around a dance floor. A tournament was in progress. The young couples danced energetically and not too well, with intense seriousness and concentration. When the prizes were announced, there was enormous excitement and interest. A crowd of shouting, gesticulating people besieged the judge like brokers around a buyer in the Chicago grain pit. The couple who won first prize walked ceremoniously around the entire room and allowed themselves to be admired. They enjoyed it immensely. The young man had a weak face and stooped shoulders. His fingernails were black. I wondered what his reactions were at that moment. And hers. And what connection they had with socialism.

The tired waitresses in brown smocks came and went, between the dances, with trays of tea and beer, and leaned wearily against the wall while the dancing was going on. They were the nicest-looking people there. They were the same girls who worked in the regular hotel dining room. They had worked in the dining room from eight in the morning until midnight. Since midnight they had been working in the dance hall. They would continue to work there until four or five in the morning. At eight they would again be at their places in the dining room, starting in on another long day's work. They earned eighty-five rubles a month, and when there was porridge left over, they were allowed to eat it. Otherwise, they had to feed themselves.

◆ ◆ ◆

On a nearby mountain several hundred prisoners lived in a camp of big tents and worked every day, under armed guard, improving a road. They were all political prisoners, from other parts of the Soviet Union. They looked healthy and well fed. I was told that they were themselves being "re-made" by those same allegedly humanitarian methods which had been applied on the Baltic–White Sea Canal.

On top of the mountain, construction of a restaurant and an observation tower was in progress. Dumpy peasant women in muddy padded coats, head shawls, and felt boots carried bricks up the runways on little wooden stretchers. One woman sat on a log in the sun and did nothing.

From the scaffolding of the half-constructed tower, there was a magnificent view. On one side the Black Sea smiled in the morning sunshine and tiny ripples lapped at the strip of beach, two thousand feet below. On the other side, across fifty miles of wooded foothills, the great white ridge of the Caucasian Alps gleamed out on the horizon. When we came down from the scaffolding, a German traveller who was with me went up to the woman sitting on the log and asked her, with ponderous German bluntness, "Are you a Stakhanovite?" The woman looked at him slowly and coldly, with an expression of bored contempt. "Of course," she replied.

I waited all one day at Sochi for the scheduled plane to Sukhum. The plane was supposed to fly there from Sukhum and back again, in one day. It never came. The airport officials were indifferent. "There must," they said philosophically, "be something the matter with it."

I later learned that the Sukhum officials had sent no plane that day because it was a "free day." They considered there should not be any service on a "free day." It had apparently never occurred to them to inform the Sochi officials of their views on these matters.

Somewhat skeptical as to the actual existence of a regular service, I hired a little special sport plane and flew to Sukhum early the next morning.

It was a beautiful sight from the plane: the whole mountainous coastline spread out below in the fresh sunshine of a spring morning. The new white sanatoriums at Gagry, strung like the beads of a necklace around the curve of the bay at the foot of the steep slopes. Off to the east, the massive snow-covered peaks, seemingly suspended, like clouds, in the sky.

At Sukhum, there was a wait of two or three hours. What was described as the regular plane to Tiflis, an open bi-plane with a single, twelve-cylinder motor, refused to start. Five or six men tinkered with the magneto and conducted a heated argument as to the cause of the trouble. It was evident to anyone who listened to them talk that none of them really had the faintest idea what was the matter. The regular mechanic of the plane was in Tiflis. The pilot lay on the grass chewing straws and making wisecracks at the helplessness of the Sukhum mechanics. I asked him if he wouldn't have certain reservations about taking that plane across the mountains after those fellows had gotten through tinkering with it. (By that time they had all the spark wires for one six-cylinder block disconnected and were arguing about the firing order.) No, was the answer, he was not concerned. If the machine started at all, it would be all right. How were things abroad, in my estimation?

Fortunately for me, the plane would not start at all, despite any amount of arguing. So they finally dispatched me to Kutais, my immediate destination, in another diminutive sport plane. Turning inland from the coast, we flew for an hour and a half over the foothills of the Caucasian range, and finally came out over a great treeless plain, bounded on the north and on the south by impressive white-capped mountain ranges.

We landed at an airstrip miles from anywhere, out on the open steppe. Here I had to wait an hour or two, before a truck came to take me to town. It was mid-day. Hot sunshine baked the plain. Not a breath of air was stirring. A little stream, carried by an artificial irrigation ditch, flowed past the small airport building. A bridge, with a concrete railing, led across it. Here I sat in the sun, together with the various members of the airport staff. Three pigs busied themselves at the side of the ditch below us. A short distance away, a young woman washed clothes over an open fire, in water from the ditch, and occasionally gave breast to a two-year-old child. It was a very peaceful little airport.

At one time we heard the thumping and whining of Caucasian music. An open droshky (or what Americans usually call a droshky; the Russians call it a *proletka*) drawn by two galloping horses suddenly appeared out of nowhere careening across the steppe, two drunks and a man with an accordion sprawled on the backseat. The drummer sat up on the driver's seat, with the driver. The wet backs of the horses gleamed in the sunshine.

The local citizens shrugged their shoulders. "Just somebody out on a party," they said. The whole affair disappeared across the fields as suddenly as it had appeared.

I talked with a garrulous, white-haired old fellow who seemed to be the butt of most of the kidding around the place. (The others had been urging him to apply to the Pioneers, the Soviet Boy Scouts, for a red necktie.) He allowed as how things in general were going better in that part of the world. Why, some of the citrus-fruit growers on the Black Sea coast were so prosperous that they were buying pianos. Some earned as much as 1,000 to 1,500 rubles a season. "But all that," he added with a touch of bitterness, "hasn't affected us yet. We are only employees."

MOSCOW, AGAIN

I picked this man up at night one time, driving into Moscow from the country. He never saw my face, nor did I see his. He sat in the backseat, while I drove. He called me "Comrade

33

Mechanic" throughout, and did not dream that I was a foreigner.

He was greatly delighted at the prospect of having a ride in an automobile.

"You're a lucky devil," he said. "Just think of being able to go joyriding all day long and get paid for it."

I asked him what his job was.

He was a bookkeeper for a collective farm near Moscow. He had an apartment and a family in Moscow, and commuted out to the farm on suburban trains every day. He got two hundred rubles a month, in addition to sixty kilograms of potatoes, thirty kilograms of milk, and some vegetables in season.

How were conditions on the collective farm?

Horrible.

What was the trouble? Wasn't the harvest enough to go around?

Enough to go around? There wasn't a penny left for distribution. Here it was March and he hadn't even made up his accounts for the year 1935. He didn't dare. The trouble was not with the harvest. The trouble was corruption. The leaders of the farm stole everything. There was nothing left for the peasants. The leaders made a practice of writing out *kommandirovki* for themselves for trips to Moscow. The peasants made paper boxes during the winter, and the leaders would obtain such *kommandirovki* on the pretext of going to town on business, in connection with the box-making. They would draw eighteen to twenty rubles each time from the treasury, to pay the expenses of the trip: train fare, meals, et cetera. They would then stay right there in the village, drink the money up, and claim their day's pay in addition. The whole cash turnover for 1935 had been only some 50,000 rubles, and these *kommandirovki* alone had cost over 5,000.

"Doesn't the Party take an interest in such a state of affairs?"

"The Party?" My friend snorted. "Why, the manager of the

farm was a Party member, and he was the worst one of the bunch. He's out now. He's gone to a raion consumers' cooperative society. He'll steal even more there. We've got a woman in his place now, but she can't do anything. She hasn't got enough authority."

"But how do they get away with this? Doesn't anyone stop them?"

"I've been trying to stop them myself for months. I got a couple of investigations started, but nothing came of it. Yesterday I was up at the Soviet Control Commission and I hope to have an inspecting committee out there pretty soon."

"They must love you out at that farm."

"Love me? Brother, it's a regular war."

We were coming into town. He was still stricken with awe and admiration at the mechanical perfection of the car.

"It's just as though it were alive. It's just like a living thing. You'd think that it did all these things of its own accord. Who'd ever believe that it was just because you push all those gadgets?"

I let him off on the Arbat, very pleased with his experience but sighing over the adversities of fortune which had made him a bookkeeper on a farm instead of a chauffeur.

From mid-1937 to mid-1938 I served in the State Department in Washington. Taking a vacation in June 1938, I bicycled across most of my native state of Wisconsin. Here: the diary account of that trip.

My jumping-off place was one of those occasional spots in the landscape of the central northern states where a touch of scenery—a rocky glen, a waterfall, or a precipitous elevation—has broken the beautiful monotony of the countryside and provided a convenient excuse for waylaying the passing motorist and extracting a few dollars from his pocket before releasing him to pursue his swift, boring drive across the plains. This place, with its aggressive tourism, its advertising, souvenirs, information booths, hotels and tourist homes, has something of the atmosphere of the religious pilgrimage points in central Europe; and I was glad to shake its dust from my tires in the bright sunshine of a hot June morning and to pedal out of town over the hills toward the east.

The air that trembled in the sunshine over the road ahead was heavy with the fragrances of early summer: of new-mown hay and of the teeming small life of the swamps. The road, although not a very important one, was broad and excellently covered with a dark oil surface.

Indeed, all the roads—both county and state—over which

I was destined to ride in the course of the following days were beautifully graded and surfaced. They led through prosperous and thickly populated farming country. They were lined with quiet, spacious farmhouses, which stood back behind tree-covered lawns and gravel driveways. Towns and villages were interspersed at intervals of roughly ten to fifteen miles.

Yet it seemed to me that these beautiful highways were the most deserted places I had ever encountered. In the course of a one-hundred-mile journey, I was destined to encounter on the open road no single fellow-cyclist, no single pedestrian, no single horse-drawn vehicle. And as for the occupants of the occasional machines that went whirring by, they obviously had no connection in the social sense with the highway over which they were driving. Slumping back on the cushions of their streamlined models, travelling at such rates of speed that the world on either hand was only a blurred, flowing ribbon of green, they had no more real association with the highway than their fellow-travellers in the cabins of the transport planes that occasionally droned overhead. They were lost spirits, hovering for brief periods on another level, where space existed only in time. To those of us who really inhabited the highway—to the birds and insects and snakes and turtles and chipmunks and the lone cyclist—these motor-cars were only an abstract danger, a natural menace like lightning, earthquake, or flood—a danger which had to be reckoned and coped with (here the turtles, whose corpses strewed the pavement for miles, seemed to be at the greatest disadvantage) but to which we had no human relationship and which only accentuated rather than disturbed our loneliness.

To anyone who complains of lack of seclusion in our modern life, I recommend walking or cycling on the highways. He may go for days without meeting any of his own kind. But I should not commend this course to anyone inclined to the feeling that the free and unrestrained association of human beings is a prerequisite for a healthy social and political life. He will think back with regret to the vigorous life of the

English highway of Chaucer's day, as depicted in *The Canterbury Tales*; and he will ponder with misgivings the extensive isolation of the modern traveller in his movements from place to place.

Be that as it may, the morning sun—to whom a deserted highway is as good as any other—began to bake lustily, and after a couple of hours of pedalling I was relieved enough to find a village by the side of a lake. The inn was a relatively new building, on the site of an older hostelry of pioneer days, and fitted out with "antiques" from the surrounding countryside. I was not sure that it was not an improvement over the black leather settees and the cuspidors of the country hotels I had known as a boy. In any event, I had a swim and—for sixty-five cents—a luncheon consisting of young onions, white radishes, broiled pike garnished with slices of apple, bread and butter, salad with cherries and pineapple, milk, ice cream and strawberries. Thus it was with an almost unpleasant consciousness of the generosity of nature in my native habitat that I set off again in the burning sunshine of early afternoon, on the second leg of my journey.

That leg was a particularly dry one. The only community along the way was a village by the ambitious name of Endeavor, through which I passed in the middle of the afternoon. Unfortunately, the manifestations of endeavor on the part of the city fathers were principally of a moral nature. The place where, according to all accepted standards, the "tavern" should have stood was occupied by a stern "gospel tabernacle." Two men in overalls, of whom I inquired concerning the possibility of getting a glass of beer, grinned widely and replied, "Not here you don't. The place is stone-dry." Their hearts were not stone-dry, however, for they caught up with me in a Ford, when I had gotten a short distance out of town, and shouted, "About a mile further, on your left." And sure enough, a mile further on the left was the ubiquitous beer sign and back of it the roadhouse with its dark, cool bar-room, and with four enormous drunks who pawed each other affectionately at the bar and inquired of each other repeatedly in tones of earnest solicitation, "Is you tough?"

Four o'clock brought me to my day's destination. This was a backwater village, abandoned by both highway and railway. The new concrete road had been put through a half mile away. The railway had discontinued service on the branch line that led to the town, and had added insult to injury, the inhabitants told me, by tearing down the "depot." So the community slumbered on peacefully, soiled but not engulfed by the flood of standard urban influence that flowed through so much of the surrounding countryside.

For me the attraction of this place lay chiefly in the fact that it was adjacent to a large piece of property which my paternal grandfather had acquired upon his return from the Civil War and much of which he had himself cleared for the plow and fenced in with a five-rail fence. I had at home the record of my father's boyhood reminiscences, written shortly before his death, and I was curious to see what had become of the land where, seventy-five years ago, communication with the outside world had still been maintained by the wood-burning steamboats that plied the narrow streams, and where the Indians and the ducks had gathered by the hundreds every year, according to my father's account, to harvest the wild rice that grew in such profusion in the marshy places.

Upon entering the village, I repaired to the saloon as the proper source of all useful information. I was not disappointed. The company consisted of the barkeep, a German farmer, and an elderly newspaper editor from a neighboring small town. They were listening to a radio account of a baseball game between Washington and the White Sox, and discussing the prospects for the outcome of the Louis-Schmeling fight. The editor, however, showed interest in my quest, offered some suggestions of his own, and then referred me to the village's oldest inhabitant.

I found the latter's house without difficulty. He was a well-preserved old man, in his nineties, with a dignified beard. We sat together, side by side, on a swinging settee on his front porch, while he told me about old times. He remembered the pioneer days, before the Civil War. His wife, who was ill and in pain, sat miserably on the side of her bed in the dark living room behind us. I could feel her eyes peering out at us from the gloom, like those of an old sick bird, full of pain and despair and resentment. The doctor came in while I was there; and before he left I heard the old woman's voice for the first time: harsh, unrestrained, and racked with suffering. "Doctor," she said slowly, "don't you think I ought to ask Kate to come up and look after me? 'Twon't be long and I'll not be around this place anymore. She said she'd come up any time I needed her." The doctor scoffed professionally. "That's all nonsense. You know where you'll be pretty soon?" he said. "You'll be back working on the farm." And he walked cheerfully out to his car and drove away. But the old woman continued to rock back and forth on the side of her bed, and no fresh hope came into the troubled old eyes.

Upon the old man's advice, I set forth to find one of the farmers who now lived on what had once been the family property. I walked through the sleepy, quiet streets of the village on the way out of town. By the side of the stream fishermen were loading huge struggling carp from a pen into crates, and heaving the crates onto a truck. I asked them what they did with the fish and they replied with scorn that it was what such city folk as myself ate for salmon.

I crossed the bridges over the stream and the marsh and climbed the hill on the other side. The knoll on the left, where the old family house had stood, was overgrown with high grass. A fat woodchuck hurried off up the slope as I passed.

At the farm on the top of the hill, they were bringing in the hay. A team of horses was working a hoist which lifted the hay from the wagons into the big barn. The farmer, they told me, was out in the fields. I rode out on an empty hay-wagon to meet him, over the sandy lanes, and he met me on the way. He was a fine-looking man, with soft blue eyes and a firm, sensitive mouth. While the wagon rolled slowly round and round the field and the young farmhand stowed the hay that rolled inexorably up the conveyor from the mechanical hay-rake, I walked alongside, in a rain of chaff, and discussed family history with the farmer.

I gladly accepted a laconic statement that I was to pass the night at the farm. The house had both bathroom and dining room, but all of us washed and ate in the big kitchen that stretched clear across the middle of the building. The dinner company included the farmer and his wife, their son, three farmhands (one of whom was a young Indian) and myself. The wife had prepared the meal herself. She had no "help." It consisted of smoked carp, onions, creamed potatoes, sweet buns with this season's strawberry preserves, chocolate cake, strawberries with cream, and lemonade.

After dinner the farmhands withdrew, and the rest of us sat in the "parlor" and talked. The son was a short-sighted, good-natured, not very bright fellow about twenty. He contributed little to the conversation. Later in the evening the daughter of the house arrived. She had been spending the day with friends in the city. She had been to college and was now preparing to become a physical-training instructor. The entry of such a person—smart, well-dressed, confident, blooming with health and energy—into the tired evening atmosphere of the old farmhouse was a breath of air from another world. It was idle to speculate whether this contrast was for better or for worse. It seemed doubtful that she would ever make a farmer's wife, like her mother. Yet she was doubt-less better educated and more wide-awake than her mother had ever been. In reality, the city, at once so menacing and so promising, had claimed her for its own as it had so many other farm children; her future lay—for better or for worse—in its copious lap, not on the farm.

I was given the guest bedroom, with its great oak bedstead and its cedar chest. On the wall, surrounded by an ornate gilt frame, was an enlargement of a family photograph, obviously taken many years before. Solemn little girls in high black shoes and ill-fitting party dresses stared stonily at the photographer. In the figure of a little boy with long ears and a self-conscious smirk I could recognize my fifty-five-year-old host. On another wall hung a picture of a youth playing the cello beside the hearth-fire, and an old man listening. "There is balm for hearts o'er-burdened in the magic of the bow," ran the legend. "Though one shall dream of days to come and one of long ago." Amid these reassuring relics of an older and familiar age, I slept well enough, and arose at six to participate in a breakfast fully as hearty as the supper of the evening before.

The next day saw me over forty uneventful miles. Again a convenient lake presented itself at midday. My destination, which I reached in late afternoon, was a larger country center, a college town of from twenty to thirty thousand souls.

I put up in a house which had rooms for tourists—seventy-five cents a night. These places, which are rapidly depriving the hotels of much of the tourist trade, served no meals, so I had to walk over to the main business center in the evening to get supper. It was the night of the big fight. Radio loud-speakers were rasping out on every hand, in the restaurants and saloons and cigar stores. A high-school band, installed on a platform in the middle of Main Street, bravely executed the overture to *Wilhelm Tell* and "The Stars and Stripes Forever," but its listeners were few and, as far as could be observed, involuntary. The town was indoors, listening to the fight.

When this brief event was over, I walked back to the house where I had my room. No one was at home, and I sat for a time alone on the porch in the darkness. The tree-lined street stretched away down the hill, under the arc-lights. The sidewalks were deserted, but a steady stream of sleek, dark cars flowed between them, moving in and out of the town. Each car had its couple or its foursome inside, bent on pleasure—usually vicarious pleasure—in the form of a movie or a dance or a petting party. Woe to the young man or young woman who could not make arrangements to be included in one of these private, mathematically correct companies of nocturnal motorists. All the life of the evening flowed along the highways in this fashion, segregated into quiet groups of two and four. There was no provision for anyone else. There was no place where strangers would come together freely—as in a Bavarian beer hall or a Russian amusement park—for the mere purpose of being together and enjoying new acquaintances. Even the saloons were nearly empty.

It seemed for a moment as though this quiet nocturnal stream of temporary moving prisons, of closed doors and closed groups, was the reductio ad absurdum of the exaggerated American desire for privacy. What was in England an evil of the upper class seemed here to have become the vice of the entire populace. It was the sad climax of individualism, the blind-alley of a generation which had forgotten how to think or live collectively, of a people whose private lives were so brittle, so insecure that they dared not subject them to the slightest social contact with the casual stranger, of people who felt neither curiosity nor responsibility for the mass of those who shared their community life and their community problems.

I recalled the truly wonderful fashion in which, as had so often been proved, these same people would rise to the occasion and subordinate their personal interests to collective efforts in the event of a natural catastrophe such as a flood, a hurricane, or a war; and I could not help but feel that one ought to welcome almost any social cataclysm, however painful, and however costly, that would carry away something of this stuffy individualism and force human beings to seek their happiness and their salvation in their relationship to society as a whole rather than in the interests of themselves and their little group of intimate acquaintances. That such a cataclysm was imminent—within the span of a decade or two—seemed probable enough; and I found myself looking forward to it in much the same way as Anton Chekhov, in the 1890s, looked forward with both hope and trepidation to that "cruel and mighty storm which is advancing upon us, which is already near and which will soon blow all the laziness, the indifference, the prejudice against work and the rotten boredom out of our society."

Before me lay another day of beautiful countryside, lonely highways, hot sunshine, and cooling drafts of beer at roadhouse bars. But nothing which I was destined to see subsequently served to weaken the relief at the thought that this sad breakdown of human association in urban America was something that could not last, and that whatever else might be sacrificed in the years to come, the spirit of fellowship, having reached its lowest conceivable ebb, could not fail to be the gainer.

From September 29, 1938, the day of the Munich Conference, until the outbreak of war in Europe, one year later, I was stationed at Prague, as second secretary of the American legation in that city. My numerous political reports from that period of service in Prague, together with some of the personal notes of that time, were published in 1968 in a volume put out by the Princeton University Press under the title FROM PRAGUE AFTER MUNICH. *The following passage, written shortly after my arrival and about a week after the Munich crisis, is an excerpt from that book.*

Prague could never have been more beautiful than during those recent September days when its security hung by so slender a thread. The old streets, relieved of motor vehicles by an obliging army, had recovered something of their pristine quiet and composure. Baroque towers—themselves unreal and ethereal—floated peacefully against skies in which the bright blue of autumn made way frequently for isolated, drifting clouds. In the sleepy courtyards, sunshine varied with brief, gentle showers. And the little groups of passers-by still assembled hourly in the marketplace, as they had for centuries, to watch the saints make their appointed rounds in the clock on the wall of the town hall.

Yet rarely, if ever, has the quaint garb of this old city seemed more museum-like, more detached from the realities of the moment, than it did during these strange days. The world had taken final farewell, it seemed, of nearly everything that these monuments represented. Gone were the unifying faith and national tolerance of the Middle Ages; gone—in large measure—was the glamour of the Counter-Reformation, the outward manifestation of the wealth and power of Rome; gone indeed were the gay dreams of the empire of Joseph II and Maria Theresa: the laughing voice of Vienna, the spirit of Mozart. A sterner age was upon us; and it was only in the gaunt spires of the Týn Church—those grim reminders of the century-long struggle of a stubborn and rebellious Bohemia against the united power of western Europe—that there was something vitally connected with the problems of this day. The ghosts of Jan Hus and the Bohemian Brethren stalked again through "blacked-out" streets that could not have been darker in the fifteenth century itself. And once again a remarkable little people, whose virtues and whose failings alike are the products of adversity, confronted what they felt to be an unjust and unsympathetic Europe.

The following letter to my sister was written from Prague during a brief official visit to that city in 1940, during the war, when I was stationed in Berlin. It gave a retrospective picture of my life in Prague during the year I had recently spent there, and one that was more comprehensive than any single diary entry.

DECEMBER 7, 1940
PRAGUE

Dear Jeanette:

This letter may arrive before I do, or I may arrive before the letter does; or one or both of us may never arrive. But when I am in Prague, I simply have to write. It has been that way ever since I arrived here on the weird day of Munich in 1938. And now when I come down here from all the sterile newness of Berlin and walk about in these venerable, shabby streets, I can't keep still.

I have written so many formal things about this part of the world that I think I have paid my due to literary discipline and decorum and am entitled to indulge just once in the "stream of consciousness" stuff. I even wonder whether it isn't possibly the only proper approach to this dreamy, poignant place, which has a thousand tales to tell and proves nothing at all, unless it be the incorrigible vanity and tragedy and futility of all human endeavor. In all the history of Bohemia there have never been any clear issues, any complete victories, or any complete defeats.

I know no place which makes more mockery of the present—no place where one is more conscious of the transience of one's self and one's own generation and of everything that is being done.

The consulate general was closed several weeks ago. I am more or less responsible for the arrangements made for the custody and preservation of the property, which belongs to the government, and I have come down for a day or two on a tour of inspection. I walk around the premises of the old palace that once housed our legation, give orders for the repair of a retaining wall in the garden, decide what shall be planted next spring, make plans for the disposal of the old, unused Renaissance wing, ponder the condition of the wooden frames of the three-thousand-odd windowpanes. All the time I am conscious of the fact that all this has been done hundreds of times before, over the ages, by innumerable counts and cardinals and custodians and architects, that each time it was done, it seemed important to the people who were doing it, that they had some sort of plans for the utilization of the great structure, and that they hoped that it would be possible to utilize the place in a way commensurate with its power and dignity. And all the time I feel that the old building is laughing skeptically at me and musing:

Man built me as a framework for great doings, for lofty decisions, for the exercise of power. I was to symbolize his strength and his grandeur. And yet in all the centuries of my existence there have not been five years in a hundred when he was able to fill my walls with anything remotely adequate, remotely representative. My rooms have stood year after year, cold and empty. No horses stamp in my marble stables. Owner after owner has either lost the means or lacked the stature to walk through my halls as one who belonged in them. Either princes of the Church have lived—for poverty—in my servants' quarters; or mean little men, awed by massive ceilings and lofty walls, lonely and uneasy in these trappings of greatness, have camped like mice in my most splendid chambers. I have been a dream to which man has never been able to live up.

And meanwhile, the seasons have come and gone. The snows of winter have sifted in onto the huge rafters of the garret; in spring, year after year, the blossoms of the fruit trees in the upper garden have fluttered down onto my window ledges; on countless days the faint showers of midsummer have swept over the hill and cooled the hot tiles of my roof; in autumn dead leaves have blown in whirlpools in the courtyards; the winds have screamed through the archways on the long black nights. The bells of the nearby churches have rung the hours for centuries. The cobbles of the street outside have echoed for untold days with the footsteps of men, marching in triumph, fleeing in terror and despair, or trudging obscurely, mechanically, up and down the hill.

All this I have seen. It has remained this way for centuries. It will remain this way for centuries to come. Nothing has changed very much; no one has lasted very long.

And now you come, clothed (apologies to my childhood friend Shakespeare) in a little brief authority; you tinker around like the rest of them; and you dream your dreams of putting me to use; and yet you are intelligent enough to know that you, too, are here only for a day, that you and all you stand for will soon be gone; but that I shall stand on, superior to those that created me, a monument to man's folly and inadequacy, a mockery of his endeavor.

I am perhaps particularly sensitive to this sort of poetic mumbling on the part of the old building, because so much, so agonizingly much, has changed and passed in the scant two years that I knew this place. It aches with memories. I arrived here, as I say, on the day of Munich. The Ambassador Hotel was crowded with international journalists. Prague was the center of the world. "Czechoslovakia"—would it stand or fall? I was put up here in the palace. That night the town was blacked out as no town has been blacked out before or since. It was silent as the tombs, over on this side of the river. We went for a walk, in the dusk, over the Charles Bridge, and had to talk quietly so that others didn't hear us speaking English.

The next morning the news [of the Munich Conference] had gotten about. An old market woman with a little stand and a big umbrella, just under my window, started in at six in the morning, delivering a bitter, plaintive oration. She kept it up until afternoon, with never a stop. For her the Republic was dead, then and there; and she was right. Her oration was the last word of the Czech people, before they were plunged back into silence and helplessness. In the morning, the loud-speakers dinned out the statement of the prime minister in the downtown streets; and the people stood weeping in a shopping passage in the center of town, where I was.

I lived on in the palace in those dark and fateful days. It was often so quiet that the silence rang in your ears. One night I found the old minister all alone in one of the vast living rooms, dozed off sitting upright on a stiff, formal settee, lost to the violent, jarring present, at one with the palace—and the centuries.

I cannot take a step in this place without wanting to laugh or cry. There, in the garden, the little white dresses of my children used to flash back and forth behind the lilac bushes on spring mornings. I could see them out of the office window. On this path I used to pace back and forth with the London *Times* correspondent deep in politics, debating issues long since settled, long since dead. Here is the bench where I often sat with the fat medical student who taught me Czech—always seating him downwind from me because he smelled so bad. Here in this windy entryway old dumb Jim, the *portier*, drunk or sober, used to let me in with the car night after night; and it was from here that the minister took his final departure, in the old Lincoln limousine, one rainy April morning, while the staff stood around and wept and knew it was the end of many things.

Wherever I go in the vicinity, it is no better. I may take a walk, as I did this morning. Here is the Wallenstein Palace: somber and magnificent. The man who built it, fearsome as he was to his contemporaries, travestied all the aspirations of Bohemian society. Born a Czech, he fleeced the Czech lands relentlessly and sold the proceeds to a German emperor for personal power. Born a Protestant, he conquered nearly all of Germany for Catholicism. Here in the garden of his palace, on a cool summer night during the German occupation, I once watched Czech actors playing old Czech fables. They did them excellently, with a studied, subtle formalism, as though they were acting in a dream; and in this detached, mechanical compliance with the formalities of the drama, they were teaching their people the real secret of self-preservation in the face of unsympathetic and unanswerable foreign rule.

Across the street is the Kolowrat Palace, the seat of the Czech government, where I watched a waiter carrying in steins of beer to the wrangling cabinet members on March 9, 1939, and failed to realize that the death-throes of a republic were at hand. Next door is the building that was the Polish legation, whose long-departed denizens were once so well informed on the passing intricacies of central European politics and now must be—if they are alive at all—drinking the dregs of a deeper and more bitter wisdom.

Beyond is another legation. Here there was a fine stuffed bird in the hall, which we always admired. Here we danced to a gramophone to the very wee hours of the morning. Here there was a minister with whom, notwithstanding the fact that we each flirted with the other's wife, I had a bond of mutual liking and respect, and whose family must also have been flung long since to the winds of ruin and separation by the war.

On up the hill; and on the left there is the strange little restaurant, clinging to the terraces of the cliff, where we drank beer on summer nights and stared out over the lights and roof-tops and bridges of a doomed city.

Through the courtyards of the Royal Castle. There, in one of those great ballrooms, the members of the diplomatic corps, assembled for the traditional New Year's reception, stood for the last time, green in the face from their hangovers, buttoned up tight in their braided, moth-ball-smelling uniforms, while the papal nuncio read his address and the new president made his rounds of greeting. The president, small in stature, made his rounds with dignity and deliberation, surveying his foreign guests with half-closed eyes, in which there was all the weariness of a small, misguided, and momentarily unsuccessful people.

On this square before the castle, the German tanks and motor vehicles were lined up on the morning of March 15, 1939. They were plastered white with the driving snow. Their hungry drivers beat blue hands against their thighs, to get the blood back in them, and muttered to the angry, weeping Czechs: "How can we help it?" *(Was können wir dafür?)*

Here, on this square, is another legation, where the unhappy minister and his American wife, unable to see anything but horror and retrogression in the events around them, brooded darkly through their own dinner parties, and saw in the Germans only the Anti-Christ incarnate. Below them lived a British secretary, who surveyed the world about him with a despairing, debonair amusement and spent his weekends visiting nobility in the country.

A few doors farther is the house where I went to comfort Alice Masaryk, in the days following the occupation, and found her washing the floors to keep her nerves in order.

And back again, down the hill, down our own street—the narrow, sloping street where we lived. Here is the building we lived in, and the cool, vaulted passageway to the courtyard with the baroque fountain, where the Czech army used to auction off its horses. Up those stairs, two flights of stairs, was our door; and beyond that there is no use my doing any more remembering. There is too much to remember, and it is all too close. For if it is sad and strange enough to think that all these other people should be scattered and gone, as though they had lived in the seventeenth century like Wallenstein; the goneness of a home is stranger still. And I am myself gone with it. I am no longer the same person who used to go up and down these stairs. The ghost of that person is somewhere up there still, together with the ghosts of all the other people who have lived there since the Thirty Years' War. It was only two years ago; but it was another time, another life. And now, we are all a little lonely. So much has died. . . .

I am afraid I am not very modern. I am afraid this would not do for the *New Yorker*. My world is neither very new nor very brave. I have no wise-cracks for Prague tonight. And it is probably just as well that it is already evening, and that my train goes in an hour, and that it is time to pack my bag and get out of this silent old building, where nobody lives anymore except little Frank, the caretaker, and Franzi, the handy-man, and where there are so many windows that we couldn't dream of closing all the blinds in deference to the blackout and consequently have had to run around at night with flashlights, through the cavernous rooms whose ceilings disappear in the gloom.

And if this letter reaches you before I do, you can put it down to war nerves, and show it no farther than to A. and C. and K., all of whom might view it with indulgence.

Yours,
George

The following is another passage from the documents published in FROM PRAGUE AFTER MUNICH; *but this one, in apposition to the entry for early October 1938, was written at the end, not the beginning, of my year of service there, several months after the German occupation of Prague and the remainder of Bohemia. Please note that the time of its writing was just a fortnight before the outbreak of the Second World War.*

Another summer is now drawing to an end—the unhappiest which this area has known since the days of the World War. It has been a strange summer, characterized by frequent and destructive electrical storms that damaged crops to the extent of hundreds of millions of crowns and seemed grimly symbolic of the rapidly alternating hopes and fears in the minds of the people. Work has gone on as usual. Even now the peasants are struggling—encouraged by the Germans and deterred by the frequent showers—to get in the harvest before the newest crisis reaches its culminating point. And the industries are busy enough trying to still the insatiable appetite of the Reich for their products. But all other manifestations of human activity seem afflicted by a strange lethargy, almost a paralysis. Everything is in suspense. No one takes initiative; no one plans for the future. Cultural life and amusements continue in a half-hearted, mechanical spirit. Theaters and public amusements attract only scanty and indifferent crowds. People prefer to sit through the summer evenings in the beer gardens or the little parks along the rivers, to bandy the innumerable rumors in which they themselves scarcely believe, and to wait with involuntary patience for the approach of something which none of them could quite describe but which they are all convinced must come and must affect all their lives profoundly. The near future should show whether this waiting attitude is the result of a sound instinct or whether it merely expresses the natural reluctance of a people which has just awakened from a twenty-year dream of independence to accept again the status of a nation of servants.

I had few opportunities to see anything of Nazi Germany in the years from 1933 down to 1939. The following glimpse was drawn from a brief passage through Hamburg, on a visit to London, three months before the war broke out, when I was still officially stationed in Prague.

By this time a second child, Joan Elizabeth, had been born and was now a lusty three-year-old.

JUNE 1939
HAMBURG, CUXHAVEN

On the train from Berlin to Hamburg, S. (the nurse) and Grace and I played impassioned games of Parchesi, and a German woman looked on in disgust because we neglected Joany.

The hotel in Hamburg being nearly empty, the director made a fuss over us and gave us a fine suite with windows looking out on the Alster. My friend, Charlie T.,* appeared while the children were being put to bed. We had whiskey and soda and gossiped eagerly while the shadows fell across the lake outside. And before Grace went to bed, I pulled her loose tooth out with my fingers.

C. took us out to eat. We drove up to the Uhlenhorster

---

*The reference is to the late Charles W. Thayer, formerly a foreign-service colleague at the American embassy in Moscow, later a well-known writer and humorist—a man of great charm and originality.

Fährhaus, arguing savagely about the character of our native land and the merits of its foreign policy, but were actually pleased in our hearts that we could still not be together a half an hour without starting to dispute in the good old Moscow fashion.

The Fährhaus terrace was packed with the nouveau riche of Nazidom. We had to take a table inside. There were fireworks over the lake, which we did not trouble to watch. Charlie got angry with the waiter because the strawberries failed to arrive. Two Italian Fascist dignitaries appeared, with square-trimmed black beards and magnificent white dress uniforms, being shown the town by local Nazi officials.

Hamburg seemed listless and empty as a city. It still went through all the motions of its ordinary activities, but the heart was gone out of it. It had lost its specific character and had become provincial, like Leningrad. It made me feel very old to think that it was twelve years since I had served there, and to realize how completely the things that I had known now belonged to the past.

JUNE 8, 1939

Saw the children and the nurse off at the station first thing in the morning. The two little faces beamed out of the train window at us, and Grace waved delightedly as the train pulled away. I was too harried and tired at the time to appreciate the full significance of this last separation. It was twelve hours later, and the sunset was fading across an impassive North Sea, when it hit me.

The boat-train left Hamburg at nine-thirty and droned along the flat meadows toward the sea. At Cuxhaven a burly Gestapo man studied our passports while two bored officials in black uniforms thumbed through the ominous volumes of the blacklist in a vain search for our names. It was a sad sailing—the saddest I have ever seen. A fresh wind was blowing out of the north, chilly and autumnal. Gulls wheeled overhead. The little port lay stretched out below us, dull and bored. The ship's band played bravely on the deck, but it was misplaced effort. There were only a handful of us passengers, and none of us smart; nor did our parting carry with it any hope of experience or adventure to warrant an accompaniment of martial music. Finally, the gangplank was taken in. The band played "Deutschland über Alles" and "Das Horst Wessel Lied," and we were off.

At the time of the outbreak of war in 1939, I was transferred from Prague to the embassy at Berlin, where I served as administrative officer until the advent of Pearl Harbor and the German declaration of war, in December 1941, at which time I, together with the remainder of the embassy staff, was taken into custody by the Germans.

There was very little travel during those years, and little time or surplus energy for the keeping of diaries. The following items, the first of them semi- (but only semi-) fictional, are all that have survived.

SOMETIME BETWEEN FEBRUARY
AND APRIL 1940
WARTIME GERMANY

The night train from Berlin to Munich stopped at Halle. It was eleven o'clock in the evening. The station was blacked out, the platform shrouded in obscurity.

The train was overfilled, as usual, and soldiers, staggering under their packs and equipment, struggled with the civilians to gain standing-room in the crowded corridors and vestibules of the cars. There was a clatter of voices, a scuffling of boots against the pavement, a panting of locomotives, and a scurrying of human forms in the darkness.

The international sleeping car which still bore, wars notwithstanding, the timeless inscription "Compagnie Interna-

tionale des Wagons-Lits et des Grands Express Européens."
It was sandwiched in at the head of the coaches. The porter
stood at the door of the car, looking down at the platform and
chewing an unlit cigarette stub. He was a wiry little southern
European, with big dark eyes and an unshaven, deeply lined
face. His crumpled uniform was open at the collar and there
were coffee stains across the breast. Standing there on guard
over the privacy of his privileged, sleeping patrons, he surveyed the scene below him—all this coming and going of the
hairless, colorless, sentimental denizens of the north—with a
vast Latin contempt.

A young woman pushed her way out of the packed crowd
on the vestibule of the adjoining car and clambered down the
steps to the ground. She was wearing a red blouse, a dark blue
skirt, and no hat. She took a long breath of air and adjusted
her hair. Seeing dimly that the porter wore a uniform and was
evidently in the possession of some sort of authority, she
addressed herself to him in a plaintive, coquettish tone:
"Can't you help me some way?" she asked. "Isn't there some
place I can find a seat, or at least a decent place to stand? I have
to be back at work in Innsbruck in the morning, and I can't
stand up in that crowd all night."

The porter measured her coldly from head to foot and
deliberated a moment. "Yes," he said in a low voice, "come
on up here." She climbed up to the platform and stood under
the pale blue light. She was apparently in her late twenties.
She had narrow-set eyes and a selfish, tight little mouth, and
there was written on her face something of the greed, the
pretense, and the narrowness of the lower-middle-class environment from which she came.

"But how about my baggage?" she asked.

"It'll be all right," said the porter, "you can go back and
look at it from time to time."

The train began to move, and pulled slowly away into the
blackness. They stood in the vestibule talking for a quarter of
an hour. She was pleased over this unexpected hospitality and

talked volubly to prolong and confirm her good fortune. Finally, the porter asked her to come into the car and sit down.

The deserted corridor of the sleeping-car was carpeted and curtained. The bright lights made her squint. In contrast to the third-class car next door, it seemed a haven of warmth, space, and luxury. At the farther end of the car the porter had a bench, covered with black imitation-leather upholstery, which could be let down into the corridor for him to sleep on; and beside it was a dirty little pantry with a wooden stool and a sink and barely room for a couple of people to stand.

First they sat on the bench, and the porter paid her elaborate compliments and told her off-color Italian stories in his broken German. She became flushed and laughed with her success and cleverness.

He took her hand and drew her into the little pantry. The air was hot. The walls of the car groaned and there was the unceasing beating of the wheels underneath. On the shelf two unwashed glasses danced and jangled together crazily from the vibration.

The porter put one arm around her and leered into her face. He had two gold teeth and an unpleasant breath. She drew back. Then she thought of the third-class car and of the people standing miserably in the corridor throughout the night.

"Aber nein," she said faintly, with a nervous giggle, "das geht doch nicht. Das sollten Sie eigentlich nicht machen." (But no . . . that won't do. You really shouldn't.)

The wheels beat on; the walls groaned; the two unwashed glasses kept up their constant jangle on the shelf.

At two o'clock in the morning the train was droning along through the blackness of Thuringia. The porter lay stretched out on his bench in the corridor, asleep. His mouth was open and his snoring was audible, faintly, above the din of the train. The woman sat at his feet, chin in hands, elbows on knees, staring gloomily down the empty corridor. She was very thirsty, and sullen with fatigue. Her skirt was soiled. She had left her comb with her baggage.

Suddenly, she got up, stepped into the pantry, seized one of the two jangling glasses and shoved it violently over to the other side of the shelf. Returning to the corridor, she sat down again on the bench and stared dully at the porter, whose lower lip trembled slightly with each exhalation. Then she put her head in her hands again and began to weep softly.

At five o'clock in the morning, daylight was sifting into the corridor through the chinks of the curtains. The train stopped for a long time at a station, and the sudden silence was oppressive. Two men in military uniforms, chattering tipsily in loud tones, burst into the car and walked through the corridor. They looked at her as they passed, and one of them said: "*Nu, nu*—just look what's here." But the woman stared gloomily past them and they moved on, laughing uproariously.

The train began to move again. The porter, who had been wakened by the interruption, slowly gathered in his legs and sat up. He sat there for a few minutes, scowling deeply and scratching in the thick black hair on the back of his head. Then he looked at his watch, got up, stretched, and disappeared down the corridor.

When he returned, she was still sitting on the end of the bench, but she had leaned over against the wall and had closed her eyes. He saw that there was no longer any room for him to put his feet.

He bent down and shook her by the shoulder until she opened her eyes. Then he grinned and said: "Now you must go back to the other car. You can't stay here any more. We are getting into Munich and the conductor will soon be coming through."

The woman stood up and gave him a look of unutterable hatred. Then, turning, she slowly made her way down the corridor, smoothing her crumpled skirt as she went, and disappeared through the door at the other end.

The porter stood smiling and watching her until she had disappeared. Then he lay down on his bench again and promptly went back to sleep.

In the pantry the misplaced glass, which had been dancing and joggling laboriously back across the shelf through the hours of the early morning, finally rejoined its fellow on the other side, and the two of them began to jangle happily together once again.

The German armies that swept over the Low Countries and northern France in June 1940 overran the American embassies in the capitals of the respective countries, cutting for a time all normal communications with the outside world. For some time neither Washington nor the Berlin embassy was able to establish telegraphic or telephonic communication with those missions or to find out what had happened to them and their personnel. But the German military authorities agreed to permit an officer of the Berlin embassy to proceed personally to the cities in question, by whatever transportation he could find, and to establish contact with the remaining American personnel. I was designated to perform this duty. Here: excerpts from my personal accounts, written at the time, of the visits to The Hague and to Paris. The reader should bear in mind that in both those places military operations had just barely ended. The German forces were still in strict military occupation of the areas they had overrun. There was scarcely any communication with the outside world.

Left Berlin shortly before one o'clock on the newly revived express train to The Hague. Prisoners, probably Polish, were working in the fields between Berlin and

Hanover. The sun beat hard on the flat, treeless fields, and the armed guards kept the prisoners lined up in neat, Germanic rows.

Beyond Hanover we began to encounter long trains of box-cars with fresh prisoners of war, presumably from this western front. The only openings for light and air were little apertures cut high up, near the ends of the cars, and through these one could see the crowded heads, the pale faces, and the bewildered eyes that stared, full of boredom and homesickness, out over the cold severity of the north German plain.

At the border two train-loads of SS, complete with motor vehicles, anti-aircraft guns, and field kitchens on flat cars, were waiting on a siding. Here, in contrast to the prisoners' cars, the sliding doors of the box-cars were thrown open; the soldiers, crowding the doorways, all looking very much alike, staring at our luxurious train, and devoured the newspapers and magazines that some of the passengers tossed to them.

There was little damage visible in Holland, at least in the district through which we passed. Now and then there was a burnt-out farmhouse or a gutted warehouse along the tracks. But everything had already been thoroughly cleaned up with true Dutch neatness, and the bridge across the Ijssel, blown up by the retreating Dutch, had already been repaired sufficiently by the Germans to permit our heavy train to crawl over it.

By the time we reached Deventer, it was dark, and the blinds had to be pulled in the cars to observe the laws of the black-out. I sat through the rest of the evening listening to a conversation between a smug Nazi businessman and a successful Dutch fifth-columnist. I had to grip the cushion of the first-class compartment to keep from butting in and attempting to blast some of the complacency and hypocrisy out of the conversation. The German, cold and pompous, merely re-echoed the *Völkischer Beobachter* editorials and was scarcely worth annoying. But the Dutchman, who had a keen, subtle intelligence and a fine command of language, put my reserve to a hard test. Professing understanding for National Socialist ideals, he told the German of Dutch tradition and of the bourgeois convervatism of the Netherlands and pointed out regretfully how hard it would be to train Dutch youth, who had only a small country to fall back on and no great conquests to look forward to, to be National Socialists.

The minister, who had heard of my approach over the radio from New York, met me at the station and took me to his home. There I bore the initial outburst of his fiery resentment (partially, but only partially, justified) at being left incommunicado for so long a time. I was then packed away, after several glasses of excellent champagne, into a comfortable bed and a slumber that lasted well into the next day.

JUNE 15, 1940
THE HAGUE

Rain—a misty English rain, smelling of spongy meadows and of the nearby sea—sifted down through the great lime trees onto the cobble-stone streets of The Hague.

In the afternoon I went for a long walk. The house-fronts of the town, prim and well proportioned, breathed Puritanism and a solid, unostentatious prosperity. The sense of formality was so overpowering that I could only envisage generations of guests arriving for tea and being scrutinized with chilly suspicion by the servants for their social qualifications. This was obviously a country where no grown-up who did not walk the primrose path could lay claim to warmth or forgiveness or tenderness. But civilization it was indeed.

I walked out to Scheveningen, getting thoroughly drenched in the process. A half a gale was blowing from the northwest. The great breakers were fighting their way in onto the sands in a melee of foam. The rain-swept boardwalk was deserted; and out at sea, in those mine-infested waters, no vessels moved.

The electric railway station was dark and empty. I was not sure at first that the trains were running. In the guard room a few German soldiers sat drinking beer, and an ugly waitress chucked one of them under the chin. On the train back to The Hague my only fellow passengers were four little Dutch school-children, who chattered cheerfully, impervious to the gray day, the rain-streaked windows, the deserted places, and all the ruin.

The train deposited us at a big station somewhere in the eastern part of the city. It took me nearly an hour to find the legation again. The search led through miles of sober streets, across bridges, along quiet canals, through shady little squares. I watched the sturdy, impassive, stubborn people trundling their bicycles and pushing their barges. Their fidelity to habit and tradition was so strong that it seemed as though nothing could ever change them. But try as I might, I could see little but ruin and decline ahead for most of them if Germany won the war. What could Germany give this country economically to replace her lost position as a center for the colonial empire or as a transit point for overseas trade? These provinces, like Norway and Denmark, lived largely off their overseas connections. They were Europe's windows to the outside world. But would a Europe dominated by Germany, confined to a continental, autarchic economic policy, deprived—at least in its northern sections—of all its colonial empires, a Europe which had killed the great economic vortex of England off its own coast—would such a Europe need much in the way of windows to the outside world? Rotterdam would remain as a transit harbor, yes. But that alone, together with the growing of some flowers and vegetables, would scarcely suffice to maintain the dense population and the high standard of living of these water-bound provinces.

One could only expect that to the spiritual misery attendant upon the destruction of a great culture and a great tradition there would be added the misery of foreign exploitation and economic decline, and that some day large parts of these

Dutch cities, sinking back into the swamps from which they had been so proudly and so competently erected, would become merely a curiosity for the edification of future generations of German tourists and would perhaps help to give the latter a sense of appreciation—tardy and helpless appreciation—for the values their forefathers had so lightheartedly destroyed.

JUNE 16, 1940
THE HAGUE

I took another long walk this morning, only to hear a German military band playing on a square to a sizable audience of placid, politely applauding Dutchmen, and to see a place, only a block or two from the legation, where bombs had wiped out most of the inside of a city block.

In the afternoon E. drove me around in his car. First we went over to a small nearby town, to see our consul at Rotterdam, who had had his office and home destroyed in the bombing and had taken taken temporary quarters there. We found him at home, and had drinks with him. The room was opened completely on one side, toward the garden. There the rain drizzled onto the rich grass and a little weed-covered canal, and everything was very Dutch and sad and peaceful. Across the canal, a stream of people passed on bicycles, and a beautiful copper beech shimmered in the rain.

From there we drove to Rotterdam. We came into town along a normal city street, with shops open, trams running, crowds of busy people on the sidewalks. Suddenly, with as little transition as though someone had performed the operation with a gigantic knife, the houses stopped and there began a wide open field of tumbled bricks and rubbish. Here and there a wall or even the gutted framework of a house remained, but in most places there was only a gray plain of devastation. The main streets leading through this great ruined area were left untouched. Trams and motor-cars ran on them as usual, and the unfathomable Dutch wheeled along on their bicycles as though nothing unusual had occurred. At one of the main corners of the city, traffic was still fairly thick, but not a building was left standing anywhere near. The impression gained was that it was a crossing out somewhere in the country, between fields that had been used as dumping grounds for debris and refuse.

Most striking of all, apart from the ghastly scope of the destruction (the number of houses destroyed must have run into thousands) was the utter absence of transitions. Where bombs had not fallen, everything seemed in perfect order. Where they had fallen, there was simply nothing left at all. I saw a shop doing business and people living in a house on one side of which there was a perfectly normal city scene and on the other side of which, beginning right at the side of the house, there stretched nothing but a desert of bleached, smoking debris as far as the eye could see. . . .

We drove back along the broad highway from Rotterdam to The Hague, where the German transport planes had landed on that first morning of the invasion. The hedges were damaged in many spots where the big machines had swung off the road to check their momentum. At the entrance to the airport near The Hague, a crowd of people were leaning on their bicycles and staring through the fence at some smoldering debris beside the gutted administration building. We too stopped to look, but an infuriated air force lieutenant screamed at the sentry to make the Americans move on, and we obediently took our departure.

JUNE 17, 1940

Got up early in the morning, to take a six o'clock train back to Berlin. The five-hour trip across occupied Holland, in the dead hours of Sunday morning, was very dull indeed. It was still raining; the towns were empty; one had a feeling of the world's being forsaken by everyone but the cows. I read the German paper, pondered gloomily the propaganda patter about the "senseless resistance" of the Dutch, and reflected that if there were anything in this war that had made any sense to me at all, it was the resistance that had produced the ruins of Rotterdam.

JULY 2, 1940
BRUSSELS–PARIS

This morning, since offers of free rides were still not forthcoming from the Germans, B. offered me one of his cars, together with the requisite quantity of gasoline; and at exactly 2 P.M. I set forth from his country place near Waterloo in a little Chevrolet bound for Paris. I had with me one of the American ambulance drivers, who was trying to get down to Paris to recover his clothes. Warned that the intervening country had been reduced by the fighting to a state of desolation which made it as uncharitable to travellers as a desert, we were armed with a bottle of drinking-water and some chocolate, to keep us alive in case we broke down on the way.

The devastation, especially south of the old Belgian frontier, was indeed formidable. All the towns were damaged; and certain large ones, particularly Valenciennes and Cambrai, were completely gutted, deserted, and uninhabitable. Here the road led through streets where the house facades were standing on both sides; but back of the facades, visible through the gaping, pane-less windows, there was wreckage and ashes and debris. In spots the odor of decomposing corpses still stole out to the streets to tell its grim message to the outside world. These communities seemed to have been entirely vacated, probably at the insistence of the military authorities, by any inhabitants who might have escaped destruction in the bombardment. They were shut off and guarded by German sentries, probably to prevent pillaging; and it affected me strangely to see these inscrutable, weather-beaten German sentries, standing guard there over their own handiwork of destruction. As though it mattered now who stood before these shattered homes and these stinking corpses! As though this tangled litter of half-destroyed human belongings had any more value when life and hope had already been destroyed!

Refugees were laboriously making their way back northwards, in search of their homes. Most were travelling on the great two-wheeled horse-drawn cart of the French peasant, which could accommodate a whole family and many of its belongings. Some were on bicycles. Some pushed baby buggies with a few parcels of belongings on them. Their faces were unforgettable, stripped of all pretense, of all falseness, of all vanity, of all self-consciousness, seared with fatigue and fear and suffering.

I saw a young girl bouncing along on top of one of the carts. Her dress was torn and soiled. She had probably not had her clothes off, or been able to wash, for days. She was resting her chin in her hand and staring fixedly down at the road. All the youth had gone out of her face. There was only a bitterness too deep for complaint, a wondering too intense for questions. What would be her reaction to life after this? Just try to tell her of liberalism and democracy, of progress, of ideals, of tradition, of romantic love; see how far you get. What is going to be her impression of humanity? Do you think she's going to come out of it a flaming little patriot? She saw the complete moral breakdown and degradation of her own people. She saw them fight with each other and stumble over each other in their blind stampede to get away and to save their possessions before the advancing Germans. She saw her own soldiers, routed, demoralized, trying to push their way back through the streams of refugees on the highways. She saw her own people pillaging and looting in a veritable orgy of dissolution as they fled before the advancing enemy; possibly she had joined in the looting herself. She saw these French people in all the ugliness of panic, defeat, and demoralization.

The Germans, on the other hand, she saw as disciplined, successful, self-confident. Their soldiers were sun-tanned, fit and good-humored. She saw them giving food and water to refugees at the crossroads, establishing camps and first-aid stations, transporting the old and the sick in their great Diesel trucks and trailers, guarding against pillaging. What soil here for German propaganda, what thorough ploughing for the social revolution which National Socialism carries in its train.

As we approached Senlis, we went through a section where the road was lined for miles with litter abandoned by the French. It seemed to be mostly paper and clothing. Almost every inch of the ground was covered with it. I could explain the paper, which consisted largely of empty cartridge boxes. The clothing remains a mystery to this time, unless it was taken off of the dead and wounded.

At one place we saw a field where the Germans had corralled hundreds of stray or abandoned horses. They had some Allied prisoners, mounted, guarding them.

In the suburbs of Paris there were a few people; but the streets looked no less normal than those of Brussels. As we drove down the rue Lafayette, the passers-by became fewer and fewer. By the time we reached the Opéra, the streets were practically empty. The city was simply dead. Policemen stood listlessly on the corners, but there was no traffic to direct and no pedestrians to guard. At the Café de la Paix six German officers sat at an outside table. They looked lonely sitting there with the empty café behind them and the empty cold street before them—no passers-by to watch; no other guests to support them; no one but themselves to witness their triumph.

The Place de la Concorde was as dead as a village square at dawn on a rainy Sunday. There was no flag or shield on the American embassy. The big iron gate was closed. I went to the side door and rang. A night watchman, who viewed me with some suspicion, told me that the ambassador and Murphy (his deputy) had left for Clermont, where the new French government was. He helped me to get through a telephone call to B., who was in charge. B. asked me to come over for supper.

I dropped my ambulance driver and my baggage at the Hotel Bristol. This building had been appropriated as a place of refuge for the remaining Americans. Much of the hotel personnel was missing; the whole place had a make-shift atmosphere; but the Americans had succeeded in keeping the Germans out and were pleased enough with the arrangement.

B.'s home was in the Étoile district. The streets around there gave the impression of an abandoned city. Houses were boarded up. The stillness was oppressive. Across from B.'s house the German army had occupied a building; and while we talked in his living room, we could hear the clatter of sentry boots against the pavement, echoing among the houses.

It was after the ten o'clock curfew when I drove the car to the embassy and then walked back through the totally deserted streets to the hotel. The sad Paris policemen and the German sentries stared at the unaccustomed sight of a pedestrian and were too surprised to remonstrate. The individual at the desk in the Bristol was no less amazed to have anyone demanding entrance at that unseasonable hour, and he unbolted his doors with all the ceremony of one opening a besieged citadel.

At the hotel the ambulance driver and I, feeling much too near to the end of the world to think of sleep, cracked out a bottle of rye. We were joined by our next-door neighbor, female and no longer entirely young. She was a true product of Parisian America and was accepting her privations with such excellent good humor that she kept us in gales of laughter with the account of her experiences.

JULY 3, 1940
PARIS

Spent the morning driving around town looking up friends of friends, none of whom were there. I wondered about the reactions of the Germans. I saw their officers in the restaurants, trying so desperately to be genteel when there was nobody to be genteel before. I heard that Goebbels was at the Ritz and thought how different that forsaken square, the Place Vendôme, must have seemed from the glamour and luxury of that place as he had pictured it. I was told that the Germans were making efforts to reopen the Casino de Paris for the benefit of their troops, but couldn't do so because all the British girls were gone and the French girls, if any could be found, were too individualistic to keep time in a chorus.

I struggled all day to find a metaphor for what had happened. Could one not say to the Germans that the spirit of Paris had been too delicate and shy a thing to stand their domination and had melted away before them just as they thought to have it in their grasp? Was there not some Greek myth about the man who tried to ravish the goddess, only to have her turn to stone when he touched her? That is literally what has happened to Paris. When the Germans came, the soul simply went out of it; and what is left is only stone. So long as they stay (and it will probably be a long time) it will remain stone. Their arrival turned the walls of a living city into the cold stones of historical monuments. And the beauties of the city had already, after a fortnight's disassociation from their own soul, begun to look faintly shabby, useless, and fantastic, like Versailles or Fontainebleau—as though they expected at any moment to be roped off and placarded and shown to tourists by guides for the rest of time.

In short, the Germans had in their embrace the pallid corpse of Paris. They will now perhaps deceive themselves into believing that the city never had a soul. That will be the most comforting conclusion for them to draw.

There follows an excerpt from a letter written to my wife from Berlin, shortly before Pearl Harbor and my own internment by the Germans.

OCTOBER 21, 1941
BERLIN

In general, life in Berlin has been much as you knew it. The major change has been the wearing of the stars by the Jews. That is a fantastically barbaric thing. I shall never forget the faces of people in the subway with the great yellow star sewed onto their overcoats, standing, not daring to sit down or to brush against anybody, staring straight ahead of them with eyes like terrified beasts—nor the sight of little children running around with those badges sewn on them. As far as I could see, the mass of the public was shocked and troubled by the measure, and such demonstrations as were provoked were mostly ones of friendliness and consideration (for the victims). Probably as a result of this fact, the remaining Jews are now being deported in large batches, and very few more stars are to be seen.

With my love to all of you,
George

In 1944, having served in 1942 and 1943 in Portugal, and then in early 1944 in London, I was reassigned as Averell Harriman's deputy in Moscow. The war being still in progress in Europe and the Far East, the only way of proceeding to Moscow at that time was via North Africa, the Near East, and Iran.

These diary notes pick up the account of the journey from Lisbon, where my wife and children were still living, and which I visited on my way from London to Moscow. From Lisbon I took my final departure, via Gibraltar, Algiers, Naples, Cairo, Baghdad, and Tehran, to Moscow. Here: the excerpts from my notes on that journey.

JUNE 15, 1944

Departure from Portugal. Took my baggage down to the airline office about noon. Annelise and I sat in an outdoor café on the Avenida for an hour and watched the curious sights of that locality: the peroxide blondes of Portugal, the women with dark underwear beneath light summer dresses, the emaciated horses pulling the heavy two-wheeled carts, the pawing cordiality of the men who met each other in the cafés. Then we drove out to the airport. At two o'clock we said one more of those tearing wartime good-byes that have now come to be so familiar.

A bored King's Messenger and myself rode in solitary state

to Gibraltar, in company only with a load of freight. The Alentejo and Algarve, revolving slowly beneath us as if on a giant globe, looked parched and barren in the baking afternoon sunshine. Later in the afternoon, after the stop in Gibraltar, I was dispatched to Algiers on a British military-observation plane, flying an operational mission over the western Mediterranean. I sat proudly side by side with the pilot, contemplated the whitecaps on the blue waters of the Mediterranean far below, and could not have been more pleased.

I was met by American colleagues at the airport and driven into Algiers. The vegetation and countryside seemed much like Portugal, but the French signs filled my heart with warmth; and the sea had a smell all its own, a keen pungent smell, different from the chilly freshness of the ocean off Portugal.

JUNE 16, 1944

Flight to Naples, in a military transport plane with bucket seats. The weather was perfect. The mountains of the Algerian and Tunisian coasts looked tranquil and deserted. Even Naples, basking in the hot June sunshine, had recovered something of the everyday boredom that is peace. To one travelling through these parts, the marvel is not the destruction that has been wrought, but rather the revelation of how swiftly the waves of war can pass over a countryside and recede, and how much, after all, *can* survive them.

Had lunch with Alexander Kirk and other colleagues, M. and O., in the big villa overlooking the bay, where Kirk has his office and residence.* After lunch I walked in the garden,

---

*Alexander Kirk, older career officer in the foreign service, had only recently been our chargé d'affaires (and my boss) at Berlin. He was now serving as a political advisor to the Allied commander-in-chief in Italy.

curious to see what an Italian garden might look like. A profusion of tiny lizards scuttled back and forth across the paths before me. The sun beat hard—but not too hard—on the high grape arbors. Sheaves of fresh-cut wheat, crisp and rich in color, lay stacked in the center of a tiny grainfield, lined with young fruit trees. A drowsy watch-dog, disturbed in his siesta, barked dutifully but good-naturedly at me, as I passed, and then, reflecting that I showed no signs of guilty conscience, dozed off again in classic repose. Below me stretched the great bay, the ships, the tall white house fronts of the city, the generous slopes of the surrounding hills; and there was no disputing the calm, graceful majesty of the place.

Later in the afternoon, I drove around at length with M. and O. in the city. It was not yet a pleasant sight. People looked reasonably well-fed, but ragged and dirty. The worst of their hardships, to me, seemed the complete lack of transportation. Once I saw a train of three incredibly dirty and battered tram cars, crawling along a street on the outskirts; and at one point an American Red Cross bus seemed to be moving civilians. Otherwise, there appeared to be no public transportation whatsoever; and the collection of ancient horse-drawn vehicles which had been pressed into service was ludicrous and pitiful.

JUNE 19, 1944

Up at the crack of dawn and off to the airport for one of the most unpleasant days of travel I have ever experienced. Bucket seats all the long, long day, in a partially blacked-out plane where it was impossible to sleep and only barely possible to read. At the stop in Malta I could get no refreshment because the British military canteen would not take dollars. Hungry and already tired, I got out of the plane in the early afternoon at Benghazi, to be met by the worst heat I have ever experienced. It was like the breath of a furnace. The atmosphere was blurred and vibrant with heat; and off across the desert there was a mirage of the sea. All afternoon the plane droned on across the Cyrenaica and the Western Desert. Hellfire Pass moved slowly beneath us, deserted and still in the afternoon glare, only a ridge of rock and sand, the signs of all the recent struggle and suffering already swallowed up in the unconquerable insistence of the desert—like the sea—on its own tremendous, boundless uniformity. At El Alamein, there were still the remains of trenches and gun emplacements, but another year or two will finish them as well.

It was already evening and getting dark when we reached the Egyptian airport of our destination. Crowded into the back of a truck, we bounced along for another hour and a half in the darkness, the diffused glow of the desert sunset filling the sky behind us. At ten o'clock at night I found myself, more dead than alive, by no fault of my own—simply by the absurdities of wartime travel—standing disconsolately in the lobby of Shepheard's Hotel. They had no room for me. I had no Egyptian money. They would change neither my dollars nor my pounds. There was no one at the legation who seemed to be able to make sense on the telephone. And the porter who had carried my bags in stood looking at me impatiently, waiting for the tip that I couldn't give him. It was a bad moment.

JUNE 20–21, 1944
CAIRO

These two days were too alike to describe separately. Egypt, that triangle of irrigated desert around the delta of a polluted stream, was suffering from a heat wave. The hot breath of the Sahara enveloped the miles and miles of brown plaster walls. The mud flats on the outskirts steamed and stunk under the fiery African sky. In the streets of the foreign quarter the glare lay, white and burning, between the blank concrete walls of the villas. People barricaded themselves in their houses against the heat; and limousines were parked in shady basement garages, lest they become too hot to sit in.

In the evening of the first day, when the sun had begun to set and the sky had cooled, the heat could be felt rising back like steam from the baked earth. Elderly Britishers, groggy from their siesta, sauntered out for the usual game of golf. Itinerant Arabs, who had lain stretched out in the shade of a wall on the pavement through the heat of the day, arose, shook some of the dirt out of their robes, and began to beat their torpid donkeys into a resumption of the interminable trek from nowhere to nowhere. Jeeps and command cars, coming down the road from the pyramids, passed a string of dromedaries plodding slowly, patiently, up the timeless hill to the timeless desert. In the Hotel Mena the doors were thrown open to the terraces. The bar began to serve drinks outside. In the music room, surrounded by elaborate Moorish gratings, the pale-faced Polish refugee woman with a dog played Chopin on the piano, and a lone rat, sick and confused with the heat, ducked miserably around on the tiled floor, among the potted palms, searching for the exit to the darkness and freshness of the garden.

On the evening of the second day the great heat ended in a sandstorm. Dry clouds rolled and turned as they swept across the city. The wind whistled in the shutters of the hotel as if in a ship at sea; and there was a steady hissing as the blown sand hit the walls and windows of the building. The palm trees of the garden tossed and moaned, their long branches clattering wildly, under the scourging by the wind. The guests sat in the lounge with the shutters closed and the electric lights on and listened, like people snow-bound in a blizzard, to the howling of the wind outside.

During the night the wind died down. At dawn, when I got up to go to the airport, it had become cool. A clean, fresh air lay over the sleeping city. But the sun was rising, great and ominous, on the cloudless sky; and it would not be long, I knew, before the heat and corruption of the day would descend once more upon the fertile, sinister land.

JUNE 22, 1944
CAIRO—BAGHDAD

Set off at 7:30 A.M. for Baghdad in an enormous old land plane of Imperial Airways. As far as Palestine, where we landed to refuel, things were smooth. From Palestine to Baghdad, across the desert, it was bumpy and cold. Emerged suddenly at Baghdad into a temperature of 110 degrees in the shade, and far more in the blazing sunshine of the airport.

L. met me and took me to the legation: a modern building with rooms of almost cavernous dimensions, provided with air-conditioning equipment which doesn't work, a swimming pool which, at the moment, cannot be filled, and bathrooms in which the water rarely runs.

JUNE 23—25, 1944
BAGHDAD

The chief impression of Baghdad in the summer, as carried away from those three days there, was one of claustrophobia. All day we were barricaded in the legation (where the temperature never fell below ninety degrees) by the much fiercer heat outside. We might look out the windows (as one looks out the windows in zero weather in the north) and see the burning dusty wind tearing at the eucalyptus trees, and the flat, bleached country enveloped in the colorless sunshine of the desert, a sunshine with no nuances, no shades, no shadows, a sunshine which does not even brown the skin, but only strikes and penetrates and dissolves with its unbending hostile power. Into this inferno of heat only "mad dogs and Englishmen," as Noel Coward used to sing, could dream of venturing. At night it cooled off considerably, and we slept in reasonable comfort on the roof. But by this time the real mad dogs and the jackals had come in from the desert, and it was not safe to walk in the outlying district where the legation was situated. The only tolerable time of day, when it would have been possible to break out of the prison walls, was the early morning.

The dryness of the heat was nerve-wracking. One had to keep drinking water from morning to night, and even then the kidneys had a tendency to cease working entirely.

In general, it was possible to keep healthy only by a very strict and scientifically conceived discipline and routine of private life.

So much for the handicaps; what of the possibilities of service in Baghdad? A country in which man's selfishness and indifference have ruined almost all natural productivity, where vegetation can survive only along the banks of the great rivers which traverse its deserts, where climate has become unfavorable to human health and vigor.

A population unhygienic in its habits, sorely weakened and debilitated by disease, inclined to all manner of religious bigotry and fanaticism, condemned by the tenets of the most wide-spread faith to keep a full half of the population—namely, the feminine half—confined and excluded from the productive efforts of society by a system of indefinite house arrest, deeply affected—and bound to be affected—by the psychological habits of a one-time pastoral life, which has ever been at variance with agricultural and industrial civilization—what, one wonders, is to become of it?

JUNE 28, 1944
TEHRAN

On Monday, June 26, I left Baghdad in a Lockheed plane operated by the British and flew to Tehran. The country seemed to consist of high, barren mountain ridges, running from northwest to southeast, enclosing long straight valleys with fertile soil irrigated by the mountain streams.

At Tehran an officer of the legation met me, a lugubrious gentleman who declared himself ill and answered all questions about Persia either in tones of black despair or with a mysterious evasiveness which was evidently somehow intended to have dire implications. He was very kind, however, loaned me money, and fixed me up with a room in a dirty and noisy hotel. At night an orchestra played in the garden, and the cars came and went with officers and officials of at least four different nationalities.

Out for a walk in the evening, I was surprised to find myself in a city that seemed, after all, very Russian. In the straight cobbled street, the high fences, the Russian signs, the crowds strolling in the evening darkness, and the cosmopolitan babble of tongues, I could even sense the familiar breath of summer evenings years ago, in distant Reval. It was impressive to think of these two capitals, so far apart and yet so near, bound together by that vast fluid influence which is Russia.

JULY 1, 1944
TEHRAN–MOSCOW

We arrived at the Russian airport at 5 A.M. There we waited nearly an hour before taking off. A horse, saddled but halterless, with an officer's sword tossing and clattering by the saddle, had gotten loose on the airfield and was capering about among the big parked planes. After the horse had been corralled by twenty or thirty of the airport officials to the accompaniment of great shouting and laughter, a Russian lieutenant, scheduled to leave with our plane, was missing. He was apparently some sort of a courier. A jeep was finally sent for him; and he arrived shortly, pale with fright over this dereliction, stammering in confusion that it was "the first time."

We flew first to Baku, over the mountains and the sea. Then we flew direct to Stalingrad: over the sea as far as Makhachkala, then overland. That leg of the trip was a rather desolate one, especially the one or two hundred miles of country north of Makhachkala, which appeared to consist chiefly of salt marshes.

At Stalingrad everything except the airport building

(which they were still working on) appeared to have been destroyed. Near the airfield there were dumping grounds of wrecked planes and tanks. There was an air of busy reconstruction about the airport building. Lunch was served in a little "stolovaya" where they had only one glass, and chairs were a little scarce; but everyone was good-natured and helpful about it. How deeply one sympathizes with the Russians when one encounters the realities of the lives of the people and not the propagandistic pretensions of their government.

On the entire four-and-a-half-hour trip from Stalingrad to Moscow, across the black-earth district, I sat glued to the window, moved and fascinated to see before me again this great, fertile, mysterious country which I had spent so many years trying to understand.

In Moscow I was met and driven to Spaso House, and with that—a new life began.

Back in Moscow I resumed, as far as I could, my old habit of
quiet expeditions into the countryside on Sundays and holidays.
Here: the account of one of them.

It was a fine July morning: Moscow summer weather at its
best. I started off bright and early, to seek out and sketch
one of the two remaining churches in the Moscow Oblast
(beside the Cathedral of St. Basil on Red Square) supposed to
date from before the time of Ivan the Terrible.

The sun rises early at this time of the year in Moscow. As
I walked over to the subway, it was already flooding into the
cobbled streets and bathing the peeling facades of the shabby
old houses that were once the homes of Moscow's upper class
and today—despite all the crowding and deterioration—still
retain the charm of all Russian architecture of the Empire
period.

From the subway exit near the Bryansk Station crowds of
people, many bearing primitive hoes and other strange imple-
ments, emerged onto the vast asphalted void before the station; blinked to adjust themselves to the glare of sunshine;
made out in the distance, across the square, the suburban
ticket windows; and broke into a competitive hundred-yard
dash towards this first objective. Frantic crowds were already
milling and pushing around at the ticket windows, and the
new arrivals threw themselves into the contest with savagery
and enthusiasm.

The suburban train was waiting at the platform. Although the locomotive had not yet been attached, every seat was taken, every aisle was full, every outdoor platform was packed, every bumper had its occupant. Even the steps of the platforms were covered with clusters of clinging humanity. Late-comers, myself included, scurried desperately up and down the platform, searching for a toe-hold somewhere on the long string of cars.

I finally found a step, a bottom step, which seemed to have room for one more single foot, and hopped onto it. A young girl, observing my success, immediately jumped up behind me and threw both arms around me to clutch the guard rail. Hanging widely out over the platform, she shouted triumphantly to an invisible companion down the platform: "Sonya, Sonya, I have found a seat!"

We waited. The locomotive was finally brought up and attached. The scrambling of the late-comers up and down the platform took on a frantic and tragic air. The locomotive whistled. A flock of ragged little boys, with burlap sacks slung over their shoulders in true hobo fashion, suddenly climbed across the adjacent empty platform under the nose of the armed guard, and, just as the train began to move, settled themselves, with contemptuous professional ease, on the brake-beams. We were off.

Slowly, almost silently, the long heavy train pulled up the grades on the farther side of the Moscow River. The skirt of the girl behind me flicked each of the switches and signal towers as we went past, but she failed to notice it and continued to beam triumphantly at the invisible Sonya, who had apparently found a similar "seat" farther down the line. Beyond the right-of-way there were endless victory gardens, chiefly of potatoes. All over the countryside you could see the backs of the women working in the fields, tilling the potatoes with their great square hoes. At one spot we passed tank-traps and trenches. Here the Russians had evidently planned to defend the railroad against the advancing Germans in 1941.

The sky was an incredibly deep blue and was lined in the distance with the rich white clouds of the Russian plain. Here and there, a poplar stood up among the fields, leaves trembling in the breeze; and off on the horizon there was always the cold, dark line of the evergreen forests.

On the crowded platform of our car, conversation was buzzing. I could hear only snatches of it. Someone had read in the morning paper the new decree about marriage and divorce, and the promise of premiums for large families was giving rise to a series of hilarious comments among the women. Just above me, a peasant girl was relating her own sufferings and those of her native village at the hands of the Germans. The tale began with the hiding of a barrel of honey and ended with the demise of her husband and her relatives. I could hear the conclusion, flung out to the sympathetic audience with all the throaty eloquence of the Russian tongue: "Who has need of me now? To whom am I now necessary?"

I tried to turn around and climb up a step, in the hopes of hearing more of these discussions. But an old peasant woman above me descended upon me with virulence: "What's the matter with you anyway, Comrade?" she shouted. "Such vulgarity. After all. That's the tenth time you've jostled me. And you with the outward appearance of a cultured man." There did not seem to be any suitable answer to this, so I stayed on my step until my station was reached.

The tower of the church could be seen from the station. I made my way to it without difficulty. The old structure stood in a little patch of woods, surrounded by suburban bungalows. Paths ran criss-cross, here and there, through the woods, sustaining a steady stream of Sunday strollers. A service was going on in the church. The drone of the choir floated out onto the sunny outdoors and mingled there with the hum of insects, the conversational voices on the paths, the sound of the breeze in the tree-tops. It was not the best church singing, but it was correct and forthright. I wondered who, in the motley population of this suburban district, had taken the trouble to learn the long variations—some beautiful, some tedious—of the traditional chants.

I sat down on a knoll and spent an hour or two sketching. Except for the trees, which forced me to sketch at an exact forty-five-degree angle, the church would have been a good subject. I have a feeling that the date of its origin was a little later than Ivan the Terrible, but it was a venerable and worthy old-timer, whatever its date.

The service was a long one. It was over just as I finished sketching. The congregation, mostly old women, emerged, babbling, and dispersed. An old beggar woman and two women with children remained on the stone porch. Then the priest, in high boots and what looked to be a new blue robe, came out the side door, locked it after him, walked around the church, chased the women off the porch, and stamped jerkily away, shaking his wispy gray beard in ill temper, complaining in a low mutter that he had nothing to eat.

I went back to the station, to get information about trains and to find something to drink. A train going back to town was apparently almost due. There was a little hut where they were selling mineral water and kvass; but you had to have your own receptacle to take it away, so I gave up.

People were already collecting on the platform for the expected train. At the end of the platform, on the cinder path, a blind woman was sitting, an old blind beggar woman. She sat patiently, intoning an endless song about the origins and trials of her affliction, singing the words like a priest in her high feeble voice. When some one put a ruble in her hand, she would start up, fumble for her little bag, put the ruble in, and then insert into her song a few words of appreciation, repeated several times for good measure: "Thank you, my nice one, my own one; thank you, my good provider. May the Lord grant you a great health." Then she would return to the complaints and reminiscences.

I decided that it was too early to go back to town, and

walked away. As I crossed the track, I could still hear the droning, cackling little voice: "I do not see the great white light; I do not see the light of God."

Near the church there was a little brick house, in old Russian style. It had a brick wall around it, and corner towers on the wall, as though in imitation of an old Kremlin. It was all very run-down. The tiny yard enclosed by the fence was high with weeds.

A soldier with only one leg was standing at the door, on crutches. I asked him what the house was. A woman in a white dress, carrying a shopping net in one hand, came up at that moment and interrupted. "He wouldn't know," she said, "it's old, the house. It's from the time of Ivan the Terrible. It used to belong to some boyar. We live in it. Would you like to see the inside?"

I followed her up the dark, winding staircase, into an upstairs room. A man was sitting there at a table, doing nothing. She introduced him as her husband. He, too, was lame, and had the undefinable look of a veteran, bored and bewildered with the humdrum of civilian life after all the adventure and comradeship of the front. The room was divided in the middle by a big cupboard. I had the impression that behind the cupboard was somebody else's apartment. The part of the room we sat in, being bedroom, living room, dining room, and bathroom combined, was crowded with objects and had the air of a storehouse. The profusion was such that all thought of attractive arrangement had been abandoned. The walls were thick. The window arches had a curious naive shape. I began to believe that they might really be old, although I still suspected the little Kremlin wall outside as being a product of the well-known passion of our grandfathers' generation for miniature.

How did she like living in a boyar's house, I asked. It was damp, my hostess said, pointing to big blotches of moisture on the ceiling. Besides, the stove didn't work. It was a calamity, that stove.

I looked with respect at the little tile and brick structure in the corner. Its antiquity seemed unchallengeable, its inadequacy scarcely to be doubted.

Did she know anything more about the house?

No, not much. It had once belonged to the church. Both buildings had originally been part of the boyar's estate. There had been a big manor house "right over there," built at a later date; and before the First World War ("in the peaceful time") it had housed a historical museum. But it had burned down, and now no one remembered much about it. Was I an artist? She had seen me sketching the church. No, I was not an artist. I showed them, in proof, my sketchbook and took my leave.

I set off to the north: along a lane, through a woods, down into a ravine, across a stream, and up the other side. Somewhere in the woods a woman was singing in a clear strong voice, a voice that you would never hear anywhere but in Russia. On the other side of the ravine two women were working in a small potato field, and a man was lying on his back in the grass and watching them. The women had broad faces, brown muscular arms, and the powerful maternal thighs of the female Slav. They laughed and joked as they worked; and it was clear that they enjoyed the feeling of the sun on their bodies and the dark earth, cool and sandy, under their bare feet. I asked them the way to the Minsk railway. After they had told me, they turned again and bent to their work with all the easy, unhurried strength of their people.

*In June 1945 the Soviet authorities permitted me, then still
serving as the number two at the American embassy in Moscow,
to visit the leading city of central Siberia, Novosibirsk, and the
major metallurgical center of Kuznetsk, near the Siberian-Chi-
nese border.*

The following are excerpts from my diary account of this trip.

L eft Moscow on Saturday, June 9, at 3 P.M., on the Trans-
Siberian express. The train, pulled for the first hour or
so by an electric locomotive, moved briskly through the Moscow suburbs; more briskly, indeed, than it was destined to
move in general on its long journey to Vladivostok. The barracks, factories, dachas, swamps, and birch groves streamed
steadily past the window. Within little more than an hour we
were stopping at Zagorsk and suffering the first of those inva-
sions of women and children selling food which were to beset
us at every station for four days and nights. Bare-footed or
beslippered, but always with clean scarves on their heads,
looking exactly the same at one station as at another, they
came bearing their offerings: milk—fresh, boiled, or curdled;
cottage cheese; cream; eggs—raw or hard-boiled; radishes;
berries; pancakes; boiled potatoes; onions; garlic; pickled car-
rots; in Siberia, butter. Some of them traded at wooden stands
set back a bit from the tracks; but most of them did business

at trainside. There, on the black cinder-track, hard-trodden and greasy with the oil and the droppings from the trains, under the feet of the milling crowds of passengers, train personnel, and station hangers-on, without regard for the clouds of soot and dust, a thriving business was done; milk was cheerfully poured from old jugs into empty vodka flasks or army canteens; greasy cakes were fingered tentatively by hands black with train soot; arguments ran their course; bargains were struck; passengers pushed their way triumphantly back to the cars, clutching their acquisitions; and timid little girls with bare feet, who had not succeeded in selling their offerings, stood by in sad but tearless patience, awaiting with all the stoicism of their race the maternal wrath which would await them when the train had gone and they would return home with their tidbits unsold.

There was little bickering. Where it occurred, it was generally over quantity, not price. In view of the great variety of receptacles used by buyers and sellers (each had to supply his own), there was considerable vagueness, and sometimes disagreement, over quantities. Strong words were passed; but they were passed, for the most part, with humor and good nature. I witnessed one scene where a soldier, surrounded by a sympathetic crowd of on-lookers, accused an old peasant woman of tricking him over a purchase of milk. "You'd better be careful, little mother," he said gaily, "not to run across me in the other world. The archangels are all my friends." To the crowd's delight, the old girl crossed herself anxiously, and the incident ended in general laughter.

About ten o'clock on the first night out, we crossed the Volga, near Yaroslavl. Seen from the railroad bridge, the great stream stretched off majestically, black and mirror-like, in the northern summer twilight. Somewhere down-stream the lights of a river boat and their reflections moved slowly on the dark surface.

◆ ◆ ◆

The next day, Sunday, found us passing through a poor forest country, like northern Wisconsin. Most of the land visible from the train window was cut-over or burned-over forest. The scrub second growth seemed to consist mostly of birch, ash, alder, and evergreen. There were many swamps. Villages were rare and poor. Except in the swamps, the earth was dry and sandy. There were few cows and only occasional goats. The villages were without churches or stone buildings of any sort. The log cabins, however, as at all points from there east, appeared to be better and more substantially built than around Moscow.

After passing Gostovskaya (770 kilometers from Moscow) there was a change and the country again became more prosperous.

In the late afternoon we stopped at Kotelnich, crossed the fast-flowing Vyatka River, and passed over the vast but beautiful swampland that lies on its eastern bank.

At eight o'clock in the evening we pulled into Kirov (Vyatka), thus completing the first lap of our journey.

The car was captained and tended by two husky and good-natured girls: Zinya and Marusya. They had a tiny kitchen where they made tea from a samovar for the passengers. They fed the samovar from scraps of wood which they picked up along the right-of-way. It was their duty to emerge with little red flags at every stop, guard the entrance to the car, and drive off the ragged little boys and other species of humanity who tried to hide on the steps, the couplings, or the bumpers. This task they performed with vigor and dignity but without exasperation. They took turns at their duties, one sleeping while the other worked. I asked them what hours they observed. The question surprised them. They had not given any thought to it. One worked until the other was slept out. Then the other worked and the first one slept. It was very simple.

I was given the end compartment. The one next to it, which shared the washroom, was occupied by two uniformed

NKVD officials: a fat and important one, and a young junior-member one with a dark, morose face. The fat one rarely left the compartment. The young one occasionally scuttled out at the stations, revolver flapping authoritatively at his side, to buy food. Sometimes when the train stopped, I could hear the younger one reading aloud to his superior from Stepanov's *Port Artur.* He read jerkily and laboriously but with commendable determination. Neither of them spoke to me at any time during the trip.

Among the other passengers there was a theater director from Irkutsk; a deputy of the Supreme Soviet from a district in the Urals; a husky man in seaman's trousers who had once been a party agitator, looking slightly revolutionary and old-fashioned; a Jewish woman who was going to fetch an evacuated child back to Moscow from Krasnoyarsk. The theater director was a real Siberian, suffered from the heat, and spent the time wandering up and down the corridor clad only in pants and undershirt. He expatiated at any provocation on the beauties of the Angara River and the virtues of the Irkutsk winter. "Real cold," he would say, thrusting out his arms in a species of deep-breathing exercise, "real broad Russian cold." The deputy of the Supreme Soviet prepared with considerable ceremony to get off at a small stop in the Urals, only to get carried remorselessly thirty-two kilometers past his station. He was furious; and I could hardly blame him, for it must have cost him plenty of effort to get back. The party organizer joked with everyone and made love—again in the old-fashioned revolutionary tradition—to the Jewish lady.

Most of the passengers were pleasant to me, but we didn't talk much. Only one evening, when I produced copies of the glossy Russian-language magazine, *Amerika,* put out by our wartime information department, a lively meeting formed in the corridor of the car. The party organizer at once took charge and made a speech about how they were worried about the future, how they had trusted Roosevelt but weren't sure about Truman, and look at this fellow Hearst. We had a lively hour of fraternization. Then suddenly everybody began to look guiltily over his shoulder and the meeting quietly dispersed. After that, Russian inhibitions claimed their own, and hardly anyone spoke to me for two days.

On Monday, the third day out, the train was at Perm when I woke up. East of Perm the country was beautiful and relatively prosperous. The meadows were bright against the dark background of evergreen forests. Cattle, horses, roads, large barns, electric power lines, were all in evidence.

We picked up the Sylva River and followed it for many miles upstream, through Kungur itself, through the long gorge at the east of it, to where the valley widened into a broad basin. The train stopped there, once or twice, in the open country, to wait for signals. The summer grain was higher in the fields here than in the district around Moscow. The lilacs were in bloom. On either side of the valley were wooded hills in the distance. These were warm, dry uplands, in the first flush of summer; and one was constrained to wonder why, in all this vast country, no place could be found where a foreigner could take a quiet country vacation.

By evening the scene was mostly forest again. Low hills (200 to 300 meters) here and there were all we were destined to see of the Urals. At eight o'clock in the evening some fifty-three hours out of Moscow, we arrived at Sverdlovsk.

I got out and wandered around the station and the adjacent streets. It was a warm, drowsy summer evening. The station and the sidewalks around it were cluttered with the usual crowds of patient, waiting travellers, sleeping amid their belongings on the tiled floors or on the pavement. The square in front of the station was unfinished, cluttered with rubbish and construction material. At its farther side a street-car occasionally passed, and frantic passengers clawed and shoved each other trying to get themselves and their bulky belongings onto its crowded platform.

On Tuesday morning early we passed through Tyumen.

Then there was flat swampland with forest, both evergreen and deciduous, and lakes in the distance. In mid-morning we stopped in the open country. There was a cry of "lilacs," and several of us rushed out into the fields to fetch them; but they turned out to be an optical illusion. In the fields the sun was hot. It was already the strong, piercing Siberian sun, which makes up during the short summer for the long winter months when it fails to deliver at all.

Soon we were in the peculiar prairie country which was to extend all the way to Novosibirsk, a country of swampland, meadow and scrub birch, more fertile, less forbidding than I had expected to see it. Much of it was rich black earth.

In these places the crops were more advanced than any I had seen. Hay was being cut. Sometimes there were more trees, sometimes less. Towards evening the prairie on either side was completely flat, treeless, shrouded in streaks of ground-mist, and the dome of the sky stretched out to tremendous distances, as though vainly trying to encompass the limits of the great plain.

In the depths of the night we passed through Omsk.

The last day, Wednesday, went slowly. We were now on the sector of densest traffic; and we were only one link in the long chain of trains, tiny trains against the surrounding distances, crawling eastwards like worms, haltingly and with innumerable interruptions, across the dusty, swampy steppes of Barabinsk. They were on their way to the Far East, in preparation for Russia's entry into the war with Japan. We stopped more than we moved; and when we stopped, we could see the freight trains piling up behind us, and hear them whistling for the right of way with the deep throaty voice which only trains in Russia and America have, and which brings nostalgia to every American heart.

There was a warm, dusty wind. Everything in the car was gritty with soot and dust. When the train stopped among the swamps, we climbed down the embankment, took off our shirts, splashed off the yellow scum from the surface of the swamp water, and washed our heads in the cool dark liquid from underneath. At nine o'clock in the evening, ninety-eight hours out from Moscow, we clattered slowly across the long bridge over the Ob and pulled up the grade into the station at Novosibirsk.

At the end of my second day in Novosibirsk, accompanied by my official host, we went to the opera, which interested me extremely. It is a tremendous undertaking. The building, completed during the war, is one of the largest, if not the largest, in the world. With an area of 11,500 square meters, and a cubic content of 245,000 cubic meters, it exceeds any other theater in the Soviet Union, and is interesting as a feat of engineering alone. The main element of the building is a rotunda, sixty meters in diameter, on the pattern of the Colosseum in Rome. A fairly flat dome, of reinforced concrete and covered with rounded iron shingles, provides the ceiling of the theater, with its chandelier. At the front of the building a rectangular entrance hall protrudes from the rotunda and faces the main square with twelve of the square columns of which Soviet Russia is so fond. (May we see in this predilection for the square column a reflection of the unyielding, uncompromising quality of all Soviet thought?)

The great vertical slab that houses the main curtains is thrust down into the rear of the rotunda like a butcher's cleaver and still protrudes above the dome. It dominates the whole building with its uninhibited functionalism, a functionalism relating solely to the internal operation of the theater and independent of the problems of weight and equilibrium which usually dictate architectural form. In this respect the slab places heavy demands on the knowledge and imagination of the outdoor spectator; but for those who can picture the internal working of the theater, it is not unnatural. It conceals behind it a lower and smaller rectangle which houses the remaining high stage equipment.

To either side of the rotunda are large rectangular wings, finished, or to be finished, in concrete block.

The theater, which began its operatic season last month with *Ivan Susanin* and *Carmen*, has a staff of one thousand, largely recruited from local sources, and including a ballet. The director hopes to wangle about two dozen of this year's graduates of the Moscow ballet school for assignment to his establishment, and eventually to operate a ballet school on his own.

I saw them perform *Ivan Susanin*. The performance seemed to me to be surprisingly good and almost up to the Moscow standard. The ballet was not as good as the singing. It happened that at the time I was in Novosibirsk there was a congress of some two thousand of the best agricultural workers of the huge Novosibirsk Oblast, and the performance which I saw was for these delegates. Many of them came from remote sections of the oblast and had never before seen anything like an opera performance. Their reactions varied all the way from complete indifference to great excitement.

All in all, the construction and operation of one of the world's greatest opera theaters in a remote and still-straggling community like Novosibirsk seemed to me to be a rather breath-taking venture. It is interesting to note in this connection that the funds for the enterprise were refused by the central government and were therefore put up entirely by the oblast itself.

At the present time the opera building is only partially completed. The streets around it are still those of a Siberian village. Log cabins and tumble-down fences are still scattered around in the shadow of the building at the rear. One cannot, in this case, attribute this to the general Russian carelessness about finishing and maintaining buildings. There has, after all, been a war. Construction had to be stopped. The one finished wing had to be filled with government offices, et cetera.

On the other hand, in all of Russia, outside of some of the

palaces of Leningrad or the Kremlin, there is no more monumental or pretentious building. It represents a complete break with its surroundings. There could be no more flamboyant a repudiation of the past, no more arrogant expression of confidence in the future than the erection of this almost mystical structure on the remote banks of the Ob.

There are undoubtedly tremendous engineering and artistic talents in the people of Siberia. I have no doubt that much more will be done in the next few years to elevate human life on the steppes and in the forests of Siberia out of the squalor of the izba. But that this life can ever be elevated—at one stride—to the grandiose conception of the Novosibirsk Opera House, I would doubt. And unless it is, the building must remain what it is today: an incongruous dream, out of all reasonable relation to its own surroundings.

Later in the week, I visited Stalinsk.* The morning following my arrival, anxious to shake out some of the effects of an eighteen-hour train journey and a two-hour banquet, I started off for a walk to see what I could of the "socialist city." Mr. Valit arrived just as I was leaving, and paled slightly at the prospect that had he been a few minutes late I might have gone off alone. He accompanied me and we had a tour around the block.

The "socialist city" lies between the railroad station and the metallurgical plant. The place, as indeed the entire municipal and industrial district on that side of the river, was nothing more than a swamp fifteen years ago. The "socialist city" of workers' apartment houses was founded in the early thirties on the designs of the well-known German architect and city planner May. Its development was obviously arrested by the war; and today there is much that has been left

---

*This, as noted above, was the metallurgical center then called Stalinsk-Kuznetsk, situated some three hundred miles southeast of Novosibirsk, near the Chinese frontier.

unfinished or has deteriorated from its original state. It is characteristic that for the resulting deficiencies the Russians blame May, accusing him of sabotage. In particular, he is reproached with having deliberately, for purposes of sabotage, designed the buildings with no entries from the street sides, all the entries to apartments being from the court. It is evident to anyone familiar with the development of modern housing conceptions that May had intended the spacious courtyards inside the blocks of houses to be attractive community parks and gardens, onto which the apartments would open. He could hardly have envisaged that the courtyards would be left ungraded and undeveloped, full of mud, piles of dirt, garbage boxes, and drying clothes. His plans, furthermore, required the careful study and approval of the Soviet authorities, who consequently had every opportunity to notice a feature as elementary as this and to express their objections to it before construction was begun. It is characteristic of the credulity and lack of discrimination of the Soviet mind, however, that this sort of rot can be—and is—unquestionably accepted by a large proportion of people whenever it bears the authority of the government.

A fine job has been done in the planting of trees in the "socialist city." The main streets have four rows of Siberian poplars, varied with the ash-leaved maple (called here the "American" maple) and the elm (called the "southern birch"). When these trees have grown, the city will have the makings of a very pleasant layout. This planting of trees is particularly important because every bit of original tree growth within sight of the city, for miles around, had been cut to obtain lumber for the plant and to facilitate coal mining.

The old village of Kuznetsk, located on the rise of the east bank, is still reminiscent of this river trade of bygone days, of guarded caravans, of fat, pious merchants, of deals concluded over innumerable saucers of the Chinese tea which constituted one of the main objects of the trade. The picturesque old log houses, however, are already being swallowed up in the industrial development of the district. In the flat valley land beyond the town the ferro-alloy plant is already working; and the first of three sections of the aluminum plant is likewise in operation. Preliminary work is being done on a large locomotive and railroad-car plant; and similar work is being carried on somewhat farther downstream, beyond the hills, in preparation for the construction of a second metallurgical combine. Thus the district around the town is already full of new buildings, dump grounds, construction barracks, et cetera.

I wanted to drive over to the nearby hills where once had stood the old fortress of Kuznetsk, in which Dostoyevski had been imprisoned and which was the subject of his *Tales of the Death House*, but my hosts showed no enthusiasm for the project. I later learned that the fortress had burned down quite recently, an event which was apparently the source of some shame and embarrassment to the city fathers, who knew that they should have taken better care of their sole historical monument.

On Thursday, June 21, I returned from Stalinsk to Novosibirsk. From the housekeepers who had looked after me during my stay in Stalinsk, I parted with a mutual show of emotion which would have done justice to a residence of months instead of days. At the station my local hosts stood among the platform crowd in the bright morning sunshine and waved faithfully until the train had finally disappeared. Stopping— in general—for longer periods of time than it moved, the train made its way slowly back through the rolling steppe country, past the straggling coal towns on the hillsides, with their great piles of slag. At the stations the usual swarms of barefooted women and little girls in head-cloths came bearing their offerings. People with enormous bundles fought with each other and with the guards, trying to get off and on the crowded day coaches in the back of the train.

The only other occupant of the coupé was a thin and lanky young war veteran who had been badly burned in a tank and retired for his wounds. His father was an old Party worker of the district; and the young man, owing doubtless to his wounds and his father's influence, now found himself suddenly appointed stationmaster in a good-sized town along the railroad. He seemed mildly pleased over this appointment, but I had the impression that he faced the future with some of that same bewilderment, boredom, and restlessness which must be the lot of war veterans like himself in any country. He was stationmaster of the station D., to be sure; but then what? Surely, that was not the end. That was all right for a few days, a few weeks, perhaps. But surely somewhere there must be something more; more excitement, some more dramatic payoff for the years of hardship, of danger, and of sacrifice.

All day the train stopped and started and rumbled across the steppe. Evening finally came. The car was unlighted. In the twilight the rolling prairie stretched out to vast distances on either side. On the station platforms, when you caught the breeze from the prairie, the air was fresh and sweet with the smell of prairie grasses. After nightfall the train moved slowly, and with interminable stops, on the approaches to Novosibirsk. During the long stops you could notice the nocturnal silence of the steppes, broken only by the barking of dogs in distant villages and the voices of trains whistling for the right of way.

At two or three in the morning we pulled into Novosibirsk. I was met by the faithful "secretary" and his girl chauffeur. Together we stumbled across the tracks in the dark with my bags and chugged off to my state suite in the hotel.

I had one day to spend in Novosibirsk before I could start for home. The secretary rather glumly announced his readiness to entertain me according to my desires. I told him I would be glad to spend the day resting. This obviously filled him with suspicion. "How come you want to rest so much?" he inquired darkly.

To relieve his mind I suggested a swim. We rattled down to the banks of the Ob in the Gorki flivver. I undressed and swam and then we sat on a rock in the stinging Siberian sunshine. Little naked boys poked along the shore in a leaky old rowboat as boys will do everywhere. Downstream, the long freight trains crawled slowly eastwards across the bridge on the main line of the Trans-Siberian, the cars and locomotives silhouetted like little black toys against the bright sky. Across the river you could see the other trains lined up and waiting for their chance to cross.

The beach we sat on was stony and unimproved. Behind us was a bathhouse, but it was run-down and faded and obviously closed. The secretary assured me that some day there would be great improvements here: wonderful parks and bathhouses and athletic facilities.

That the effort would be made, I did not doubt. I only wondered whether again, as in the case of the local opera house, Russian imagination and Russian dreams of grandeur, unencumbered as usual by any desire to connect past and future, would not cut loose from all connection with reality and begin some fantastic colossus of a project, build part of it hastily and with bad materials, never finish it, and then leave the beginnings to rot away or be used for other utterly incongruous purposes. Meanwhile, the Ob, of course, would continue to flow its tranquil course towards the northern sea. And probably, regardless of what marvels had or had not been constructed on shore, for countless further summers naked little boys would continue to find leaky old rowboats and to pole their way up- and downstream on summer days, shouting and splashing, cutting their feet on the rocks, and making astounding discoveries about the nature of rivers and the contents of river bottoms.

I had decided to return by air. It was Saturday when I left. The plane was originally scheduled to leave at five in the morning and to reach Moscow in one day. Actually, it did not get away until noon; and the journey took three days. For two or three hours we flew over the swamps and lakes of the steppe country. I sat next to a little old working woman who had the hands of a man, who was a member of the Central Committee of the Union of Building Trades, and who was going to Sverdlovsk for a meeting. She was illiterate but bright and alert. She talked at length during the flight to Omsk; and her observations on the flight and on life in general had all the pungency and charm of the mental world of those who had never known the printed word. When we stopped for an hour or two at Omsk, in the blinding heat of mid-day, I shared my picnic lunch with her, sitting in the grass under the shade of the tail fin of the plane. She made me read aloud to her from Tolstoy's *Peter the First*, which I happened to have been reading in the plane. Gradually, we were joined by other passengers, and before the time finally came for the take-off, I found myself reading to half the plane's company—a most attentive and respectful audience.

We arrived at Sverdlovsk in a pouring rain. For a long time we remained in the plane out on the field. It was a Russian-built Douglas, and the roof leaked. After a long delay we were bundled into an open truck, where we got thoroughly drenched, and were taken into a sort of a dormitory hotel on the edge of the airfield, where we were told that we would spend the night. One of my fellow travellers was the Party secretary, Mr. B., with whom I had "done" Novosibirsk one evening. We had encountered each other again in the plane like old friends, and he now stuck by me loyally. He succeeded in wangling a room with four beds for the two of us, and then in keeping out several other importunate passengers who were looking for a place to sleep. His method was very simple. Looking them quietly in the eye, he would say, "You just take those bundles of yours and get out of here." There must have been something in the tone of voice which revealed the nature of the authority behind this demand, because the invaders invariably withdrew silently and without complaint.

The following morning the rain was still streaming down. It was a cold and dreary Sunday morning. The window of the room revealed nothing more exciting outside than a wet field, a barracks, a truck splashing around in the mud, and in the distance, woods. Inquiry failed to reveal anyone in the building who had the faintest idea what was to happen to our company. It appeared that there might be a technical possibility of finding transportation to Sverdlovsk for the day, but there was no assurance that one could get back.

The hours of the morning wore on. B. and I got fed up with the uncertainty, and he decided to turn on the heat. He found a telephone and for half an hour he jiggled the receiver and shouted. His efforts were herculean, and successful. About an hour later the crew appeared from somewhere, looking slightly shamefaced. The truck was rolled up. We drove out to the leaky Douglas, got the motor started, and soon were off into a solid bank of cloud, destined for Kazan. There was no assurance that we would get to Moscow. But the director of the airport at Sverdlovsk had clearly concluded that his Sunday would be more peaceful without us.

At Kazan we were bustled off once more to an airport hotel. Moscow, it seemed, was having a victory parade; and the Moscow airport would accept no more planes that day. We would have to stay overnight. Again B. and I snatched the best room and barricaded ourselves against all comers.

In the late afternoon we were sitting in the "commercial buffet," which was a room with two or three tables, a little buffet stand, and a few stale cakes for sale at staggering prices. A lady passenger of middle age, in a well-cut gray travelling suit, who had quietly and without question associated herself with B. and me as the most privileged and influential element among the passengers, casually undertook to raise—by a mere telephone call—a car which would take us around Kazan and show us the sights. This rash boast brought the buffet girl to her feet, from behind her little table. "And just where in hell," she asked with crushing weariness, "do you think you would raise a car in the city of Kazan?" Our travelling companion looked at her challenger with a steely eye. "From the NKVD," she replied. The buffet girl quickly disappeared again behind her cakes.

The telephone call was made—to the head of the NKVD in person. But an hour went by and the car failed to materialize. We decided to start out on foot. We walked as far as an amusement park. Evening was upon us, and the crowds were gathering there for what was scheduled as a "popular stepping-out." We borrowed twenty kopek pieces from numerous strangers, and there were more laborious phone calls to the NKVD from a public telephone. It was finally decided that the car should come to the amusement park.

We bought sunflower seeds to eat and started into the park, but soon decided that it was too crowded for comfort and that we would rather see the center of town. We set out down a long, broad, tree-lined street, with fine big buildings that reflected clearly the pre-revolutionary university town. Some of the buildings had been made into military hospitals. The soldier-patients, clad in the frightful flannel garments peculiar to all Russian hospitals, sat out in the front gardens, with their accordions, playing, singing, talking, making remarks through the iron fence at all the girls who passed by. It was pleasant and homelike, if slightly vulgar, to be sauntering on the streets of a Volga River town on a summer evening, spitting the husks of your sunflower seeds philosophically before you as you walked. Eating sunflower seeds gave you the same sense of bovine calm and superiority as chewing gum. For a moment I could almost forget that I was a foreigner in a country governed by people suspicious and resentful of all foreigners. But not for long.

We spied a jeep which the lady thought was the promised car. It passed us before we could stop it. We walked all the way back to the amusement park and found it. It was the one, all right. The head of the NKVD was there in person, with a chauffeur. He greeted the lady with great respect. But he was embarrassed to shake hands with me and refused to accompany us in the car, preferring to depart on foot rather than to ride publicly with a foreigner.

The jeep drove us around through the center of town. I was charmed with the place: with its atmosphere of the wealthy river-merchant town and university city, with its white buildings, with the towers of its Kremlin glistening in the moonlight. I was struck by the fact that while it is far more of a place than Novosibirsk, you hear far less about it. That is, I suppose, because it is first and foremost a tsarist, rather than a Soviet, city. Perhaps also because it is the center of the Tatar Republic; and the political reactions of the Tatars have not been all that could have been desired in recent years.

The chauffeur, in the uniform of a private in the NKVD troops, declined to give me any information about the population of the city. I had to return to Moscow to learn that it was now in the neighborhood of two and a half million, having been only about a million before this war. It must, at the moment, be the third-largest city in the Soviet Union. But there seems to be little tendency to show it to foreigners.

The following day I sat for a long time on a suitcase in the stern of our Russian Douglas, looking out at the forests and farm country between Kazan and Moscow and trying to gather together into some sort of pattern the mass of impressions which the past fortnight had left upon me. It was clear that here, spread out below us on the enormous plain, was indubitably one of the world's greatest peoples: a talented, responsive people, capable of absorbing and enriching all forms of human experience; a people strangely tolerant of cruelty and carelessness yet highly conscious of ethical values; a virile, fertile people with great endurance and vitality, profoundly confident that they are destined to play a progressive and beneficial role in the affairs of the world, and eager to begin to do so.

Dividing them from the world outside their borders stands a regime of unparallelled ruthlessness and jealousy. This regime knows better than anyone else what riches, what possibilities, what dangers lie in the people of Russia. It has these people completely in its hand. It is determined that no outside influence shall touch them. For this it is important that they should be taught not only not to fear the power of external forces but also not to look to them for favors. The Soviet government must always be made to appear the sole source of gracious bounty for the faithful and of righteous wrath and punishment for the incredulous or the undutiful. For this reason the entire system is so designed as to obviate every last possibility of foreign influence on the popular mind and to turn to the advantage of the Soviet government itself every act of foreign governments or individuals which might affect the people of Russia.

The American man in the street, reading of the struggles and sufferings of those Russians who were so recently his allies, feels the urge to help them, subscribes to the Red Cross or the Russian War Relief, does not demur at the extra labor and taxes involved in lend-lease to Russia, and accepts with goodwill the arguments of those who advocate great credits for the Soviet government. How much more must the traveller feel who sees with his own eyes the deprivations of the Russian people and the heroism: the young people working twelve hours a day without comfort or relaxation, the middle-aged people who can recall no security and no peace in their lifetimes and who have ceased to expect any for the future, the widows and war-cripples, the crowded homes, the empty cupboards, the thread-bare clothes, the pitiful substitutes for comfort and convenience—and with it all the wistfulness, the hope, the irrepressible faith in the future. Surely here, it would seem, in this gifted, appealing people, purged by hardship of so much that is vulgar and inane in the softer civilizations, organized and prepared as no great people has ever been before for the building of a decent, rational society— here if anywhere would be a suitable outlet for the practical genius and the yearning to feel themselves helpful to others that are signal traits of the American people.

But the fact is, there is no way of helping the Russian people. When a people finds itself in the hands of a ruthless authoritarian regime which will stop at nothing, it finds itself beyond the power of others to help. Gifts presented to it can be given only to the regime, which promptly uses them as weapons for the strengthening of its own power. If these gifts are passed on to the people at all, it is with the innuendo they were concessions the regime was clever enough to extract from a crafty outside world while foiling the evil designs which lay behind them, and that those who would share in the benefits of them had better keep on the good side of that omniscient power which was so ably defending their interests. On the other hand, blows aimed in exasperation at the regime itself are no help to the people it dominates. Such injuries are promptly ducked and passed on to the people, while the regime, breathing sympathetic indignation, strikes one fiery attitude after another as the protector of a noble nation from the vicious envy of a world which refuses to understand. And if then, in the train of policies of arrogance and provocation, real catastrophe finally overtakes the nation, the regime promptly identifies itself beyond all point of distinction with the sufferings of the people and takes refuge behind that astounding and seemingly inexhaustible fund of patriotic heroism and loyalty which human nature seems to reserve for all such occasions. The benevolent foreigner, in other words, cannot help the Russian people; he can only help the Kremlin. And conversely, he cannot harm the Kremlin; he can only harm the Russian people. That is the way the system is geared.

This being the case, what does he do? The answer is anybody's. But I, for my part, should have thought, with the sights and sounds of Siberia still vivid in my mind, that in these circumstances he would be wisest to try neither to help nor to harm—to make plain to Soviet policy-makers the character of his own aspirations, the limits of his patience, and the minimum conditions on which he can envisage polite neighborly relations with them—and then to leave the Russian people—encumbered neither by foreign sentimentality nor foreign antagonism—to work out their destiny in their own peculiar way.

There follow excerpts from the account of a journey from Moscow to Helsinki in September 1945, only shortly after the cessation of hostility in the European theater of the Second World War.

Left Moscow with the congressmen at 2:15 P.M., in the American DC-3. The first part of the trip was taken up in conversation with the congressmen. Later I got some time to myself to stare out the window and to watch, with a sense of growing excitement, the approach to the strange and incomparably dramatic city which I had not seen for nine years. The broad waters of the Volkhov, where once the Hanseatic merchants floated their goods to and from the markets of Novgorod, passed under us, broad and slow as in the days of the Hansa, but now barren of craft. Lake Ladoga became visible only as a remote patch of light on the eastern horizon. We picked up the great cold Neva, on its way from Lake Ladoga to the Gulf of Finland, and followed it a piece downstream. Now we could finally see, far to the left of us, the masses of clustered buildings which were the city.

At four-fifty we landed on a field to the northwest of town. There was no one there to meet us, or even to help us out of the plane. The Intourist girl, it turned out, had gone to the wrong airport. We stood for ten or fifteen minutes at the open door of the cabin, looking out at the field and waiting for something to happen. Rain was falling gently. The grass was the rich grass of the rain-swept country near the sea, thicker and longer than around Moscow; and there was no mistaking the fact that the sea—the lonely chilly sea of the north—was near at hand.

A big bus finally drove up, splashing wildly through the puddles at the edge of the field. It bore the inscription "Finland Station—Putilov Works," and I wondered anxiously whether because of the arrival of us nincompoops some thirty Leningrad proletarians had probably had to walk home from work for lack of an autobus.

We set out in the bus across the islands. I had been in Leningrad three days of my life, and yet it was like coming home. I had read so much about it; and through the years spent in the Baltic states I had come to love the flat horizons of the north, the strange slanting light, the wintry bleakness of nature, and the consequent accentuation of all that is warm and rich in human relationships.

We were driven across the Kamenny Ostrov [Island] and the bridge, along the Kamenno-Ostrovski Prospekt, past the Hermitage and the Winter Palace, across the Nevski Prospekt, to the hotel. The others immediately set out again to see the exhibition of the defense of Leningrad. I went out by myself to walk around the center of town.

I walked past St. Isaac's Cathedral to the Summer Garden. The weeds and grass were high between the paths, under the oak trees. The equestrian statue of Peter the Great, just recently freed of its wartime sandbags, reared high over the riverbank.

The river stretched out tranquilly to its bright, far horizons. The surface of the water was smooth, but if you looked at it carefully, you could see that it moved rapidly with that silent, majestic current which Pushkin noted.

Up past the Admiralty, near the bridge, the ice-breaker *Sibiryakov* was lying at the quayside, gleaming in a coat of fresh brown paint. On the bridge, men were laying new electric cables under the pavement. There was little traffic across the bridge. Occasionally, a three-car train of street-cars, bursting with human beings, would groan up the incline to the center of the bridge.

The Winter Palace was being painted, but many of the windows still gaped vacantly. The surrounding streets were quiet, almost deserted. On the empty embankment, under the shadow of the palace, two children rode bicycles up and down—as impervious to the past glory as to the present ruin about them.

I walked up the Moika Embankment, behind the General Staff buildings, to the Nevski Prospekt, sat on a bench before the Kazan Cathedral and watched the people. They looked sober, a bit tired, but still vigorous. There were swarms of them waiting for the street-cars and trolley-buses that still made up most of the traffic along the famous old street.

Alone, I made my way back to the hotel—behind the cathedral, down the gloomy Gorokhovaya Ulitsa, and again along the Moika Embankment. Here, near Mariinskaya Square, two of the long rows of poplar trees had fallen over into the canal, bending and twisting the iron fences in the process. The tops must have broken off and stuck in the mud, for many of the branches were still alive with green leaves.

This walk brought up countless associations of the past: of the picture of Pushkin and companion leaning on the embankment looking at the river; of Kropotkin exercising with his stool in the Fortress of St. Peter and St. Paul; of Alexander I looking out of the Winter Palace during the flood of 1823; of Prince Yusupov throwing the body of Rasputin into the Moika; of the crowd moving across the square towards the Winter Palace on the night the place was stormed; of the generations of music teachers and pupils going in and out of the conservatory; of the Italian opera of one hundred years ago; of the unhealthy days of Leningrad's spring thaws, with little groups of black-clad people plodding through the slush behind the hearses to the muddy, dripping cemeteries; of the cellar apartments of the gaunt, dark inner streets, full of dampness, cabbage smell, and rats, and of the pale people who manage to live through the winters in those apartments; of the prostitutes of the Nevski Prospekt of the tsarist time; the people cutting up fallen horses in dark, snow-blown streets during the time of the siege. This is to me one of the most poignant communities of the world: a great, sad city, where the spark of human genius has always had to penetrate the darkness, the dampness, and the cold in order to make its light felt, and has acquired, for that very reason, a strange warmth, a strange intensity, a strange beauty. I know that in this city, where I have never lived, there had nevertheless been deposited by some strange quirk of fate—a previous life, perhaps?— a portion of my own capacity to feel and to love, a portion—in other words—of my own life; and that this is something no American will ever understand and no Russian ever believe.

The train for Helsinki left in late evening. The only other Intourist guest who was going there was a somewhat gloomy Mexican in a beret who spoke with a perfect Texas accent. Just as we went out the front door of the hotel, the bus that was to have taken us to the station started up and disappeared without us into the darkness, to the amazement and consternation of the Intourist girl who was to accompany us. For a long time I stood out on the square, looking at the stately outlines of St. Isaac's Cathedral looming out faintly in the darkness, while the Mexican described to me the course of his diarrhea. Another bus, not ours, stood empty and deserted by the curb. A drunken Soviet soldier came weaving along out of the darkness, hammered indignantly at the door of the empty bus, and then asked the white-bearded doorman when it was to leave. "That's not your bus," replied the doorman. "Where in hell do you want to go, anyway?" The soldier scowled and staggered around in a little circle, bringing up again before the doorman. "I want to go west," he said, "as near as you can get to the Soviet border." The Intourist girl, who had arrived on the scene just in time to hear this last crack, quickly hustled us back into the lobby, where we waited until another bus could be made ready.

When I woke in the morning, we were just pulling out of the totally ruined and deserted (formerly Finnish) town of Vyborg. It was overcast, and there was a strong cold wind. Rays of early-morning sunshine, slipping through the clouds, slanted across the earth, caught the gutted shells of apartment buildings, flooded them momentarily with a chill, pale gleam. Below us lay the port, quiet and empty. An abandoned boat washed gently beside the remnants of a pier. But the light of morning was fresh on the harbor. The water rippled gaily in the breeze, as though it were not bounded on three sides by the mute testimonials of men's incredible capacity for destruction. And a gull, wheeling and circling over the inner basin, rejoiced in the new day, in the prospect of fish below, and in its own graceful strength.

We moved slowly through a war-devastated and deserted country. Weeds and scrub trees were growing on the abandoned farms. The houses, doorless and windowless, were obviously sinking gradually back into the new vegetation around them. When you occasionally got a glimpse into the interiors, you saw that the floors were full of rubbish and offal. And you knew that the rank new vegetation still concealed thousands of live land mines.

After an hour we reached the new Finnish border and stopped at the first Finnish station. Here everything was suddenly neat and cheerful. A new station building had been erected, simple and of wood, but with a certain distinctive modern touch. The platform was in good repair, and clean. There was a freshly painted kiosk where newspapers were on sale. Food was the only essential not in evidence. But the station was almost deserted. The sky was gray. And everything was a little sad.

Our Russian locomotive retired, leaving our sleeping-car, together with two "soft" cars full of Russians bound for the new Soviet naval base at Porkkala, to wait for the Finnish train. We had long to wait. I paced up and down the platform in the wind, a slave to the Anglo-Saxon habit of exercise. The Russians stared vacantly out the windows of their car; and on their faces was written the same stoical emptiness with which Russians stare out of train windows all over their vast, melancholy Russian world.

The sidings were full of freight cars loaded with Finnish goods being shipped to Russia as reparations. Little cars, wheels, and tracks for a narrow-gauge logging railroad, bright with shiny metal and new paint, were carefully stored and lashed on big gondola cars. On others there were piles of clean-sawn lumber, neatly cut and carefully stacked. All these contributions bore the mark of orderly, conscientious Finnish workmanship. I wondered at first whether such offerings did not sometimes rouse pangs of shame among the inhabitants of the great shoddy Russian world into which they were moving. But on second thought I was inclined to doubt this very strongly.

Except for myself, the station platform was almost deserted. A young, lithe Finn, with a knife in his belt, gave side glances of hatred and contempt at the Russian cars as he went about his work as a switchman. Woodsmoke from the little switch engine was torn away by the wind and carried across the clearing, its odor reminiscent of the north woods at home. A Finnish railway-man in uniform rode sedately up to the station building, parked his bicycle, and went inside to transact his business. A peasant cart drove up with a family in the back. The family might well be hungry, but the horse was fat and sleek, and trotted with a happy briskness no Russian horse possesses. Over the entire scene there lay the efficiency, the trimness, the quietness, and the boredom of bourgeois civilization; and these qualities smote with triple effect on the sense of a traveller long removed from the impressions of a bourgeois environment.

The Finnish locomotive finally appeared, picked us up, and

started off with us through the forests at a pace that seemed positively giddy after the leisurely lumbering of Russian trains. There was a dining car. There was not overly much to eat, but what there was was well prepared; the place was well run and inviting; the other passengers were friendly, unafraid, and unsuspicious. All day long we moved through a beautiful northern country, the forests broken with lakes, farms, meadows, and herds of cattle. The Russians continued to stare out the window with impassive faces. By evening we were in Helsinki.

I spent the years from mid-1946 to mid-1950 in Washington, first at the National War College, then as director of the Policy Planning Staff in the Department of State, and later, in the first months of 1950, as counselor of that department.

In March 1949, being then director of the Policy Planning Staff, I paid an official visit to the American and British zones of occupied Germany. It might be noted that Berlin, where I had lived for some five years before and during the war, was just then enduring some of the hardest and most harrowing moments of the Soviet blockade, and was being supplied and supported only by the American-British airlift. Other cities visited on that journey included Hamburg and Frankfurt.

My official reports on both of these journeys are in the government files. Here are some excerpts from the private accounts.

No one can doubt that in the midst of the National Socialist regime, and in sharp opposition to its young revolutionaries, there lives a great Christian, Western, German nation, deeply suffering, desperately biding its time.

—HERMANN RAUSCHNING,
GERMANY'S REVOLUTION OF DESTRUCTION, 1938

For us, Europe after the war is a question of how the picture of man can be re-established in the breasts of our fellow citizens.

—FROM A LETTER FROM HELMUTH VON MOLTKE
TO A FRIEND IN ENGLAND IN 1942

Arrived in the evening and was driven through dark, deserted streets to Harnack House—now an American club and guesthouse. The city seemed dead—a ghost of its former self.

Harnack House, brightly illuminated, stood out in the darkness like a garish honky-tonk that has stayed open too late in a sleepy provincial town. It was Saturday night. The thumping of dance music oozed out with the shafts of light from the windows of the building. Cars were lined up on the street and the little band of German chauffeurs, stamping up and down and muttering in the cold night air, seemed like an evil caricature of the bundled Russian coachmen of olden times, waiting for their masters outside the night-clubs of St. Petersburg and Moscow.

Inside, the lounge had that deserted and unappreciated air of most club-rooms in the evening; but the dining room had more life. It was equipped with candles in recognition of the festivity of the occasion (Saturday night). A German band was faithfully whacking out American dance tunes which they knew by heart. The faces of the musicians were drawn and worn, and so wearily deadpan that you could not tell whether they failed to see the colonels and the OMGUS [Office of Military Government, U.S.] civilians and their ladies who danced before them or whether they saw them and just didn't care. Plainly, they were interested in neither the occasion nor the music they were playing. Both were something inflicted upon them by others. Not theirs to reason why.

The patrons were decorous and well behaved. Only at one table, where they were having a birthday party, a major was raising his voice to command attention and his monologue cut through the music and the murmur of conversation: "Look what's on de menu. Tuna fish. Tuna fish, for God's sake. We been feedin' it to the dog. He don't even like it anymore. He jes' looks at me and say, 'Jeez, tuna fish again.' "

Late in the evening I took a long walk. The streets were

silent and empty and utterly dark. This was the once-fashionable suburb of Dahlem. The private villas—those that had escaped the bombing—stood out dimly in the shadows. What pretense, what eager hopes, what plans for personal happiness and prosperity lay behind the building of each of these houses? Whatever these hopes and plans were, they were now dashed. Today the villas stood mute and dark and cold. If Germans lived in them at all, they camped in them like barbarians in the palaces of Italy. There seemed little prospect of doing anything else. It was hard to tell whether this was in itself good or bad, deserved or undeserved. Whatever it was, every one of those dim architectural forms spelled a broken dream, spelled one more bit of frustration for people who had once felt the call of hope and initiative. However you looked at it, it seemed a pity. I had lived in this city many years, in its better days, and the immensity of the ruin overwhelmed me.

Back in the club I could not sleep. From my window I watched the events of the night. In little groups the guests emerged and departed in their cars. The last lingering lieutenant found his way into his jeep. Finally, the musicians assembled, with great grumbling and scolding of their own late-comers, and rode off in an incredibly overloaded jalopy over which they appeared to dispose. And then the tall bare poplars, the same patient poplars which had waited and watched through the final years of the Weimar Republic and the Nazi era and the war and the bombings and the arrival of the Russian army, stood alone again through another night, until the battered cars of the first early subway train came clattering past through the open cut a few yards away and the sky lightened to the dawn of a gray, soggy March Sunday over airlift Berlin.

MARCH 18, 1949
HAMBURG

In the morning my colleague drove me around Hamburg. We first drove out to Altona, then back along the river. The dock area across the river was fearfully damaged. The islands in mid-stream, once crowded with warehouses, industries, and installations of all sorts, were now flat, gray fields of desolation.

But the real destruction we did not come to until we had passed the harbor and the business district and entered the large residential districts east of the Alster. Here was sweeping devastation, down to the ground, mile after mile. It had all been done in three days and nights in 1943, my host told me. Seventy-five thousand persons had perished in the process. Even now, after the lapse of six years, over three thousand bodies were estimated to be still buried there in the rubble.

In the ruins of Berlin there had seemed to be a certain tragic majesty. Berlin had been a great cold city, an imperial city, haughty and pretentious. Such cities invited the wrath of gods and men.

But poor old Hamburg: this comfortable, good-humored seaport community, dedicated like so many of our own cities to the common-sense humdrum of commerce and industry— for Hamburg, it seemed a great pity.

And here, for the first time, I felt an unshakable conviction that no momentary military advantage—even if such could have been calculated to exist—could have justified this stupendous, careless destruction of civilian life and of material values, built up laboriously by human hands over the course of centuries for purposes having nothing to do with this war. Least of all could it have been justified by the screaming nonsequitur "They did it to us." And it suddenly appeared to me that in these ruins there was an unanswerable symbolism which we in the West could not afford to ignore. If the Western world was really going to make valid the pretense of a higher moral departure point—of greater sympathy and understanding for the human being as God made him, as expressed not only in himself but in the things he has wrought and has cared about—then it had to learn to fight its wars morally as well as militarily, or not fight them at all, for moral principles were a part of its strength. Shorn of this strength, the West was no longer itself. Its victories were not real victories; and the best it would accomplish in the long run would be to pull down the temple over its own head.

The military would stamp this as naive, and would say that war is war, and that when you're in it you fight with every means you have, or go down in defeat. But if that is the case, then there rests upon Western civilization, bitter as this may be, the obligation to be militarily stronger than its adversaries by a margin sufficient to enable it to dispense with those means which can stave off defeat only at the cost of undermining victory.

MARCH 20, 1949

Flew back to Berlin at mid-day, only to discover, upon arrival, that both of my official hosts were out of town until evening and that I was blessed with a Sunday afternoon all to myself. I therefore set out joyously alone, on foot and unattended, feeling like a bird out of a cage, to see the sights in my own way.

Took the subway downtown and went for a long walk in the once-familiar "western area" between Fehrbelliner Platz and Wittenberg Platz.

Despite occasional snow flurries, the weather was brighter than last week. It was suddenly the difference between winter and spring. The heavens were no longer all one tone. There were dark clouds, and light clouds; and between them gleamed a new sky—the pale blue sky of spring, in the existence of which one had almost ceased to believe in the endless, dragging northern winter.

Even the children noticed it. On my way to the subway station I passed three of them, walking an Airedale dog. "Oh look," the little boy was saying, "the dark cloud is the night-fairy and the light cloud is the day-fairy." The Airedale caught the hope and excitement in the boy's tone, and looked eagerly at the others and strained at the leash, to show that he was one of the gang and ready for anything.

(You are right, my little fellow—I thought to myself—there is a day-fairy and a night-fairy, a light cloud and a dark cloud. And which of these clouds will hang over you and over-shadow your life in the days of your maturity—which fairy you get will depend partly on you, since none of us is without will and responsibility who is not completely a prisoner. But it will depend even more on us Americans. For we have won great wars and assumed to ourselves great powers. And we have thus become the least free of all peoples. We have placed upon ourselves the obligation to have the answers; anyone can come up and put a nickel in us and ask for an answer, and the rules of the game require us to give one. This, too, you will eventually discover. And according to the answer we give, you may get mostly the day-fairy or mostly the night-fairy, hovering over yourself and your future. And I'd watch that one, if I were you, come to think of it; because we aren't too sure about all these things ourselves.)

The children were out in force on the streets, enjoying the Sunday afternoon. For them there was no question of adapta-tion. What other children, after all, had so vast and variegated a play-field, with so many possibilities? What other children had infinite supplies of bricks and other building materials for building dams in the flowing gutters? What other children had such magnificent settings for hide-and-seek? Where else could you, if the policeman wasn't looking, detach one of the little steel dump cars on the rubble-removal tracks and roll it down whole city blocks to a make-believe railway station far away? Who else had such natural embattlements and redoubts for conducting snowball fights?

All these, and other things, children were doing on this Sunday afternoon, when winter was lightening into spring. And it was plain that if only somehow the inward influ-ences of health and hope could be brought to them, if it could be shown to those children that somewhere, at the end of that faint rainbow that actually hovered over them on this afternoon whenever the March sun penetrated the snow flurries, there were such things as freedom and security and rewards for work accomplished and the chance to walk down the broad vistas of beauty and warmth in the human spirit: if these things could be done, then the ruins, like the charm of a wicked sorcerer, would lose their power over these children, and the day-fairy would once again come into her own.

But whence was all this to come? From the parents? The parents were stoical and hardened and purged of many of their erstwhile illusions. But they were still bewildered, unenlightened people, with a terribly restricted field of vision. From us Americans? We were doing our best. But we had no answer, yet, to the great political insecurity which hung over this area. And our own vision was clouded by our habits, our comforts, our false and corrupting position as conquerors and occupiers.

MARCH 21, 1949
FRANKFURT

In the evening I drove down out of the hills to Frankfurt to take the train to Paris. It had been a fine sunny day—the first day of good weather since I came to Germany. Now, although darkness had fallen, the sky was still bright in the west and the stars were out. In the villages people were out strolling, enjoying the first evening of fine spring weather. There was brisk vehicular traffic all along the road, and most of it German. I thought of the whole bizonal area stretching off behind us in the dusk, and it seemed to me that you could hear the great low murmur of human life beginning to stir again, beginning to recapture the rhythm of work and life and change, after years of shock and prostration. Here were tens of millions of human beings, of all ages and walks of life, reacting, as human beings always have and must, to the myriad of stimuli of heredity and education and climate and economic necessity and emotion. Whatever we did, they would no longer stand still in thought or in outlook. Nothing could keep them from seeking again some outlet for the basic need of the human being to feel that he is doing something important and fruitful and necessary.

Would we be able to feel our way into this sea of human reaction and human will, heretofore so repugnant, so little interesting to us? Would we be able to realize that we are the doctor on whose understanding the recovery and health of this patient depend, that recovery and that health without which there may be no unity and no success for the Western world? Would we be able to roll up our sleeves, to overcome our own distaste, and to study with cool objectivity the anatomy and pathology of this tremendous body politic known as Germany which had wrought so much havoc in our Western world? Would we be able to steer its development into cooperative and constructive lines? Would we be able to give it the sense of participation, the sense of being needed, which it so desperately required? Or would we turn our backs upon it in anger and revulsion, and leave it no choice but to grow again outside of us and against us, in the spirit of those bitter lines by Goethe with which the German Communist Party once used to close its meetings?

Du musst herrschen und gewinnen,
Oder dienen und verlieren,
Leiden oder triumphieren,
Amboss oder Hammer sein.

You must rule and win
Or serve and lose—
Suffer or triumph—
Be anvil or be hammer.

In the darkened streets of the suburban villages, in the bustle of the Frankfurt station, in the lights of the little station platforms of the plundered French zone as they slipped past the train windows, there were no answers to these questions; and the misty darkness which hung over the sleeping countryside of the Rhineland was heavy with uncertainty.

Scribblings on an airplane, approaching the coast of England at night, en route from Germany to Washington.

MARCH—APRIL 1949

Beneath us, from the shadowy recesses
Enshrouded by the twilight's silken tent,
Where map-lines blankly hint the coast of Kent,
Where sea to cliff and cliff to heath progresses,
Where unseen surf on unseen shoreline surges,
And cries of sea-birds mingle with its roar—
Breathtaking, wondrous, like the first faint urges
Of child-hope after child-grief, there emerges
The spider-thread of lights on England's shore.

And now the dim black table of the land
Turns slowly, massively, before our vision,
As though impelled, with ponderous precision,
By some gigantic and relentless hand.
Here fire-strings, defiling through the night,
Trace out the darkened snake-path of the highway.
And there—a modest needle-point of light
Marks out, perhaps beside some lonely byway,
Something to which the deepest English yearning
At last returns—will never cease returning—
That coldest and yet coziest of places:
The English home.

Good light, long may your flashing,
Like friendly beacon on a storm-swept shore,

Tell those who travel by the airplane's roar
That their suspended loneliness is passing,
That somewhere, on the earth's forgotten floor,
A sleeping form in childish crib is turning,
A candle on a window-sill is burning,
An open latch-string marks a waiting door.

In February 1950, no longer director of the Policy Planning Staff but now counselor of the State Department, I was sent on another (and last) official journey—this time to a number of Latin American capitals. The trip began with a train journey from Washington to Mexico City.

Here: excerpts, once again, from my personal account of this train journey and of the stopover in Mexico City.

FEBRUARY 18, 1950
WASHINGTON–MEXICO CITY

The train pulled out of Union Station into the early darkness of the February evening, carrying a traveller who felt slightly silly to be embarking, at his age, on so long and spectacular a voyage—to be abandoning the solemn legitimacy of the routine of the Department of State—to be leaving his family for so long—to be imagining that he could see anything or learn anything in the course of such a tour which others had not seen or learned before him.

A couple of hours later the train was passing through York, Pennsylvania. The traveller's farm-home was only sixteen miles away, off there to the west, across the darkness; and he had it now much in mind. It would be quiet there now. A. and M. would have finished the evening chores, and supper. It being Saturday evening, they would probably have gone to town. No light would be on about the place. The winter night would be cold, for the sky was clear. No domestic animals would be out. Even the cats would have crept into the barn for comfort. Only the old drake would be standing, motionless, on the concrete water trough in the barnyard, his white silhouette gleaming ghost-like in the darkness, a tragic, statuesque figure, contemptuous of the cold, of the men who had neglected him, of the other birds and beasts who basked in the warmth of human favor—contemptuous even of the possibility for happiness in general, human or animal.

He would be standing there through the hours of darkness; and the crisp silence of winter night would be about the place. There would be only the crunching and stomping of animals in the barn behind him, the rustling of some wild thing down in the meadow, the drone of a distant truck, and perhaps the sudden and thunderous rumbling occasioned by my neighbor B.'s car, as it rattled—home-bound—over the loose planks of the little bridge, down by the pasture.

Well, the train was moving on now—increasing with every minute the distance between us, destined soon to become so great. Might God help us all, I thought. . . .

FEBRUARY 19, 1950
SUNDAY

I woke up early, raised the curtain in the sleeping-car berth, and looked out. We were crossing a river. It was just the beginning of dawn. The half-light reflected itself in the oily scum of the water, left in kindly obscurity a desolation of factories and cinder-yards and railroad tracks along the shore, but caught and held, in its baleful gleam, the cold, mute slabs of skyscrapers overhead. It was the business district of some industrial city: what city, I did not know, nor did it matter.

And it occurred to me that for cities there is something sinister and pitiless about the dawn. The farm, secure in its humility and its submission, can take it. It can even welcome it, joyously, like the return of an old friend.

But the city, still sleeping, cowers restlessly under it, particularly under the Sabbath dawn. In this chill, calm light, the city is helpless, and in a sense, naked. Its dreams are disturbed, its pretense, its ugliness, its impermanence exposed, its failure documented, its verdict written. The darkness, with its neon signs, its eroticism, and its intoxication, was protective and forgiving—tolerant of dreams and of delusions. The dawn is judgment: merciless and impassive.

In the Fred Harvey restaurant of the St. Louis station there were nostalgic murals of old river scenes. Canned music ("The Rustic Wedding") mingled with the clatter of dishes, the shrill cries of waitresses, and the murmur of a cross-section of that rich stream of oral exchange which embellishes and characterizes the life of the Midwest: "Yessir, the president of our company is only forty-four. . . . We got five o' the best girls in the business. . . . They put him in the hub-nut division, an' he wasn't there more n' a month before the others went to the old man and said if he stayed there they'd all quit. . . . I goin' to eat kinda light, today. . . . Eleanor'll run for president, sure as you know. . . . The Hub Ice Fuel Company is a big company; you move at a fast pace over there. . . . First time I ever seen a woman walkin' along towin' a cat; the cat ain't used to it, don't know what to make of it. . . . Now what on earth d'ya suppose he's goin' to do with that nightgown? . . ."

Outside the station, a pale winter sunshine—Sunday afternoon sunshine—fell on the blank fronts of the station-district joints: Pop's Pool Hall; Hotel Rooms $1.50 and Up; Danny's Tavern; Pressing and Cleaning While-U-Wait; Julio's Place.

I caught a bus on my way toward the Mississippi River. Infected by the customs of the nation's capital, it also sported canned music ("Rose Marie").

The last two or three blocks had to be covered on foot. There were blocks of saloons and rooming-houses, with seedy-looking men slouching in front of the windows of the closed stores, leaning against the walls, in the sunshine, waiting. (What are they waiting for? What are they looking for?

What is it that they expect to happen in this dried-out street in down-town St. Louis on a Sunday afternoon in winter? That a girl will pass? Or that there will be a fight? Or that some drunken bum will get arrested? Could be, could be.)

Here was the Court House—mid-nineteenth-century style: heavy stone, tall blank windows. In it, a placard said, the Dred Scott case was tried. Beyond the Court House—parking lots, and then the great cobbled incline towards the river. The lower part of it, near the water, was covered with mud which looked dry but was really slimy; and there was an occasional stick of driftwood.

On this particular afternoon the riverbank was inhabited by six stray dogs, a bum who sat on a piece of driftwood and held one of the dogs in his lap, two small colored children with a bag of popcorn, and a stranger from Washington who sat on another piece of driftwood and sketched a cluster of four abandoned craft tied up by the shore: to wit, one scow with gasoline drums, one dredge, one dirty motor boat, and one genuine old show-boat, still in use but slightly self-conscious. The colored children hovered over my shoulder, chattering pleasantly and dropping popcorn down my neck as they watched the progress of the drawing. Railroad trains clattered along both sides of the river and across the high bridge upstream. A gull came ashore to dabble in the slime between the cobble-stones. And the river moved lazily past: a great slab of dirty gray water, gleaming here and there in the sunshine, curling and eddying and whispering quietly to itself as it went along.

I walked back through the old business district: a district of narrow, dark streets, of sooty, fortress-like bank buildings and hotels that once were elegant. (The trouble with American cities is that they have grown and changed too fast. They have never had time to clean up after themselves. The new is there before the old is gone. What in one era is functional and elegant and fashionable survives into the following era as grotesque decay. These cities have never had time to bury their dead; and they are strewn with indecent skeletons, in the form of the blighted areas, the abandoned mansions of the Gay Nineties, the old railroad and water-front vicinities, the "houses by the railroad tracks.")

On the train from St. Louis to Texas the lounge car had canned music ("Ave Maria") emerging from somewhere in the roof. We used to say: "The customer is always right." But what of the man today who doesn't like "The Rustic Wedding" or "Rose Marie" or "Ave Maria," or who has heard them too often, or who doesn't like music at all through loudspeakers, or who just doesn't like music at all? I raised this question in my mind as I fled back to the sleeping-car; and the wheels of the train, which used to clatter in so friendly and reassuring a way on the railroad voyages of my boyhood, seemed to be clicking off the words: "That-to-you; that-to-you; that-to-you."

FEBRUARY 20, 1950

On the sleeping-car from San Antonio to Mexico City, I was seated across from a gentleman from Indiana, with spouse. Feeling deeply disloyal to my own midwestern origin, I found that I could take no pleasure in any of my neighbor's characteristics. Neither the penetrating voice which boomed relentlessly through the cars in the service of an unquenchable loquaciousness, nor the toothpick which never left his mouth except at meal-times (I'm sure he slept with it), nor his breezy curiosity about the rest of us ("What-cha carryin' that ink around fer?"), nor the incessant talk with fellow-Indianians about things back home ("Yeah, I remember him; he used to run the bank at New Cambridge; and his uncle had a real-estate business over at Red City"), nor about marriage ("Now I'll tell you what you want to do: you and your wife git in that there berth with your clothes on, and then when she kicks you out, you ain't in such a fix, hee, hee, hee"): none of these characteristics excited my local pride. Why, I found myself muttering, did he come to Mexico if all he wanted to talk about was Indiana? And why, in general, do people have to act like caricatures of their own kind?

FEBRUARY 22, 1950
MEXICO CITY

Washington's Birthday reception—spilling out from the main hall onto the veranda, and thence into the garden. It all seemed achingly familiar. We stood there in the garden, clutching our drinks with the left hand to keep the right one dry and available for hand-shaking. Those who finished drinks looked desperately for some place to put the empty glasses, and finally put them on the stone steps (over at the side, where they wouldn't get stepped on). The local Mexican employees, dressed in their Sunday best, clustered shyly together for comfort. I found myself next to the wife of a senior colleague and made the mistake of telling her I had been in Russia. "Oh, have you really?" she was saying. "What are the Russians like? Do you like them? They're all slaves, aren't they? Why don't we *do* something about it?"

As we talked, little leaf-shoots from the tropical tree above us fluttered softly to the ground. Although the tree was deciduous, the shoots had tiny needles, like evergreens. I wanted to pick one up and examine it, but thought it would be impolite, and refrained.

Like all Latin capitals, Mexico City is noisy. By day, there is a blasting of horns, and a great deal of whistling and calling. At night, locomotives scream in the suburbs; church bells ring the quarter hour; a parrot utters a strange sort of whistle, a signal which he could have learned in no good company; towards morning a military post pierces the air with artillery and anti-aircraft fire. Altogether, the night is restless, uncertain. Violence seems just around the corner. The city sleeps the uneasy sleep of the threatened animal; and its dreams are troubled.

After the meeting with the president, C. and I left by car for Cuernavaca, where we were to spend the night, by arrangement, in the private home of a kind and hospitable American resident, whom we had never met, and who was, at the time of our arrival, himself absent.

The road wound up the sides of one of the mountain ridges which rim the high basin containing Mexico City. At the pass, about 9,000 feet in elevation, we came suddenly upon a village which appeared to consist exclusively of gin shops—their fronts entirely open, like the tents in a county fair at home—inside: colored lights, juke boxes, and walls lined solidly with bottled liquor. From there, we descended steadily, over miles and miles of serpentines, to the outskirts of Cuernavaca, at about 3,000 feet.

I cannot pretend to describe our host's estate. The house, only one or two years old, was not unlovely. It was in the style of a Moorish palace, and successfully conceived: with patio, cloisters, and terraced gardens. It was decorated with magnificent and unbelievable antiques from the Hearst collection, of which my host had purchased roughly one-half for this purpose. ("When we got done," he later told us, "we had seven carloads left over, and you can't imagine what trouble we had getting them back home.") The dining-room set was composed of ceiling, panelling, murals, and furniture allegedly from the Doge's council chamber in Venice. The ceilings of the cloisters were from old Spanish and French monasteries. An Elizabethan trestle table of enormous length, the board cut from a single gigantic piece of oak, graced the side of one of the cloisters. In my host's bedroom hung original Breughels and Gainsboroughs. All the beds were the great four-posted canopied affairs of kings and grands seigneurs.

It was all too much for me. I lay sleepless, through the long night, under the huge crimson draperies that had once served a prince of the Church and still bore his insignia—while mosquitoes buzzed around my pillow. Outside, the fountain tinkled softly in the patio, and a fitful night breeze searched aimlessly back and forth among the cloisters, like a ghost, murmuring, as it seemed to me, "Lost, lost, lost." By this it referred, I was sure, to all of us: to my restless hosts, who had come to live so far from their native soil; to myself, the guest, who had wandered where he did not belong; to the unhappy antiques, crowded together, like creatures in a zoo, in such incongruous diversity; finally, to itself, the wind, imprisoned in such beautiful walls and failing to find the concomitant of all this beauty.

And it finally occurred to me, in the wee hours of a sleepless night, that this was the same wind that could always be found moving through the places of the lost people. It was the wind that blew through the Riviera and the Bahamas and the Sierra de Sintra: the wind of exiled royalty, of the hopelessly rich, of the tortured intellectuals; the wind of King Carol and the Windsors—the wind that gave its name to the Palace of the Seven Sighs. It was the wind of the last refuge, which turned out to be no refuge at all—the companion-wind of human pretense and despair, accompanying its charges, like an earnest, faithful animal, in the quest of that which was never there—troubling their dreams at night with its frantic, naive searching for that which would never be found.

The square before the cathedral was taken up by a street fair; bedlam of booths, hawkers, and customers. Souvenirs, religious trinkets, food for the pilgrims, were all being dispensed. Slowly, the big limousine edged its way into the dense mass of people, who accepted its invasion without indignation. We got out and pushed our way into the cathedral. Though packed with people, it was cooler and dark in there. A ritual procession was moving around the edge of the building, past the side altars: priests, acolytes, choirboys, and lay deacons with white silk cross bands over their dark suits and banners held above their heads. Priests were chanting, the choirboys responding over and over again with the same group of four notes.

We had to edge back towards the wall, with the crowd, to make room for the procession. Women worshippers, scurrying along on their knees and trying in this way to keep up with the procession, squirmed past our feet.

In the scene of the procession, as it moved past us, there was an overwhelming electric starkness that rocked the spectator like a bolt of lightning: the gross, bleary faces of the priests; the desperate intentness of the kneeling, scurrying women; the heads of the choirboys thrown back and their faces uplifted as they sang, their child eyes glancing upward at the great Roman columns and vaults with their gold ornamentation; the dirty, bursting shoes sticking out from under the priestly and choral robes and shuffling over the worn flagstones. Here was the full-throated utterance of the human mass, with all its age-old vitality, with its spiritual dependence, its will to believe, and its readiness to submit to the organization and regimentation of that same will.

I drove back to the airport still saturated with the penetrating eloquence of this scene. I have never taken offense at the thesis of the Roman Church that many men require a spiritual as well as a profane framework of law: a moral order, founded on an appreciation of the dilemmas of birth and death and of the requirements of social living—together, a moral order drawn up by those who are wiser and more experienced than the great masses of humanity and are capable of channelling into the body of spiritual law the ponderous experience of millennia of human progress. For many people it is always better that there should be *some* moral law, even an imperfect or entirely arbitrary one, than that there should be none at all; for the human being who recognizes no moral restrictions and has no sense of humility is worse than the foulest and most savage beast.

ACADEMIA

My career as a foreign-service officer may be considered to have ended (although there were to be two periods of ambassadorial service in later years) in the summer of 1950, at which time I moved to Princeton. At the outset of the year 1951 I was reminded that I had, before leaving government service, lightheartedly accepted an invitation to deliver a series of lectures at the University of Chicago in April 1951. I set forth for Chicago at the appointed time, but with only two of the six lectures completed, the remainder having to be scratched out on the spot. They were published soon thereafter under the title AMERICAN DIPLOMACY. *Here: the account of the arrival at Chicago.*

APRIL 8, 1951

The train got in at 1 P.M. I had had some discomfort on the train and ate no lunch.

There was a milky sunshine here, but it was still prespring, in contrast to the East.

The taxi, battered and dirty, pounded south on the outer drive, in the broad stream of Sunday afternoon traffic, and brought me to a huge hotel on the drive, several miles south of the Loop.

Later in the afternoon I went for a walk. The hotel, viewed more closely from the pedestrian's angle, was a great brick box, trimmed with some stone casing and metal ornamentation on the ground floor, for elegance' sake. Altogether, it gave the impression of shaggy, besooted, but robust ornateness, springing like a mushroom out of a sea of cinder lots, traffic, filling stations, and long streets of one-floor brick saloons.

I walked over onto the point by the lake. It was a little park, with lawns, a stone administration house, a public toilet, and an embankment braced by tiers of great concrete blocks against the attacks of the lake. At the stone building two soldiers were trying to pick up a couple of little teenagers in blue jeans and flowing shirttails. The girls, hardly more than thirteen, leaned against the wall, chewed gum, and spewed profanity at their admirers. On the south side of the point, students were ensconced on the steps of the embankment, sunning themselves and reading. One was reading *The New Yorker*. Up on the lawn a young man and his girlfriend were trying to take pictures of each other, and she was staggering around; you couldn't tell whether she was hilarious or just drunk.

I left the park and went inland. The streets were dirty and unreceptive—only the saloons and the drugstores and the flashiest motorcar sales agencies were open. You met men with no hats, blue overcoats, no ties, hair uncombed, shoestrings dragging. They all looked as though they had hangovers. On a street corner three older men stood silent and motionless staring up a side street. I looked, too, but could not see what they were staring at.

I went into a drugstore thinking that, having had no lunch, I ought to get something to eat. The soda-fountain counter was wet and dirty. There was no one serving—only a man pushing litter off the floor with a wide pushbroom. I waited until his little heap of paper cups, cellophane wrappers, and cigarette butts had passed under my feet. Then I gave up the idea of eating and went back to the hotel.

On the way, I thought of the things I had seen, and of the *Chicago Tribune* I had been reading in my room. I had read an article on communism at Harvard, among other things, which I wanted to clip and send to Grace. I also reflected that my grandfather and my mother had come from this town. I heard some boys on bicycles screaming at each other across the street and realized that even the language was unfamiliar to me.

So I shuffled along back to the hotel, in the depression born of hunger plus an overpowering sense of lack of confidence in my surroundings; and a small inward voice said, gleefully and melodramatically, "You have despaired of yourself; now despair of your country!"

I knew that the challenge, however melodramatic, was not unfair, and that this, too, I would have to learn to bear in my wanderings in these once-familiar regions.

In the summer of 1951 the Kennan family made the first of many postwar trips to Kristiansand, Norway, where my parents-in-law, then still alive, resided. They were then installed at their summer home, situated in the islands some miles from Kristiansand. These were still the days of ocean liners rather than transoceanic air passage; and on this occasion the liner, one of the fine old Norwegian-American Line ships, proceeded first to Bergen, and thence, with stops at Stavanger and Kristiansand, to Oslo. The calls at the first three of those places were made on the same day.

JULY 1951
NORWAY

Yesterday was a long and strenuous day. We came into Bergen at six in the morning. A sharp cold wind was blowing, churning up the smooth surface of the fjord into the straight, tight seas that I remember so well from my sailing days here. By nine o'clock we were away from Bergen again. For four hours we moved at high speed down through the islands to Stavanger. The sun had come out. The wind was behind us, which made it possible to enjoy being on deck (for the first time since we had left New York, incidentally). The gulls wheeled around us and behind us by the thousands. And Norway simply took my breath away—not just, or even primarily, the colors of the mountains and sea and sky, but rather the places where the hand of man had softened and ordered this hard nature: the little docks, the villages at the foot of the rocks, the white cottages, the hay drying on fences around the tiny green pastures, an old stone monastery church on a treeless, rocky island near the sea—stubborn, hard, defiant, braving century after century the long winter bleakness, the gales, the loneliness, the rain and the cold—living the poetry of windswept rock and sky and sea and only that.

At eleven o'clock there was a Fourth of July ceremony on the ship. The children paraded around the deck, waving little American flags, led by the ship's orchestra, which had constituted itself a band for the purpose. Then an unfortunate Norwegian diplomatist and myself made speeches in the tourist lounge.

Shortly after lunch we were in Stavanger. It was blowing great guns by this time, but still brilliant sunshine. We docked in what seemed to be the very center of the town. Seen from our high decks, on a level with the rooftops, the little cobblestone quayside street below us looked like a stage setting—everything so compact, so neat, so sedate, yet so full of life: warehouses, offices, stores, all doing business before our eyes; bicyclists, horses and carts, people standing in the sunshine just looking at the great ship above them, piles of cargo piled up on the street at shipside. This was a harbor street as harbor streets were meant to be, teeming with life, with sociability, with the intimacy of ship and shore.

Looking across the slip to the street on the other side (for our berth seemed to be right in the middle of town), I found myself conscious of the subtle but amazing difference in the form and perspective and plasticity of objects that still divides the old continent from the new. There were two or three old warehouse buildings on the quay. How they could have differed from American buildings, I cannot say; and yet there was an expressiveness and eloquence and meaning about them, combined with naiveté and simplicity, that simply caused one to gasp. That it could have lain in the dimensions of the buildings themselves I doubt. It was something connected with the entire pattern of shape of quayside, of skyline, of space arrangement. I doubt that any of it was deliberate, or even a part of consciousness, with those who had created it. Perhaps it does not even have any relation to the present generation.

It was midnight when we reached Kristiansand. In the early nocturnal dawn of the white night, we walked over to the motorboat harbor, whence we were to be taken, in the family's boat, out to the archipelago. The red dawn was reflected in the water, as I remember it being reflected from the Duna, at Riga, in other days. A row of little sailboats was silhouetted in it, and the effect was overwhelming.

B. and myself were let off at the fisherman's house on the south side of the point, where Annelise and I were to stay, and I left the baggage there. Then for half an hour we stumbled around the paths of the peninsula, trying to find our way over to the main house. There was a loveliness about everything that surpassed any memories I had retained: the early dawn, the freshness, the cleanliness of air and land and water, the fragrance of evergreen and rock and grass—a little of Bermuda, a little of Maine, a little of Portugal.

When we got to the main house, the children had been put to bed. We sat up with the old people* and drank vermouth with brandy until nearly four o'clock. Then A. and I dragged ourselves back to the fisherman's cottage, in the morning light, and went to bed.

---

*The reference here is to my wife's parents. Mention of them was made in my memoirs (Princeton University Press, 1967, vol. I, p. 39) in the following words: ". . . her mother, a warm, open-hearted person, capable at times of childlike gaiety, but always against the background of a great maternal dignity and purity, a woman from whose lips I never heard an ungenerous or spiteful word; and her father, gaunt, gnarled, and taciturn, an oak root of a man, destined . . . to endure and survive mistreatment and concentration camp punishment at the hands of the Nazis—a stubborn and difficult person, but one from whom, again, over thirty years I never suffered a discourtesy or unkindness. No one who knew it could fail to love Norway for its nature; but even had the landscape been of the dreariest, one could not have failed to love it for such people."

Liberated in 1950 from my official duties in government, I naively thought there would now be time for everything, and I accepted commitments in many directions. One of these was for service on the Board of Trustees of one of our great national foundations; and this brought me to meetings in Southern California, where I had scarcely ever been before. Here: one of the first impressions.

The reader might care to bear in mind that, as of the date of this entry, of the past twenty-four years—since I was twenty-three—I had spent only five years in the United States. I was seeing my country, consequently, with new eyes.

NOVEMBER 4, 1951
PASADENA

I have today that rarest of luxuries: a day of complete leisure, with no obligations, away from home where not even family or house or neglected grounds can lay claim to attention. I am out here for three days on business and am the guest of a friend whose home, swaddled in gardens, looks down from the hill onto the rooftops and foliage of Pasadena. It is strange, and somewhat enervating, after watching the death of the year in the growing austerity of the East Coast autumn, to sit now in a garden, to listen to the chirping of birds and the tinkling of a fountain, to watch the foliage of the eucalyptus trees stirring in a summer breeze, and to feel the warm sunshine on the back of one's neck.

It is Sunday, and I am apparently being left to my own devices—than which nothing could please me more.

I have learned that whenever pressure is suddenly removed from me, it does not leave me serene and contemplative. On the contrary, the fragments of thought surge back and forth in my mind aimlessly and futilely. There is a feeling of empty agitation, and the attention flits distractedly around the chambers of experience and impression, like a restless person in a house, touching objects here and there for no reason at all. Peace of mind and serenity, like most other human attributes, are apparently matters of habit.

My thoughts are full of this Southern California world I see below me and about me. It is easy to ridicule it, as Aldous Huxley and so many other intellectuals have done—but it is silly, and a form of self-condemnation, to do so. These are ordinary human beings: several million of them. The things that brought them here, and hold them here, are deeply human phenomena—as are the stirrings of anxiety that cause them to be so boastful and defensive about it. Being human phenomena, they are part of ourselves; and when we purport to laugh at them, as though we stood fully outside of them, it is we who are the ridiculous ones.

I feel great anxiety for these people, because I do not think they know what they are in for. In its mortal dependence on two liquids—oil and water—which no individual can easily produce by his own energy (even together with family and friends), the life of this area only shares the fragile quality of all life in the great urban concentrations of the motor age. But here the lifelines of supply seem to me particularly tenuous and vital. That is especially true of water, which they now have to bring from hundreds of miles—and will soon have to bring from thousands of miles—away. But equally disturbing to me is the utter dependence on the costly, uneconomical gadget called the automobile for practically every process of life from birth through shopping, education, work, and recreation, even courtship, to the final function of burial. In this community, where the revolutionary force of motorization has made a clean sweep of all other patterns of living and has overcome all competition, man has acquired a new form of legs. And what disturbs me is not only that these mechanical legs have a deleterious effect on man himself, drugging him into a sort of paralysis of the faculty of reflection and distorting his emotional makeup while they are in use—these things are not too serious, and perhaps there are even ways of combating them. What disturbs me most is man's abject dependence on this means of transportation and on the complicated processes that make it possible. It is as though his natural legs had really become shriveled by disuse. One has the feeling that if his artificial ones were taken away from him, he would go crawling miserably and helplessly around like a crippled insect, no longer capable of conducting the battle for existence, doomed to early starvation, thirst, and extinction.

One must not exaggerate this sort of thing. All modern urban society is artificial in the physical sense: dependent on gadgets, fragile and vulnerable. This is simply the apotheosis. Here the helplessness is greatest, but also the thoughtlessness. And the thoughtlessness is part of the helplessness.

But alongside the feeling of anxiety I have at the sight of these people, there is a questioning as to the effect they are going to have, and the contribution they are going to make, to American society as a whole. Again, this is not conceived in terms of reproach or criticism. There is really a subtle but profound difference between people here and what Americans used to be, and still partly are, in other parts of the country. I am at a loss to define this difference, and am sure that I understand it very imperfectly.

Let me try to get at it by overstating it. Here it is easy to see that when man is given (as he *can* be given only for relatively brief periods and in exceptional circumstances) freedom both from political restraint and from want, the effect is to render him childlike in many respects: fun-loving, quick to laughter and enthusiasm, unanalytical, unintellectual, outwardly expansive, preoccupied with physical beauty and prowess, given to sudden and unthinking seizures of aggressiveness, driven constantly to protect his status in the group by an eager conformism—yet not unhappy. In this sense Southern California, together with all that tendency of American life which it typifies, is childhood without the promise of maturity—with the promise only of a continual widening and growing impressiveness of the childhood world. And when the day of reckoning and hardship comes, as I think it must, it will be—as everywhere among children— the cruelest and most ruthless natures who will seek to protect their interests by enslaving the others; and the others, being only children, will be easily enslaved. In this way, values will suddenly prove to have been lost that were forged slowly and laboriously in the more rugged experience of Western political development elsewhere.

Governmental service in periods and places where great political tension prevailed was not conducive to the sort of leisurely and detached diary-keeping of which this volume is the reflection; and if any time and place ever fell squarely within that category, it was the months spent as ambassador in Moscow in 1952. But there were occasional attempts (not, apparently, greatly appreciated) to convey to officials in the State Department by personal letter something of the atmosphere of Moscow and its environs in that strange final year of Stalin's life. The following are excerpts from one of those letters.

JULY 15, 1952
AMERICAN EMBASSY
MOSCOW, USSR

Garden plots exist around Moscow by the hundreds of thousands, some leased out for the summer by the suburban municipalities from public lands (roadside strips, stream bottoms, etc.) but without accompanying buildings, others leased out as the grounds of summer dachas, others belonging to what are, in effect, private suburban properties. These areas on the edge of the city virtually hum with activity, and the activity is one having little or nothing to do with the "socialized sector" of the economy. Houses are built with family labor (log houses still, but stout and warm and not bad housing); gardens and orchards are laid out; poultry and livestock (cows and goats) are traded and cultivated in great number, though all trading must be done in individual animals, or at the most, pairs, not in herds.

I would guess that the number of people participating in the pursuit of such part-time activities just around Moscow alone runs into the millions. And around their activities there has grown up a sort of commercial servicing establishment: people who make their living by growing seeds and hot-house plants, breeding animals, etcetera. All these people have to keep their operations to a small scale. They must be careful not to employ labor, or to be found owning anything so magnificent as a truck. Everything must be masked as individual, rather than highly organized commercial, activity. But there are ways and means of solving all those problems.

The result is that on the outskirts of Moscow there has grown up a veritable world of what you might call "miniature private interest," a world in which people devote themselves to, and think about, everything under the sun except the success of communism, and appear to be quite happy doing so. I know, in fact, of no human environment more warmly and agreeably pulsating with activity, contentment, and sociability than a contemporary Moscow suburban dacha area on a nice spring morning, after the long, trying winter. Everything takes place in a genial intimacy and informality: hammers ring, roosters crow, goats tug at their tether, barefoot women hoe vigorously at the potato patches, small boys play excitedly in the little streams and ponds, family parties sit at crude wooden tables in the gardens under the young fruit trees. The great good earth of Mother Russia, long ignored in favor of the childish industrial fetishes of the earlier Communist period, seems once more to exude her benevolent and maternal warmth over man and beast and growing things together; and only, perhaps, an American ambassador, stalking through the countryside with his company of guardians to the amazement of the children and the terror of the adults, is effectively isolated, as though by an invisible barrier, from participation in the general beneficence of nature and human sociability.

The spiritual breach between the rulers and the ruled is one of the things that most strongly strikes a person returning to Russia at this juncture after a long absence. Somehow or other, the betterment of material conditions for the mass of the people seems to go hand in hand with a certain sort of withdrawal of these masses from emotional participation in the announced purposes of the regime. This is not to be confused with political discontent. On the contrary, it is attended by the steady disappearance of those age groups which have any sort of recollection of prerevolutionary times or any ability to imagine any other sort of government than this one. It even is attended, I think, by an increasing acceptance of Soviet power and, in general, Soviet institutions as a natural condition of life, not always agreeable or pleasant, sometimes even dangerous, but nevertheless something that is simply "there," like the weather or the soil, and not to be removed by anything the individual could possibly do—something that simply has to be accepted and put up with.

But in this very acceptance of Soviet power as a sort of unchangeable condition of nature, there is also implied the very lack of living emotional and political relationship to it, about which I am speaking. Thirty years ago people were violently for it or against it, because all of them felt Soviet power as something springing from human action, capable of alteration by human action, and affecting their own lives in ways that raised issues of great immediacy and importance with respect to their own behavior. Today most of them do not have this feeling. Their attitude toward it is one of increasing apathy and detachment, combined with acceptance—acceptance sometimes resigned, sometimes vaguely approving, sometimes unthinkingly enthusiastic. In general, I think it fair to say that the enthusiasm varies in reverse relationship to the thoughtfulness of the person and to his immediate personal experience with the more terrible sides of Soviet power—such things as the experiences of collectivization, recollections of the purges, or personal unhappiness as a victim of the harshness of the bureaucracy.

It is my feeling that the regime is itself in large measure responsible for this growing emotional detachment of large masses of the people. For one thing it has rendered itself physically and personally remote from the rest of the population to an extraordinary degree. One had a feeling fifteen or twenty years ago of a much greater personal impact of the members of the Politburo on the actual running of the country, an impact which created a certain sense of intimacy between them and their subjects, and even such of their subjects as were suffering at their hands. More was known and felt by people of the personalities, the views, and the moods of the top rulers. Today these rulers sit in inscrutable isolation behind their Kremlin walls. For most people they are only names, and names with a slightly mythical quality at that. The relatively few changes in personnel in the top bodies in the past fifteen years have meant that even that link with the public which is provided by the normal flow of advancement into prominent position of people who once had normal ties with friends and neighbors and coworkers is now largely missing.

The fact of the matter is that the bottom has been knocked out of the internal ideological position of the Soviet regime by the immoderate and "all-out" glorification of Stalin and exaggeration of the regime's own successes in the past. A vacuum has been created in this way which it will not be easy for anyone to fill. The country lives today, ideologically, in a species of Wagnerian twilight, characterized by the rosy, ethereal reflections of great deeds once accomplished, breathing an atmosphere of well-deserved relaxation and smug self-congratulation over the tremendous achievements of the parting day. The real reason why Soviet plays are bad plays in the year 1952 is that all have to be written on the assumption that the happy ending has already taken place before the dramatic happenings begin: witnessing them, the Western observer has the impression of seeing a family of actors sitting around on the stage after the last curtain has fallen, still congratulating each other on the fortunate outcome of all their adventures, those who were once in error having now seen the light and started on proper paths, the others glowing with a veritable surfeit of rectitude. There can be no real negative characters in the Soviet drama, except agents and dupes of the menacing outside world; for how could such people be produced by the influences of Soviet society alone, which has been correctly conducted for thirty-five years?

This relative stability in social relationships seems again to stem directly from conditions in the top ranks of the regime, particularly the congealment of personnel at the very top, the stagnation in promotions at the Central Committee level, and the general atmosphere of wary hesitation and inactivity which is no doubt a reflection of the delicacy of all personal-official relationships in the light of Stalin's increasing age and the growing problem of succession. The connection of these things with the growth of social distinctions was clearly symbolized for some of us, the other evening, by the sight of Stalin's son sitting with two other air force officers in solitary splendor in the government box at the ballet and ogling the prima ballerina in the best regal tradition. I cannot imagine that this young man conceives of himself as a crown prince. Despite his general's rank, he is not a person of any position in the Party, as far as any of us are aware. I should suppose that any bid for power on his part would set all sorts of fireworks in motion. But the quiet ostentation of his appearance at the ballet is eloquent testimony to the fact that distinctions other than ones of Party or police position now have raised their heads and achieved recognition in the Soviet Union and find the crowning expression in the immediate vicinity of the august presence itself.

We have seen that the emotional withdrawal of the mass of

the people from an identification with the life and experience of the political power was a reflection of the policies of the government itself. We see that the stratification of social groups in the country likewise has as its origin conditions at the top of the regime. These things, to my mind, warrant our most minute attention. The very essence of the domestic policies of the Stalin regime has been to attempt to abolish the factor of elemental and natural evolution in the development of Russian society—in fact, to abolish change itself except insofar as change might represent one of the deliberate temporary zigzags of Party policy. We now see two changes taking place before our eyes, neither of which was presumably desired by the regime, both of which even bear in themselves considerable potential danger for the regime, and yet both of which the regime has found itself obliged to stimulate. One is the detachment of the people from the supreme political purpose; the other is the growing rigidity of caste stratification in Soviet society.

Both of these phenomena, in deepest essence, are reflections of the life and works of a single man. The first is the reflection of his infinite jealousy and avidity for political power—qualities that carried him to his absurd pretensions to an earthly divinity and actually killed the ideological sense and function of the political movement of which he is the head. The second is the reflection of his increasing age and approaching death. No great country can be identified as closely as this one is with the life and fortunes of a single man—so bent and attuned to his personality, his whims and his neuroses—without sharing to a degree his weaknesses and his very mortality. The Party has tried to rule out change; but the Party is hoisted here on the petard of its own lack of genuine democracy, of the loss of organic connection with the emotional forces of the people themselves, of its dependence on, and beholdenness to, the life cycle of a single individual.

I see no early revolt in the Soviet Union. I see no likely dramatic or abrupt ending to the phenomenon of bolshevism.

Least of all do I see in the minds of the people any new or revolutionary alternative to the present system. I cannot rule these things out, but they are not in the cards as they appear to me today. I *do* see that the Party has not succeeded in ruling out change. I see that there are great forces operating here which are not really under the control of the regime, because they are part of the regime's own failings and its own mortality. I see that the original glamour and emotional meaning of the revolution have largely exhausted themselves, and that the regime faces a dilemma in the need for filling the resulting vacuum. I would warn against drawing any primitive and oversimplified conclusions from the observations I have just made. But I think they have sufficient force to stand also as a warning against the assumption into which many people have drifted: that the Soviet leaders have somehow found some mysterious secret of infallibility in the exercise of power and that it is no problem for them to hang on indefinitely and to mold Soviet society to their hearts' desire. What is coming in this immediately approaching period may very well be a crisis of Soviet power quite comparable in scope and seriousness to the original civil war or the death of Lenin or the purges of the thirties—but entirely different in form.

Very sincerely,

George F. Kennan
AMBASSADOR

As related in my memoirs, the sad months of ambassadorial service in Moscow in 1952, ending with my expulsion from that country, were followed by Mr. Dulles's decision that I should no longer remain a member of the American Foreign Service. The final separation from the service, in which I had spent twenty-seven years, came on a day in June 1953. The following account of the events of that day, based on diary notes, appeared in the second volume of my memoirs; but it belongs, in spirit and in significance, in this collection as well.

The farm in question, I may explain, was one situated in south-central Pennsylvania, acquired during the war in 1942. It was our first, and for some years our only, real home.

Finally, the day arrived—a day in June—when the three months were up and the retirement became formally a fact. I busied myself that morning in the department, collecting such personal papers as I had about me and making arrangement for the receipt of my appointed pension. By early afternoon I had completed these final chores and was ready to leave.

It occurred to me then that one would normally, on completion of twenty-seven years of service with a great organization, say good-bye to someone before leaving it. My connection with it had, after all, been something more than wholly casual. I had enjoyed the most rapid advancement, as a Foreign Service officer, of anyone of my generation. For two years, in the exciting days of the Marshall Plan and the rescue of Europe, I had occupied the office next to that of the Secretary of State. Only three years before, I had been Counselor of the department and president of the American Foreign Service Association.

I cast around, in my mind's eye, to discover someone to whom I might suitably say good-bye. At first, I was unable to think of anyone. The friends from earlier Moscow days had either left the service entirely or had been sent to posts abroad. The housecleaning conducted by Mr. Dulles's minions as a means of placating congressional vindictiveness had been thorough and sweeping. The place was full of new faces—many of them guarded, impassive, at best coldly polite, faintly menacing. But I persisted in my quest. Surely, there must, I thought, be someone somewhere in this great building—the institution that had been the center of my professional life for twenty-seven years—to whom it would be suitable and proper for me to say good-bye on this occasion.

Then suddenly a light dawned on me: there was Mrs. Mary Butler—the receptionist who guarded the approaches to the offices of the Secretary and his senior aides on the fifth floor. A southern lady in the finest sense of that term, beautiful, courteous, warm and competent, her lovely face and cheerful greeting had heartened me on many a morning in the years of incumbency as head of the Planning Staff and had strengthened me for the trials of the day ahead. She had happily survived the purge that followed upon Mr. Dulles's assumption of office. I did not know her really very well, but I knew she would be interested, and possibly even sorry, to know that I was leaving for all time.

I went up, therefore, and took leave of her. I then went downstairs, clutching a briefcase full of personal papers, got into my car, and drove slowly northward, for the last time, through the familiar meandering byroads of central Maryland, to the farm. Again I had a feeling—misleading, of course, as on the occasion of my arrival in Princeton three years before—that the great effort of life had now come to an end, that nothing of consequence remained, that there was now plenty of time for everything.

The farmhouse was deserted when I arrived. The farmer's family, as I recall it, had gone off for the afternoon. Without even bothering to remove my bags from the car, I strolled around our own house, seated myself on the open front porch, sat there an hour or two and, looking out over the two lovely fields that stretch off below the house to the east, tried to take stock of the change that had, that day, been wrought in my life.

There was plenty to think about, but someone else, I knew, would have to strike the balance, if one was ever to be struck, between justice and injustice, failure and accomplishment. I myself could not. I cannot today.

The farm was the gathering place for the family, and remains so to this day. The following two vignettes are accounts of trips to the farm, the first from Washington, and the second from Princeton.

Heat. I was in Washington on business. Went out at 2:15 P.M., to drive back to the farm. The heat beat down fiercely onto the helpless city. The streets were almost deserted, though twenty or thirty thousand people were at work, all around, in the government offices. At the parking lot there was a Negro in attendance. He was stripped to the waist, streaming with perspiration, and complained of the heat. I drove up Connecticut Avenue, but then cut over to Wisconsin Avenue and drove to the farm via Highway 240 and then Highway 27—the way we used to take between Washington and the farm in earlier years. On the way, I passed many places which, I realized, meant something to me—or had once meant something to me—from these past trips: the place where the man was building the new dairy barn (now looking shabby and worn and somehow as though people were disillusioned with it); the place where we once asked about the crop the men were harvesting in the field beside the road and found out it was wormwood (we were traveling in Ronny Allen's new Buick, and he could not go more than thirty miles an hour, and the trip went fast never-

161

theless, and Ronny is now dead); the place where Grace and I once had a flat tire (there was then a little brick schoolhouse there, in a grove of trees; the schoolhouse is now some sort of a store or a pop joint, and people dump tin cans in the little woods next to it); and the place where the roof had blown off the house; and the place where the view is so lovely; and the place where they bulldozed everything down and put the cement-mixing plant and later somehow there was something faintly beautiful about it after all. All of these things had meant something to me, and it was perfectly silly that they had. I meant nothing to them. They didn't know they had meant anything to me. Perhaps they didn't even mean anything to themselves. Well, anyway, they would now mean nothing to me anymore. Something had happened to me now. I realized their emptiness, their indifference. But God, the world was dull, and still, and hostile—lying there in the heat.

DECEMBER

The men are at work, building clapboard surfacing on the front of the house at the farm. I drove down alone from Princeton, to have an eye to what they are doing. It was pouring rain all the way to the Susquehanna district, where it turned to snow. But the ground had been warmed up by several balmy days, so it didn't stick.

I ate in a diner near Dillsburg. From its big chrome-glass windows you could see out over the valley, leading upward into the mountains to the west. As I was eating, the late-afternoon sun suddenly emerged, triumphant, over a great jagged-edged bank of cloud, and flooded the valley, bringing out a mass of glorious winter color. The fat waitress went over and kneeled on the window seat, staring out. "Say, ain't that just the purtiest thing you ever seen?" she said. "I don't know whatcha talkin' about," said the frizzy-haired one; and the pimply-faced boy with whom she was flirting said, "Aw, she's jes nuts." I said to the fat one, "It *is* pretty." "Ain't it, though?" she said, still enraptured. "It's like Grandma Moses or sumpin'."

All the way from Dillsburg down to our village, the sun shed its slanting watery light on the brown grass fields and the lush winter grain. The white barns and silos, clean and glistening from the long rain, gleamed out from the distant hillsides. But suddenly, as I came into our village, it was all over. Darkness was falling fast; the night cold was already creeping over the landscape; and the puddles, shining with the reflection of the bright western sky, had the stillness that told you they were freezing. Out at the farm the little creek was foaming and gurgling with its minor torrent of muddy water; the sky between the big barn and the corn barn was a fiery red. When you walked on the thick winter grass of the lawn you could feel the spongy wetness underneath a faint freezing crust. Above, to the southeast, over the big creek, the first cold winter stars were out, and a sliver of a moon.

*In 1955, driving with my sister through my native Milwaukee,
I paid the first visit I had ever had occasion to pay to the graves
of my parents: my mother, who had died two months after my
own birth, and of whom I had no recollection; and my father,
who had died while I was accompanying Ambassador William
C. Bullitt to Moscow in 1933.*

Today was a day of dreams. We left in midmorning and drove (rather slowly, in the dense Sunday traffic) to Milwaukee. Wisconsin Street looked almost exactly the same, as did much of the lakefront, but the parks were smarter, more extensive, and more populated.

On our way into town we passed the Forest Home Cemetery and stopped off there to visit our parents' graves. The cemetery was huge: hills, valleys, miles, it seemed, of curving, crisscrossing roads, in which we got quite lost. We had no idea where the graves were; and there was no one to tell us. But at one point we all sensed the nearness of them. I got out of the car, and walked away alone, dazed and excited, among the headstones, a little panicky, like a lost child. (Father, Father, where are you?) And it was as though, if I did not find the grave, we would be forever lost and separated.

Jeanette finally saw the family name on a stone, a little off the road. We got out and walked in. There they lay—the tombstones still sturdy, respectable in a Victorian sort of way; the inscriptions uncompromisingly legible and specific; the mounds still showing where the bodies had been laid.

First—my mother, Florence James Kennan, whom I never knew, struck down by death only two months after the birth of the fourth of her children. Here, buried and helpless, lay all the love that could not be expended—all the tenderness that could not be bestowed. (Dear Mother, it must have been hard and bitter for you to leave your little children. We have all held you, in retrospect, in a sort of awed adoration—our ever-young, dead mother, beautiful, unworldly, full only of love and grace for us, like a saint. In imagination, we have received all you would have given us. Pity, only, that we with our youth could not have borne some of your frailty—could not have breathed back into you some of the strength you once gave us. May our love, somehow or other, reach you.)

Next to her—my father, Kossuth Kent Kennan. (God be praised that they lie side by side.) It was a real marriage, full of difficulty, embarrassments, and pain—family differences, differing social origins, and what not—but full of real love and a total mutual commitment. My father: awkward; shy almost to the point of cowardice; often putting his foot in it; unable to explain himself; oversensitive; proud; slightly boyish to the end of his days; always in some ways a yokel, in others a man of noble intellect; capable of being utterly broken up and disintegrated by too much beauty; a sentimentalist like the rest of us; a man from whose taut, severe, lawyerlike face the love of someone else could suddenly shine forth with great warmth and intensity; a man of much loneliness and much suffering; gaunt, tough, abstemious, scarcely knowing illness after his youth, living life to the very end—to a dark and tortured and lonely old age. Myself a moody, self-centered, neurotic boy, as shy as he, and confiding in no one, I must have given him little solace in his old age; but I loved him as I have loved no other man but my son; we never grated on each other; I appreciated his silence and his forbearance. And I understood, perhaps better than anyone in the family, but only later and in retrospect, his loneliness, his unhappiness, his despair, and his faith.

On his grave, too, the mound looks little and pathetic and slightly helpless.

I still dream from time to time, with tenderness and affection, of my father, and long to be reunited with him (now that I am in my prime and could lend him strength and understanding). Yet he lived out his life. And the sight of his grave, though I had never seen it before, was somehow more expected; and I could look at it with greater equanimity than I could at that of my mother.

May the God in whom he believed so desperately give him grace and respite and healing in the afterlife—above all, peace, and the sense of communion with others.

Ray, a villager and former truck driver, had for years been an enthusiastic caretaker, and invariably a cheerful, pleasant companion, on my Pennsylvania farm.

On Tuesday I went in the village and saw Ray. Lying in a high hospital bed in the dining room of his house, he was in pitiful shape: both his arms now twisted and useless, speech and eating possible, but with difficulty. He looked at me with a face full of anguish and worry and suffering. It seemed to him, I knew, so unjust. He had worked so hard and done so well with his one good arm. It had been a source of such comfort and pride to him that he could manage so well—that he could drive his Model-T Ford with the one good arm and tend the grounds beautifully. Now even that was gone, and death, I understood, was near. His face seemed bigger, drawn out by suffering; the usual cheerful, sly little lines—the mask of brisk, shrewd country good humor—was gone; and looking now at this new, defenseless, unveiled sort of face, I realized how little I had ever known him, how rarely I had ever looked at him behind his mask. And I also realized how all the usual attributes of life—age, sex, status, and the acquired habits of personality—retire and stand aside in the presence of the proximity of death, leaving the soul naked and alone and helpless, as it was when it came into this world, full only of the great agonized question "Why?" but dimly conscious that in the very ability to ask that question there lay a measure of ascendancy over the mere matter in which the soul had been clothed and by which it had been surrounded, and that there was, in that ascendancy, the justification for hope beyond life—and for prayer.

California again, this time for research at the Hoover Library in Palo Alto.

My mind keeps plucking and tugging at the riddle of this California area, trying to capture its essence, to define its differentness, to establish its relationship to that which exists elsewhere in this world. From this process nothing emerges but fragmentary thoughts and insights—irreverent, exaggerated for purposes of illustration, none of course adequate to the purpose.

California reminds me of the popular American Protestant concept of heaven: there is always a reasonable flow of new arrivals; one meets many—not all—of one's friends; people spend a good deal of their time congratulating each other over the fact that they are there; discontent would be unthinkable; and the newcomer is slightly disconcerted to realize that now—the devil having been banished and virtue being triumphant—nothing terribly interesting can ever happen again.

California is outwardly one-dimensional, in the emotional sense. Looking at the faces, listening to the snatches of conversation, one wonders whether such a thing as anguish exists at all—whether, in fact, there is even any anguish in love, or whether this, too, comes, is experienced, passes, and dies with the same cheerful casualness that seems to dominate all the other phenomena of existence.

◆ ◆ ◆

These people practice what for centuries the philosophers have preached: they ask no questions; they live, seemingly, for the day; they waste no energy or substance on the effort to understand life; they enjoy the physical experience of living; they enjoy the lighter forms of contact with an extremely indulgent and undemanding natural environment; their consciences are not troubled by the rumblings of what transpires beyond their horizon. If they are wise, surely the rest of us are fools.

On a Saturday afternoon the inhabitants spread out from San Francisco by the hundreds of thousands: to the hills, to the seashore, to rivers, to cottages, to golf courses and tennis courts and fancy outdoor grills and a thousand other forms of pleasure. In the vegetable and berry fields of the Santa Clara Valley, at the same time, wetbacks, working in gangs, move their hoes with endless monotony along the crop rows that stretch out to the horizon; their faces under the big straw hats are turned with sullen impassiveness to the ground; they do not see the endless cars of the weekend pleasure-seekers, streaming along the highway at the edge of the field, past the battered yellow bus in which they came—in which, in fact, they live—and which is now parked, leaning sharply, in the steep ditch.

Milwaukee and St. Louis.

Went up to Milwaukee yesterday. After lunching with the J.'s I drove back via Cambridge Avenue, stopped the car there, and sat for a long time looking at the old house in which I was born and reared. There it stood, looking just as it always did. The trees and shrubs around it were higher, and the neighborhood had deteriorated badly; but the whole place seemed strangely serene and timeless—as though it were glad that the civilization of this age had passed it by—as though it were content now to live by its memories and to await, without either complaint or haste, the day—which cannot now be so far off—when it will disappear from the face of the earth, and all that once transpired in it and around it will be swallowed up in the forgotten past. Looking at it, I had the same feeling I had when, a half hour later, I sat, once more at the head of my parents' graves, and wept my heart out, like a child. The graves were immensely peaceful, lying there in the thin late-summer sunshine of a cool August day, with the breeze murmuring in the tops of the two double-trunked elm trees that rise above them. They seemed to say: "We have reached a reality beyond all your strivings and sufferings; on your terms it is neither good nor bad; you cannot conceive of it. You cannot help us now, any more than we can help you. But we are serene and timeless, and you are not. We have our secret, infinitely sad to your mind, no doubt, but in tune with nature. We have known all the suffering you now know, and then some; we are beyond your sympathy, as you are beyond our pity. Look: we give you the breath of peacefulness—we are a part of the long afternoon of life; take the hint, go your way as best you can; do not ask too many questions; it will not be long before you join us."

AUGUST 26, 1956

It was hot after we left Chicago. The landscape, flat as a tabletop, was as monotonous as any in the world: cornfields, cornfields, cornfields; long double ribbons of concrete highway paralleling the railway for tens of miles at a time; occasional farms; occasional villages, with sheds and sidings, and grade crossings, and little wooden houses with spacious lawns behind the tree-lined streets: the essence of the Middle West. As we approached St. Louis, things looked dusty and still, and there was a thunderstorm brewing over half the sky. The miles of freightyards and factories and warehouses and sidings on the outskirts of St. Louis were very deserted, motionless, on a hot, late Sunday afternoon in August.

Looking at all this, and at my fellow passengers, I suddenly thought for a moment that I understood the message of the strange stillness that struck me so on the part of the old house in Milwaukee and my parents' graves. I realized that I, too, belonged back there somewhere in the past. I had always thought of the present as morning—as prologue. Now I realized that for me, at least, it is not. It is afternoon—the afternoon of a day that will bring nothing more than the fatigue and, perhaps, the peace of evening. For a moment I saw this age and its doings as my father might see it from the grave: blind, willful, doomed, and not very interesting. I am living in the world my father despaired of, and rightly so. Why should I take it too seriously, hurry and worry and bustle around in it. It is, after all, late afternoon; the main happenings of the day are over; not much more is going to happen today. In this way I may acquire something of that same peace that the house and the graves have, recognizing, too, without complaint, that my day is past, that I am as much of an anachronism as the house, that I, too, have been passed by and do not really mind too much—because the present is too uninteresting. We of the past have a secret; and we need never worry about its being betrayed—for no one now is curious about it. No one would understand it even if he tried.

*Accompanied by my wife and the two youngest children, I spent
the academic year 1957–58 in Oxford, as Eastman Professor at
Balliol College. Here: some of the impressions of my first days
there, before the arrival of the other members of my family.* *

After eleven days in Oxford, I finally get a moment—
in a rather moth-eaten and genteel old London hotel
(where a grandfather's clock in the lounge gives out the
chimes of Big Ben)—to write a line, once again, in this record.

How does one gather together the impressions of one's first
days in a strange place in a foreign country?

Oxford! Serene courtyards. Magnificent old towers, graceful but strong, seeming to swim against the background of the
blowing clouds. Breakneck traffic plunging incongruously
through the streets. Great phalanxes of bicycles, sweeping
down the High Street, ridden by young women with strong
limbs and healthy complexions, not delicate but not unattractive. At home: a chilly, empty apartment in a huge empty
house. Endless loneliness—days without the exchange of a
single social word. Long walks in the fresh, damp wind;
through the parks; along suburban streets which have the

---

*Two of the children, Grace and Joan, had been born in the 1930s, before
the war. The other two, Christopher and Wendy, who were with us in
Oxford, both born after the war, were now eight and five years of age,
respectively.

prim, rectangular bluntness and blankness of so much of the modern urban scene in England; along the banks of quiet rivers, where lovers lie in the deep grass, as lost, as desperate, as helpless as the heroine and hero of *The Forsyte Saga.* (Ah, love in England, so frail, so handicapped, so overwhelmingly without a chance, and so terribly poignant by consequence!) Meals in tiny little hotel restaurants, where there are only two waitresses, where the menu never changes, and all is so quiet that people whisper in order not to shatter the churchyard stillness. Old common rooms of the colleges, with the paneling, the candles, the port, and the feeling of people clinging, clinging, to what is really past, and for how long? The contrasts of the English personality in the casual encounters, running all the way from the most beautiful politeness and helpfulness to occasional ferocious flashes of rudeness or condescension. And everywhere the little groups of summer tourists, camera and guidebook in hand, dragging their feet, duty written into every line of the visage.

During the Christmas vacation, totally exhausted from the strenuous autumn in Oxford, I was hospitalized briefly in Zurich.

Zurich is somber, overcast, the bare trees silent and submissive in their winter rest, the unfrozen lake, so inviting in summer, now forbidding and deserted, its surface covered with a sinister, wintry gleam. The town has grown tremendously, is now unbelievably smart and prosperous and well ordered. What, one wonders, would be the position of Switzerland in a world controlled by the Communists? Nowhere has the capitalist system, superimposed on a wise and sturdy democracy, produced such results as here, unless it be in Sweden. Whether human happiness has really been promoted thereby, I do not know. Man is still an animal, whose physical nature demands danger and combat; and whether he can ever find self-expression and peace in these gleaming, well-ordered stables, where the discipline of good social behavior is demanded of him as in no other place, seems doubtful. But if merit resides (and somehow I think it does) in eliminating squalor, in treating nature with respect, in making human habitation clean and strong and attractive, my hat goes off to the Swiss. And this is not to mention their foreign policy, which, along with that of Finland, is the only sound and sensible one in the world.

An afternoon's excursion in Denmark.

Wishing to disembarrass my hosts of my presence, I proclaimed my intention of going away for a day's excursion. There were errands to do in Copenhagen in the morning. It was early afternoon before I could get away. A suburban train took me to Hillerød. There I changed to a local train (what the Germans call a *Bummelzug*) filled with a mixture of country people and weekenders from Copenhagen going out to visit their country relatives. Sedately, with countless little stops, the train pursued its leisurely way toward its terminal point, Hundested, at the very northwest tip of the large island on which Copenhagen is situated.

It was a warm, sunny afternoon, with thundershowers in the air—a bit heavy and clammy. To both sides the ripening grain, high and heavy in the fields, waved to the breeze of the passing train. The bright sky to the northwest and west bespoke the nearness of the sea. At the tiny little stations the postmasters—sleek, well-fed, roly-poly Danes—scurried out with their handcarts to receive the last of the week's mails; bicycles were removed from the baggage car; family groups welcomed relatives, loaded with bundles from the big city, and disappeared with them down country roads and lanes, on carts or bicycles or on foot. I, hanging out the window, watching these scenes, felt very lonely, in the silly way one does in foreign lands; and every time one of the passengers, to whose countenance I had now accustomed myself during this brief hour of anonymous companionship on the train, disappeared down the station platform and out of my life, it was a tiny wrench and a tiny parting—a symbol of the underlying impermanence and loneliness of the human state.

Hundested—the end of the line, except for a spur that went on to the ferry slip. It was already after 4 P.M. I had coffee in a deserted konditorei on the little main street. Why, I wondered, were all little seaside towns—maritime towns—somewhat alike, from Norway to Portugal, from Denmark to New England: small houses, wall-to-wall, narrow streets, but not too narrow, and fairly regular? The sea as a livelihood never afforded, I supposed, the substance for pretension, or, if it did, this was only for people who lived in the great turn-over ports, not in these fishing and ship-captain villages of Hundested, Arendal, Cascais, Stonington, or what you will.

Across the street two teenaged girls, wearing the tight jeans and sweaters that have become everywhere the mark of protest against my own generation, lolled against a wall and waited hopefully for some boys to come by.

I paid my bill and strolled on down to the harbor. It was not necessary to ask the way. In a seaside town everything points to the harbor. It was, as I had hoped it would be, a spectacular little place: a basin, several hundred yards long and fifty to a hundred yards wide, protected by moles at the narrow entrance, and sheltering, in addition to the ferry slips, a whole fleet of the sturdy Danish fishing cutters, very much like their fine Norwegian counterparts.

I settled down to sketch. On the dock opposite me a small crowd had collected, and as I saw what drew them, I realized that a sinister shadow hung over the little port on this heavy Saturday afternoon. An ambulance was drawn up on the dock; below, there was a motorboat with a black flag; people were lowering something into the motorboat. It was, as I was soon told, the body of a little boy, the missing one, who had gone beyond his depth in the surf and simply disappeared from sight.

Through how formidable a series of perils, I reflected, the average little boy must move; his hope, his curiosity, his eagerness for experience, render his life, if he is a healthy, outdoor boy, as precarious as that of the seaman-adventurer of antiquity. In all of this he is guilty of nothing more than an enthusiastic response to his own instincts and nature. What justice lies in the never-ending succession of happy coincidences by which most little boys survive these perils while others do not? And is there not some special heaven into which those are received around whom, as around this little fellow, the black waters have closed prematurely?

Passage by liner from Southampton to Le Havre, en route to Hamburg.

Early Friday morning, the eleventh, just as the dawn was breaking, we came into Southampton. Chilled and sleepy, I followed our progress from the upper deck, drank in the magic of the lights and shapes of anchored vessels in the half-dawn, then went down again to sleep fitfully for another hour before breakfast.

When the ship sailed again, it was bright daylight. The shores of the Solent and the Isle of Wight, now bathed in a misty late-summer sunlight, revealed the usual English mixture of shabby sordidness and a verdant, upper-class beauty. At Cowes the striped awnings of the Royal Yacht Club still blazed out in defiant exclusiveness from the mass of trees and housefronts. A converted Thames barge, dark and awkward with its ponderous sprit boom, rode uneasily at anchor among the graceful yachts, like a fresh-baked Labour peer at a royal levee. All along the shore, on both sides, were the remainders of the days of Victoria and Albert—of a civilization that not long ago (within the memory of living man) seemed, and believed itself to be, of a solidity unequaled since the days of the Roman Empire, and is yet today so wholly undermined that almost nothing remains of it except in the universities, in the pretenses or habits of a few older people, and in these physical Victorian relics: hospitals, castles, private houses—

romantically imitative, ostentatiously solid, wholly un-ashamed, blinking contemptuously from the banks of the river at us denizens of a new and insipid age.

In the afternoon, having glided all morning across a sea as calm as oil, we came into Le Havre. The *plage*, the hillside, the prim modern villas along the top—all was in a golden, relaxed late-summer sunshine. On the mole, as usual, people were fishing. Behind them were the new buildings of the recon-structed city—very modern, functional, and uninteresting in their gray concrete. The tug that brought us in was steered by a figure that could not possibly have been other than French, with his slippers, his beret, the cold cigarette dan-gling from his lips, the contemptuous taciturnity and touch of Gallic abandon with which he swung his craft around—a misanthrope, unquestionably, a man who did not think highly of humanity, who hoped for nothing from humanity, who had made his terms with a benighted and ridiculous world. Just let the world attempt to break those terms—he would know how to stand up for his rights. At the great ship he was guiding to the dock, he never once glanced up. We meant nothing to him. He had seen it all, known it all. "Je m'en fous."

En route by train, through Jutland (Denmark), to Hamburg.

The day wore on. The train clicked its way southward hour after hour over the flat, thrifty Danish landscape. The weather was still of that unnatural perfection—cloudless sky, golden sunshine, and mild dryness—which is the blessing of all northern Europe in this unprecedented year. The fields looked prosperous but slightly dry.

A young Englishman got on. He was a student at an agricultural college in the north of England—had been working all summer on a Danish farm. Now he was on his way back to England for another year as a student. He said his ambition was to be a farm manager. He had been impressed with the long hours of Danish farm work, with the number of processes still done by hand for traditional reasons, and with the dullness and drudgery of farm life there as compared with England. He divulged information on his agricultural experiences readily enough, but I was caused to reflect, after talking with him for an hour, on the fact that he was still personally a complete cipher. How deeply the Englishman, and particularly the middle-class Englishman, buries the soul beneath a protective covering of conventional personality. Some Americans do, too, but not nearly so many. It is in some ways an admirable trait, and better than its opposite; yet it involves a discipline almost inhuman, and a loss of spontaneity and enthusiasm which, it seems to me, could hardly be made up in any other way.

◆ ◆ ◆

We reached Hamburg in early evening. Having four hours to wait there, I treated myself to dinner at the Vier Jahreszeiten, which I have always thought of as the best hotel in Europe. The rest of the evening I sat on a café terrace across from the main railroad station, watching the people move along the sidewalk and the stream of traffic coming and going before the station, and pondering the nature of this new Europe—this materialistic, impersonal, semi-Americanized (but in some ways more modern than the U.S.) Europe—with which I have so little to do. Never had I realized more keenly the extent to which the Europe of my youth, and the Europe about which I had cared, had left me and receded into the past, just like the America of the same description. A man's life, I reflected, is too long a span today for the pace of change. If he lives more than a half century, his familiar world, the world of his youth, fails him like a horse dying under its rider, and he finds himself dealing with a new one which is not really his. A curious contradiction, this: that as medicine prolongs man's span of life, the headlong pace of technological change tends to deprive him, at an earlier age than was ever before the case, of the only world he understands and the only one to which he can be fully oriented. For it is only the world of one's youth, the nature of which is absorbed with that tremendous sensitivity and thirst for impression that only childhood and early youth provide—it is only this world that answers to the description. The Western world, at least, must today be populated in very great part by people like myself who have outlived their own intellectual and emotional environment, and who are old not only in the physical and emotional sense but also in relation to the time. We older people are the guests of this age, permitted to haunt its strange and somewhat terrifying halls—in a way part of its life, like the guests in a summer hotel, yet in a similar way detached from it. We sometimes talk with the hotel staff. We are listened to with interest, amusement, or boredom, depending on the relevance of our words. Occasionally, whether by officiousness or indiscretion, we get fouled up in the life of the place. But guests we remain: it is not our hotel; we do not work there; we never fully understand what goes on in the pantries and the kitchens; we shall be leaving it; the personnel, who will remain, is youth. And the faces of the personnel, while sometimes cheerful, sometimes competent, sometimes strong, are nevertheless terrifying to us for the things that are not written on them.

Written in Rheinfelden, a town on the Swiss side of the Rhein, not far from Basel, where I was attending an academic conference.

SEPTEMBER 18, 1959

One afternoon just before departure I took my passport along and crossed the bridge to the German side. I was overwhelmed by the contrast. Here, more clearly than anywhere I had ever been, one saw the difference between a country that had involved itself in two world wars and one that had not. On the Swiss side one had in every way this wonderful feeling of intactness, both in space and in time. One felt that the generations had merged imperceptibly into one another, that values of the present had been erected carefully and reverently on the foundations of the values of the past, that families had remained families. On one old house in the Swiss part of the city I had noticed, in fact, an inscription:

> Lasset uns am Alten,
> So es gut ist, halten.

> Where the old is good,
> Let us hold to it.

And the fact that the tail end of a late-model Mercedes protruded from a garage in the same building somehow failed to destroy the force of the motto.

On the German side, all was different. Whether or not there had been physical destruction by bombing, I do not know; but the place had the air of a town that had been torn to pieces and was being reconstructed: no harmony, no center, little beauty. And the people were as different as night from day. There was, compared with the prim Swiss, a ravaged, desperate, and brutal quality to their faces. One saw at once that here was a place which had been through moments of something like a breakdown of civilization. There was still a tinge of wolfishness in the way people viewed each other: the memory of a time (the final years of war and Nazidom) when man was enemy of man, as in the Russian Civil War. On the other hand, there was, as compared with Switzerland, a certain wide-flung, careless energy on the German side. The Swiss, too, were energetic, but with them this force was contained, well-bred, bourgeois to the core. In Germany, these middle-class values had disappeared, so that one had, along with the sense of coarseness and brutal competition, a sense of greater scope and power and ruthlessness of action.

Curiously enough, the women on the German side had also been in some way affected by the disintegration and looseness of values. They had the sheer, coarse, sexual attractiveness of primitive women, which again contrasted strongly with their prim and repressed sisters across the Rhine. Surely, one thought, this cannot be just the force of environment: this must reflect the fact that in Switzerland, over the course of generations, the discreet influence of parents, interested less in the girl's physical attractiveness than in her qualities as a person and a member of society, has been important in shaping marriages; whereas in Germany the children of this age are the products of the catch-as-catch-can sexual mores that have prevailed in that country for the past forty years. Here, by consequence, the sultry belle of the streets has taken a prominent share in motherhood. Her children show it.

In October 1959 I returned briefly to Oxford for an academic conference.

I was in Oxford for three and a half days. Again: the incredible blue sky, the golden autumn sunshine, dry leaves, dusty paths, water lying almost stagnant in the streams that normally flow in such abundance. For the first time, being relatively free of the responsibilities of normal residence and of a guest professorship, I could really enjoy the city as it should be enjoyed. I walked a great deal, through many of my former haunts. I found I could have a more kindly eye toward the place, now that it put less demands on me. It was quite unchanged: beauty living in the midst of drabness; a bit too many walls, too much privacy, too little sense of space and perspective; above all—too much motor traffic. Surprisingly to me, who had expected to be reminded in Oxford mostly of his own struggles and sufferings, or of the place as an objective phenomenon of experience, I found that it was, at every turn, the two little children who shared our life here two years ago who were called to memory by these familiar scenes. There was the children's bookstore to which Christopher used to repair after school, to read the books on the shelves as though it were a library; here was the park bench under which the children used to play with their Dinky Toys; here was the place on the towpath of the Thames, where they cheerfully puttered about in the mud on a raw and infinitely desolate Sunday morning, while I huddled for protection against the wind in the lee of a pile of building sand destined to become part of a new boathouse for one of the colleges; here was the place in the High Street where we always lined up to make the right-hand turn on the way to school in the morning and where Wendy always complained of having a stomachache; here was the traffic island in the middle of the High Street, to the safety of which I taught Christopher to leap, amid the charging buses and bicycles, when he crossed this fearful thoroughfare on his way home; there, looming up over the wall from the masters' lodgings at University College (where, on this occasion, I was graciously housed) was the window from which Christopher used to lower things on strings to the courtyard many feet below. These and dozens of other sights brought to mind the miseries of that arduous winter, but primarily from the standpoint of the intimacy with the children: the endless weekends in which there was nothing for them to do; their constant squabbling as to the merits of Linnie's (the female symbol) or Bobbie's (the male symbol); the bleak picnics in the surrounding hills; the dutiful walks through the paths of the wintry meadows; the loathsome visits to the shopping district for toys and other sources of amusement. Thinking back on all these episodes, I realize for the first time how much this intimacy with the children meant to us, and how enormously we loved them—through it, despite it, because of it.

As I say, I look back on Oxford now with a greater mellowness. I do not think it a very good place to bring up small children, unless one has one's own house and garden and servants. As a center of teaching, it is incomparable. As a center of residence, full of contrasts and contradictions. Within the walls of the colleges it is a bit stuffy and ingrown, but still a place of immense and almost unparalleled distinction, rich and full of human color. Were I to be told that I had been condemned to spend the rest of my days there as a scholar, I would feel that it might involve some physical problems; I would want to know how I was to get away for longer periods two or three times a year; I would also look forward to a long and dreary battle with the climate and the food, as well as to endless reactions of irritation over the way the place is being engulfed by modern industrialism and the automobile; but basically I should not be unhappy. I could think of few places, in fact, where I would feel more at home—not, of course, as a native of the place or the country but as a permanent intellectual visitor in a town geared to visitors of precisely that sort.

The one thing that frightened me in Oxford on this occasion was the tendency I think I saw emerging: to mingle intellectual life with the sort of compulsive social life among married couples that is common in the diplomatic world: dinners, lunches, cocktail parties of all sorts, involving people in and out of the university. Obviously, Oxford has to move with the times; but if the original tradition of cloistered and celibate scholarship within the college compound is ever wholly abandoned, these lovely old quadrangles will simply become annoying hangovers of the past, inadequate physically to the needs of the modern age. It is the penalty laid on Oxford by its own great tradition that it must learn to resist, in some measure, the habits of the day.

Berlin again, fifteen years after the war.

JUNE 16–22, 1960

Berlin was bright, open, sprawling—with its character-istic energetic air, in which one burns one's self out (at least I do) with the sheer output of energy, on first arrival. The rubble had not been all removed, in the western sectors at least; clusters of buildings were still separated by wide gray fields on which scarcely anything grew. The new Hilton Hotel where I was installed (a curious mixture of mid-century America and Germany, as modern as anything in Texas or Southern California) stood alone, with the wide expanse of the Tiergarten on one side and a desert of such cleared land on the other, so that one had the sense of being somewhere on the periphery of town, not in its center.

Now, for the first time, one had the impression of a wholly new Berlin, with a quite different arrangement of functions, arising—or, better, superimposed—on the skeleton of the old one, the street pattern being largely unchanged. It was a shock to reflect how much of the old city, particularly the parts of it that had once been so central and so imposing, so seemingly timeless and indestructible—the great, teeming business center between Potsdamer Platz and the Friedrich-strasse and the old residential Tiergartenviertel—had passed utterly into history, so that coming generations, in fact even today's young people, would not even know that these quar-ters had ever been there, and would be unable to picture them even if told. Five years ago the old Berlin, if only in the form of its ruins and rubble, had still prevailed: the new life had only camped, tentatively and almost apologetically, on what was left of it. Today the new Berlin has taken over. The old one, the scene of such vitality, such pretensions, such horrors and such hopes, is being thrust down into the oblivion of history, before the eyes of those of us who knew it.

Never before have I been so impressed with the sheer grandeur and scale on which this city is laid out. One wonders where such generosity of concept came from in the Gothic complexity of the Wilhelminian outlook. Imitation of Paris, presumably; but compared to this, even Paris seems to me somewhat cramped and confined. If, in some remote future, this does not become the greatest of world cities, it is not because it was not designed for it.

Today a great air of relaxation hangs over this vast urban area. There is little of the hustle and bustle that marked it in the prewar period. There is space. There is time. Everyone is waiting for something. They do not know when it will happen; they only know: not soon. Meanwhile, there is not much to do but to live and to wait.

My first day in Berlin was the seventeenth of June, the seventh anniversary of the day when the workers of the eastern sector revolted and the East German government came within an inch of destruction. Toward evening I attended a mass commemorative ceremony on the square before the Schöneberger Rathaus. In 1928—thirty-two years ago—I had lived on this square. It was then a marketplace. My windows had looked down on the canvas roofs of the stands. The place was then the end station of one of the double-deck bus lines that combed the city; and all night you could hear the chugging of the idling motors of the buses waiting to start uptown again. Now the apartment house where I then lived was gone, destroyed in the bombing—gone with all the life that then had filled it. Even the eager, nervous, bewildered boy of twenty-four, who once sat at that window on the fourth floor, was really largely dead. Little remained of him but some silly habits and memories in a graying man of fifty-six.

But now, today, at the commemorative ceremony, we all sat or stood, in great masses, on the square where the market had once been, and watched the long streamers that hung on the sides of the Rathaus flutter in the fresh evening wind, or stared up at the tremendous tower that loomed overhead. There was a high podium and massed flags. Runners in track suits—German kids of high-school age—arrived with a torch they had carried from somewhere (the last 110 miles, of course, had to be traversed by airplane), and a girl presented it to Willy Brandt, after which it served to light a fire in a tall urn. The *Regierungspräsident* of Schleswig-Holstein then made a tactless speech, in which (to the annoyance of the politically more sophisticated Berliners) he dwelt on the German-Polish border problem. He was followed by the ex-president, old Professor Heuss, whose Schwabian good humor and old-world charm went right to the Berlin heart. Then came Willy Brandt: young, strong, confident, a little too much the candidate for the chancellorship, I thought; but who are we Americans to speak of such things in an election year.

Later that evening I sat with a group of Social Democratic personalities—Brandt and his Norwegian wife (he was himself a Norwegian citizen at the end of the war); the vice president of the parliament, Carlo Schmid; Erler, head of the Social Democratic opposition in Bonn; Richard Löwenthal; and others—in a restaurant, and whiled away the hours of the night. I had feared they would embarrass me with questions about international affairs, but they appeared to accept me largely as one of themselves. No pressure was put on me to contribute; and I had the feeling conversation would have been much the same had I not been there at all.

On Monday evening I went to the theater, over in the Communist eastern sector of the city with M. It was the former Theater am Schiffbauerdamm—the theater where, until his recent death, Brecht had directed. The area around the theater, once the very teeming center of this entire city, was now empty, silent, almost deserted. Across the parking plaza and the river loomed the huge corpus of the Friedrichstrasse railway station, once the main station of Berlin, now dark and empty, witness only to the passage of an occasional half-empty elevated train.

The play was a dramatization of Sholokhov's *And Quiet Flows the Don*—translated, obviously, from the Russian. The acting was good. The house was not full. In the corridors people whispered and glanced furtively at one another. One had suddenly the feeling that we—the actors and the little band of spectators—were the only living people in the great, ruined, and deserted area that stretched for miles around, that we were going through a ceremony of sorts in the midst of this great void, as in a dream, as though some menacing spirit were mocking us, putting us through our paces. Fear—guarded, concealed, nameless fear—presided over the whole performance, and we, the hushed, defensive, haunted audience, were as much a part of the strange spectacle as were the actors.

M. and I sat, in stony silence, in the second row, behind two silent figures in some sort of Communist officer's uniform. Even when the curtain was down, there was not a sound among the audience. A whisper would have been heard all over the hall. It was clear: I was back in Russia—not the Russia of today, but Stalin's Russia. The dreadful, furtive spirit which Khrushchev had largely exorcised among his own people had found refuge here in this distant Russian protectorate, and it now presided, like a posthumous curse of the dead Stalin on the "faithless" Germans, over the ruins of the "eastern sector."

The first of the two parts of the play—one and three-quarters hours of the wretchedly primitive ideology of the early Stalin period—were all I could take. We left during the intermission. The square in front of the theater lay empty and barren as we emerged. On the nearby railway station there was a moving band of electric writing: the words of a Tass news program fleeing out of the darkness to the right and disappearing into the darkness at the left; but there was no one but ourselves to read those words, and we had no interest. A street running off of the square, narrow like a chasm, between two rows of undestroyed apartment houses, was brilliantly lighted, yet utterly empty, like the corridor of a prison. One wondered whether the houses behind these frowning facades were real, or whether they were only papier-mâché, and the whole thing some evil, mocking trap.

We drove across the bridge and turned left along the river, behind the university, heading toward one of the great squares that fronted on the one-time (now destroyed) Imperial Palace. Suddenly, we emerged onto this vast open area from the little park in front of the ruins of the old Zeughaus. We got out of the car, walked out onto the deserted square, and were suddenly overwhelmed—but utterly, profoundly, as I have not been in many years—by what we saw and felt around us.

It was now late twilight—the long-drawn twilight of the northern night. Under the trees it was dark, but the sky was still partly bright. There was a touch of gold in the air. Before us, there was only the great square confronting the ruins of the enormous Wilhelminian Romanesque cathedral. The entire area was unbelievably silent and empty. Only one pair of lovers, standing under the trees by the Zeughaus, moved uneasily away at our approach. All about us were the ruins of the great old buildings, semisilhouetted against the bright sky. And what ruins! In their original state, they had seemed slightly imitative and pretentious. Now they suddenly had a grandeur I had never seen even in Rome. We both become aware that this was, somehow, a moment like no other. There was a stillness, a beauty, a sense of infinite, elegiac sadness and timelessness such as I have never experienced. Death, obviously, was near, and in the air: hushed, august, brooding Death—nothing else. Here all the measureless tragedy of the

Second World War—the millions of dead, the endless seas of bereavement and sorrow, the extinction of a whole great complex of life and belief and hope—had its perpetuation. So overpowering was the impression that we spoke only in whispers, as though we were *in* a cathedral, instead of standing in the open, before the ruins of one. Not a soul was now in sight. But no—far up, at the top of the enormous flight of steps leading up to what was left of the cathedral, on the pedestal of one of the huge marble columns, we saw half-hidden in the shadows three adolescent boys—motionless, themselves like statues, themselves silent, endlessly alone and abandoned; and their lost, defiant figures burned themselves into my vision to the point where I see them still today—elbows on the knees, chins resting on the palms of hands—the embodiment of man's lost and purposeless state, his loneliness, his helplessness, his wistfulness, and his inability to understand.

We drove back, in silence, down the dead space of what was once the great Unter den Linden, to the Brandenburger Tor and through the Tiergarten; and when we got back into the bright lights and the busy normality of West Berlin, it all seemed toylike and trivial: an officious little busybody of a civilization, fussy and impermanent. None of it seemed to matter. Neither of us could forget the great awesome ruins, standing so patiently and majestically and sorrowfully, under the night sky, four miles away.

Journey from Norway, via Hamburg and Innsbruck, to Venice,
for an international conference marking the fiftieth anniversity
of the death of Leo Tolstoy.

Three days in Hamburg. Lovely sunshine; strong, cool breeze. On the Aussenalster (the larger of the two lakes that lie in the center of the city) there were more sail-boats than ever; the little white passenger steamers still plied along the shores; the parks that line the lake were more ver-dant, more beautiful, more richly used and enjoyed than ever. The constant procession of trains still moved, night and day, along the causeway dividing the lakes. The harbor once again was a teeming, dramatic place, not quite as much so as it was in the twenties (for the Iron Curtain now cuts the river off some fifty miles upstream) and no longer the greatest port on the Continent (Rotterdam has passed it), but almost so. The glistening black tugboats still lined up in solid phalanxes at the foot of the *Landungsbrücke*, and once again the great pier was the scene of an incessant coming and going of small passenger craft. The town still smelled of coffee. The hotel (the Vier Jahreszeiten) was still, for my money, one of the best in the world.

I roamed with my sketchbook over the wide rubble fields (broken by an occasional new glass-and-steel building), in the area where once the old town stood with its maze of narrow streets and its fine old Hanseatic houses. I walked miles in the countryside of an evening, with M., talking international affairs, trudging along hedge-rimmed lanes with the wheat standing man-high in the fields alongside and the air heavy with the smell of the rank, rich coastal grasses. I lunched, as a guest, in the paneled gentility of the director's dining room at the old Warburg Bank. Annelise, coming from Norway, joined me on the second day. We went to dinner at the consul's and were thrust back for an evening into that stilted, isolated, yet kindly world of the foreign service which now strikes me as so sterile, so colorless, so unreal. On Saturday afternoon we sat with M., as of old, on the high restaurant terrace at Blankenese, with the river spread out far below us, and watched the stream of ocean-going ships putting out to sea to take advantage of the weekend.

All these things we did; and yet, when I think back on those days, I realize that I have nothing interesting to say about this sturdy Hamburg of 1960, with its startling material success, its heavy motor traffic, its relatively egalitarian style of life, its lack of slums and great houses, its better-dressed, semi-Americanized girls, its relative placidity, its absence of social tension, of ideology. Whenever I am there, my mind goes back constantly to the memories of the Hamburg of thirty-three years ago, in which I lived. Here, I say to myself, was the place I had my office; there was the spot where they found the body buried in the lawn of the fashionable villa; here was the square where I watched the Communist demonstration in the rain on a Sunday morning and wept for the people who marched in it; there, across the lake, was the grand hotel where we had that ghastly foreign-service wedding; here was the tennis club where I once played tennis with the wife of my chief and failed to recognize her; and there were the dolphins in the harbor where the tanker lay when the captain and I, both tight as ticks, boarded her by top ladder at 2 A.M., before setting forth on a rough twenty-three-day passage to Norfolk, Virginia. This old, roaring, passion-ridden Hamburg had meaning for me, as the present one does not. But was it really more meaningful? Or was it just that I was younger? Was it in the city that the mystery resided? Or was it in me?

There was a one-night layover in Innsbruck on the journey south. Shiny blue overland tourist buses from Frankfurt stood parked in front of the hotel. In the lobby swarms of American girls stormed the *portier*'s counter for mail, made cracks about the inanimate elevator, gave various signs of a wearied boredom, shouted to each other: "What place did he say this was?"—while shapeless middle-class Englishwomen, like Agatha Christie's Miss Marple, ensconced in the armchairs, fingered their embroidery and watched them with pursed-lipped disapproval.

Down in the old town, the Sunday afternoon crowds surged slowly through the arcades. The sky was overcast. It was muggy. Everyone was tired. Spatters of rain chased us under the portico of the cathedral. We returned to the hotel and slept, like stones, through the late gray afternoon.

At night there was cheese and beer in a cellar restaurant of the old town. An Italian couple at the next table tenderly fed the baby on pickles and wine. The waitress was jolly. Sounds of raucous singing drifted up from a cryptlike cellar, still further down in the earth. A pretty little waitress tripped endlessly up and down the stone steps with mugs of beer. Obviously, and reassuringly, a bit of the old Austria had remained.

We reached Venice in the evening and made our way from the station, amid swarms of piratical porters and gondoliers, to the dockside, where we boarded a crowded vaporetto for the Lido. Here was the city again in all its watery confusion and timeless glory, still too beautiful to feel suffering or shame at its degradation into a tourist attraction: the Grand Canal, teeming with the evening traffic; the fading reddish facades of the palaces glowing in the soft twilight; the Piazza di San Marco ablaze with light and music and architectural magnificence; warships moored in the roadstead; massed ranks of gondolas tossing in a sort of undulant unison before the quays, among the gaily colored pilings; tall square towers rising, like mirages, from distant islands across the lagoons, the canals stretching back, fetid and sinister, into the narrow chasms between tall buildings.

Our hotel was not in Venice proper but on the long sandspit of an island called the Lido that separates the lagoons from the sea. Our windows looked out on the little quayside square, facing the lagoon, where the vaporettos land and where the buses and trolleybuses take their departure for the more remote parts of the island.

It is a noisy spot. Here, on the Lido, automobiles are permitted. They arrive hourly, in triumph, on a ferry boat, thumbing their chromium-plated noses, as they pass, at the arrogant city of Venice, which still resists their incursions as stubbornly as it once did those of the Turks (and, in my opinion, with no smaller reason). All day, the little square by the hotel is filled with the parked Vespas and motorcycles of the commuters (who are obliged, with gnashing of teeth, to abandon them here and to pursue their journey into town by boat). Toward evening the square trembles to the clatter and whine of these little vehicles as they take off on the homeward trek. Every morning at five-thirty the refuse barge, carrying yesterday's litter from the nearby market, emits a shattering, machine-gun-like roar, as it moves past the hotel on its way to some watery dump. By six o'clock, the Vespas are once again whining and sputtering; men are disputing loudly on the quay; people are screaming, in hoarse Latin voices, at the bus drivers; the vaporettos are tooting and banging against the landing stages; the buses are shaking the hotel as they rumble past. This goes on all day.

But it *is* beautiful. The windows look out, across the lagoon, to the spires and towers of the city. All day there is a going and coming of boats, large and small, along the channel that leads to the sea. The aspect of sky and water is constantly changing—never the same for more than three or four hours at a time—always beautiful, often startling.

The Tolstoy conference took place on the island of St. George, just across the channel from the Piazza, off the mouth of the Grand Canal. The island is taken up mostly by the monastery of the same name, now owned by an Italian foundation, which has restored the whole place. The monastery, built partly by Palladio, is Italian Renaissance at its best: severe, spacious, rigidly symmetrical, very serene.

We were a motley band who assembled in the old refectory, under the great Tintoretto, to celebrate the fiftieth anniversary of Tolstoy's death by giving voice to reflections about his life and work: Italian professors and the writer Silone; several Indians, wearing the homespun cloth that Gandhi taught them to wear; the Spaniard Madariaga; Madame de Proyard, the translator of Pasternak; an old French beekeeper who had known Tolstoy in his youth, who was a "follower" and who looked like Maxim Gorky; from England Lord David Cecil and Sir Isaiah Berlin, and also a very brilliant lady don from Cambridge and her don-husband; three Soviet Russians, accompanied by an interpreter whom everybody took for the police escort; several members of the Tolstoy family from Paris (all grandchildren); my friend Nicolas Nabokov (Vladimir's cousin) with his eighty-four-year-old uncle, also from Paris; a young Polish Jew who had been for six years in Soviet prisons and concentration camps; from the American side: John Dos Passos; Professor Ernest Simmons, Tolstoy's biographer; Marc Slonim, a left-wing émigré and literary critic from New York; and myself.

The Russians were an interesting group: aside from the soft-eyed little interpreter, there were Professor Ermilov, of the University of Moscow, a Party-line critic and the veteran of innumerable literary-political intrigues, a man whose owl-like head was sunk down between his shoulders, as though for protection, giving him something of the air of a turtle; Markov, the new secretary of the Writers' Union, reserved and suave; and old Professor Gudziya, editor of the new, complete ninety-volume edition of Tolstoy's works which the Soviet government is now publishing, and an unregenerated representative of the old regime, untouched by the forty-year episode of communism which he has so miraculously survived, a man full of sardonic humor and natural human feeling.

For three and a half days we chewed over Tolstoy: hailing his artistic greatness; deploring or defending, according to our respective temperaments, his philosophic and religious speculations. In general, we kept off East-West differences. On the last day we were all happily and miraculously united by the presentation made by one of the Tolstoy grandsons, a youngish doctor from Paris, a man of such gentleness and innocence of character that he reminded me of Dostoyevski's "prince" in *The Idiot*. For nearly an hour he talked, quite simply, about the family, and did it in so disarming a manner that he held us all, Soviet Russians and foreigners alike, in a state of sympathetic and respectful attention. It was at this moment that I realized that the figure of the old Tolstoy himself, with his massive literary and moral authority, was one of the few images imposing enough to bridge even the overriding ideological conflict of our day: neither side could afford to disown him—both of us had to do our obeisance to him and claim him for our own—a sure sign that there were things in life more fundamental than the differences between communism and capitalism. And while we were all agreed that he would personally have snorted with disgust over the whole idea of such a conference as that which we were holding, I also thought it would have given him a certain satisfaction to know that he had provided in his person one of the rare common grounds on which both sides of an ideologically torn world could find a meeting place, fifty years after his death.

Outside the conference hall there was the usual number of interminable restaurant meals, and one or two social events that brought the various members of the conference together.

One evening we were entertained by the municipality of Venice, on the great gallery of the Doge's Palace. In all the world there is, I think, no more spectacular place for a party. I came into conversation with the Soviet critic, Ermilov, who turned out to be, on such an occasion, entirely human. Together we stood looking out over the balustrade, onto the square, with its blaze of lights, its armies of café tables, its strolling crowds, its orchestras, its statues, the lights of ships bobbing and weaving offshore; and Venice, for the moment, had associated itself with Tolstoy in uniting the two worlds.

Later that evening, after the reception, several of us (the ones who spoke Russian) sat with the Soviet Russians at a café across the square. It was late now; the square had emptied. Only a bunch of young rowdies disported themselves, over by the quayside. In the emptiness of the vast, nocturnal piazza, surrounded by a sea of empty tables, our little party sat, like a group of actors on much too large a stage, before an empty theater, playing out one more wistful, futile attempt to bridge in some way the chasm that lay between us. At one end of our table a frozen silence reigned. At the other end young Tolstoy, two of the Soviet people, and I succeeded, for some reason, in forgetting the barriers that divided us, and we poured out our thoughts to one another, like friends reunited after years of absence—until something in the stares of the people at the other end brought us back to reality. Humbled, appalled at our violation of all the Cold War conventions, we hastily said good night, shook hands, and disappeared out of each other's lives again, slinking back to the protective custody of our respective ideological worlds.

In July 1964, upon returning to Norway after several weeks of
lecturing in Japan, I went to a place on the Norwegian west
coast to take possession of my first seagoing sailing vessel, which
had just been built for me there. This fragment describes the
journey, by train and coastwise steamer, from Kristiansand to
the yard where the boat had been built.

An afternoon train took us as far as Stavanger. It crossed inland, through a cold and rain-drenched but utterly lovely countryside: hills, forests, innumerable lakes and fjords, little farms with intensely green pastures bedded down between the rocks; and on these farms, as in the towns, the appealing white wooden cottages of southern Norway: little Cape Cod–like structures, built so obviously with a view to protection against the elements that I cannot live in one without wishing, for sheer coziness, that the storms might blow—a wish, I may say, that seldom has to wait long for fulfillment in this strenuous climate.

At Stavanger, in early evening, we changed to the night boat for Bergen. There was supper on board, with the usual generous smorgasbord, the ship rolling to the stretch of open sea off Stavanger. Then we were in among the islands again. I stood for a time, after supper, on the deserted top deck, bundled up against the cold, trying to familiarize myself with the marks and contours of the great rugged coast along which, only a few days hence, I should myself have to be the navigator. When I finally succumbed to weariness and went below, we were stopping briefly at one of the tiny harbors in the islands. The tidy little dock, deserted but for a solitary stevedore and one other man leaning, with his leg over a bicycle, against the shed, was illuminated by a single arc light. Freight was being swung down from the fore-hatch. Beyond, in the gloaming, the masts of fishing vessels, swaying in response to the slight swell from the sea, showed above the roofs of the town.

Morning—Friday, July 10, Bergen. Rain was pouring on the crowded, busy harbor, and on the fish market at the end of it. Much trouble finding a taxi. Finally, one was discovered, and it took us twenty miles out of town, to a great yellow barn of a summer hotel, looking much like an American lakeside hotel of the turn of the century, and standing on the shore of a wide and rather deserted fjord. Here well-to-do English and Scottish people on summer holiday drank their whiskey in the little bar, read week-old copies of the *Daily Telegraph,* and stared disconsolately through the windows at the rain-swept fjord, the soggy tennis court, and two little "for-hire" sailboats tossing wildly at anchor in the gray seas.

Leaving our baggage at the hotel, we all set off at once, again by taxi, this time over some seven miles of fresh, wet countryside, to the boatyard. It turned out to be a small establishment, standing isolated beside a ferry landing on an otherwise uninhabited fjord. There at the end of the quay, gleaming under blue and white paint, lay the object of so many dreams and efforts. I was so excited I could scarcely pay the taxi driver. She was a beautiful sight—impressive with her high freeboard and powerful, fishing-boat lines—sturdier, in fact, than I had dared to hope.

By invitation of the History Department of Ripon College, I
visited that institution in the winter of 1965 to deliver one
public lecture and to conduct discussions with students. My
father had attended Ripon College in the 1870s, working his
way through by doing various chores around the place. I natur-
ally had this circumstance much in mind in accepting the invita-
tion, and the consciousness of it did not leave me during the visit.

FEBRUARY 9–14, 1965

I took a train in the early evening, from Trenton. When I woke up the next morning, it was still very early, and we were somewhere in Indiana. The sun was rising. A golden half-light bathed the little towns that streamed past. There were glimpses of empty early-morning streets, glistening from the night's rain, of wind-ruffled puddles, of little wooden houses, shabby, patient, and half-asleep, and above all, the strange, still flatness—a flatness like no other flatness, subdued and yet exciting, as though filled with deep unspoken implications. This was not my country; but it was already in no sense the East. I knew I was close to home.

As the train pulled into Valparaiso, Indiana, a bank of clouds to the northwest (over the lake, no doubt) created the perfect, even disconcerting, illusion of a range of low mountains. What, one wondered, would life and people have been like had there been such a mountain range there? Life, presumably, would have been more varied, more violent, more interesting; but the massive inert power of the midwestern cultural tradition, with all its virtues and all its weaknesses, sufficient to constitute the spiritual heart of a nation, would not have survived.

My youngest sister and her husband, with one of their grown sons, met me at the station in Chicago. We breakfasted together in the fancy station restaurant, darkened now and with soft, crumb-covered carpets, and huge menus, after the fashion of the age.

When I speak of my sister Jeanette, I have to take care not to say that she is "one of those people who. . . ." Jeanette is not one of any people who. . . . She is as midwestern as the little houses of those Indiana towns; but there is no one like her. To a degree, of course, this is true of everyone. In Jeanette's case it is decisively so.

The center of her concern and effort in life is that things should go well and cheerfully for everyone around her, that there should be no unpleasantness, that people should not lose heart. She has her own solitary moments of discouragement, even of black frustration and despair. But the presence of others arouses her to an unfailing exertion of moral responsibility. In the company of others she cannot tolerate a bleak, silent, failing moment. When this occurs, it seems to her it is somehow her fault. Harsh words, acrimony of all sorts, distress her as though you had hit her with a whip. She can be stern, on occasions, with ill-behaved children, or with adults who take advantage, who carry things too far, who try to load their troubles on others beyond a point. But I cannot recall her ever saying a spiteful or an angry word. The moment itself is her charge, her responsibility. It is her mission in life to save it. Buoyant sociability, optimism, and conciliatoriness are the essence of her being. She does so desperately want that people—at least at this unique, precious, unrepeatable moment that is the present—should not lose hope, that they should take heart and believe in life. If the Beatitudes are to be credited, she belongs among those who are to inherit the earth.

Jeanette has been the center and the strength of the family for forty years. Whenever I think of the family, in the way one does, as of an intimate circle of people for whose reactions and opinions one has a special concern, it is Jeanette whom I picture as its representative and leader. Without her, half of the rest of us would lose touch with one another; the family, as a living reality, would cease to exist.

On the train from Chicago to Milwaukee I sat in the observation car, looking out in the direction of the near but not visible lake, across the flat countryside, littered now with the debris of our overelaborate, wasteful civilization: highways, junkyards, power lines, filling stations, housing projects, and what-not. I fell to wondering what, for the likes of me, was, after all, "home." From the time the family came to Wisconsin, in 1850, to the time when I myself left for good, in 1921, barely seventy years elapsed. Was this span of residence, for a family, enough to make a place "home"? Roughly, it was a span of two generations. True, so far as I knew, the family—the paternal line, at least—had never lived any longer than that in any other place, at least not since they left Scotland, which was presumably in the time of Cromwell. They had lived successively in Ireland, in Massachusetts, in Vermont, in upper New York State, and finally in Wisconsin, but never anywhere longer than those two generations. If Wisconsin, then, was not "home," what was? Well, there was now Princeton, and the farm in Pennsylvania, and the cottage in Norway. But there was more than that. There were those curious places—parts of Rhode Island, certain sections of Moscow and of Leningrad—where I had felt so overpowering a sense of familiarity as to evoke the mystery of a former life. Home, then, was the whole great arc of the northern and western world, from Moscow across Scandinavia and the British Isles to Wisconsin. One was, in other words, a sort of Nordic cosmopolitan, truly domiciled only in the natural beauty of the seas and countrysides of this northern world: in its seasons, its storms, its languid summers, but occasionally also in its vanishing urban settings, the half-remembered ones, pictured as they were before the inundation by the automobile.

The Illinois-Wisconsin border is more than just a political division. It is one of the great geographic, climatic, and atmospheric divisions of the country. South of it stretch the great plains of black earth. North of it the country is gravelly, rolling, heavily glaciated, dotted with lakes and moundlike hills. Technically, Wisconsin is, I suppose, in the Midwest, but it is not fully *of* it. It is the vestibule to the great Northwest, which is different. The climate changes, too, as one crosses this border. Illinois was snowless and thawing. As we approached Milwaukee, snow streaked the furrows of the winter fallow, and the puddles were already half-frozen in the fields.

Milwaukee, the area around the station—the sooty little park, the Public Service Building from which the interurbans once departed, the various pubs with the Blatz signs—looked just as it always did. A raw, dirty wind sneaked out of the railway yards and the dim alleys, bringing clouds of stinging dirt; and over it all lay the familiar flavor of cheap, sinister sin—of back rooms in saloons, of sailors in bus stations, of the stage doors of burlesque theaters, and of dirty picture cards—the same flavor that hung over it, so repulsively and yet so unsettlingly, when I was a youth arriving and departing from this square on my trips to and from the military academy.

Shortly after arrival, I stood with my cousin on the top floor of the new office building his firm had built. We looked out over the deserted harbor mouth, and the icy gray bay beyond. "An affirmation of faith in the future of Milwaukee's business district": this is how the company had described the new building when it was opened a year and a half ago. My cousin was still mildly optimistic. Other office buildings, he pointed out, were now rising around them. I was silently skeptical. New York City came to mind. I had just been reading on the train Victor Gruen's *The Heart of Our Cities*. Few of us, I reflected, really understood the complexity and subtlety of the reasons for the decay of these city centers. Not many of us were prepared for the far-reaching changes in habit, above all in transportation and the arrangement of life, that would be necessary to restore them to vitality.

Three youngish men from the Ripon History Department met me on the little brick station platform at Columbus, Wisconsin, and drove me the intervening forty or fifty miles to Ripon, over wide straight roads, past frozen, snow-covered fields and prosperous dairy farms with beautiful red barns and less beautiful houses done in the dirty yellow brick of the region. My companions were solemn, correct, and amiable, but a bit intimidated, I suspected, and guarded.*

The face of Ripon is overwhelmingly that of a New England town: wide streets lined with tall trees, spacious lawns, quiet, well-worn wooden houses back behind the trees; but the houses here, instead of being New England houses of the eighteenth or early nineteenth century, are New England houses of the late nineteenth century. I saw no single beautiful one among them.

Wisconsin is not alone to blame for this architectural emp-

---

*I had not, at the time, given thought to the fact that the invitation to lecture at Ripon came only from the History Department, not from the college. Nor did I attach any significance to the fact the the president of the college was not in evidence during my visit. I learned only later that the invitation was the subject of some controversy and tension in the college, I being viewed as too liberal, if not worse, for the political atmosphere of that part of the late Senator McCarthy's state. If this was true, the college, I may say, made up for it handsomely some years later by conferring upon me, in 1968, under the presidency of Dr. Bernard S. Adams, an honorary degree, as it had upon my father in 1907.

tiness. The designs of these houses, like that of the house in which I grew up on Cambridge Avenue in Milwaukee, are standard builders' designs straight out of Connecticut; and if they are plain and uninteresting with their dreary touches of Victorian pretension, the plainness and pretension were alike imported. For their builders the problem of design was one of custom and convention, not of aesthetics. These men took uncritically what came to them from an older, richer, and more authoritative culture. In their oblivion to genuine aesthetic values, even to such as they might have been surrounded by in their own youth, they were only being true to the mysterious compulsions of their generation. They built what was wanted and accepted, and like so many other Victorians, they put their pride in quality of workmanship and material, rather than in outward form.

Ripon College itself is dominated by three old stone structures. They are the original buildings. They were already in existence when my father came to the place ninety-five years ago. They stand, in conformity with the tradition of the region, on the ridge of the highest hill in the vicinity, and constitute the center of both town and college. The land in front of them, as I could see from old photographs, was originally a meadow, stretching off down the hill. Today, it is tree-grown and turned into campus. Other buildings have been added to form the traditional college quadrangle.

The three old buildings, built of the yellowish sandstone of the region, severe and without architectural ambition, their walls enlivened only for utilitarian purposes by occasional buttressing ribs, stand—tall, gaunt, and forbidding—on their hilltop. True children of the age and taste of General Grant, they preside stubbornly, self-assertively, without apology or compromise, over their changed and changing environment. Only the tall trees that have now grown around them mitigate in some degree their austere authority. I was assigned to a guest apartment upstairs on the top floor of one of them. It was, they told me, the one in which my father had lived in his senior year. Even today, looking at its scuffed floors, its blank, graceless windows, and the battered tongue-and-groove of its interior partitions, it was not too difficult to imagine what it must have been like when my father inhabited it. I wondered only how it had been heated. By stoves, of course, and more comfortably, let us hope, than by these fearful radiators—clanking, dusty, burning with dry heat—so dear to the hearts of many American builders. (The ones in the guest apartment I was mercifully able to turn off entirely, without detriment, it seemed, to the comfort of the place.)

I went, the first evening, to call on an old friend of the family: a spinstress ex-teacher, no longer young, whose parents had been friends of my parents, who had taught at the grade school I once attended in Milwaukee, and who had occasionally visited at my childhood home. In a cozy, old-fashioned living room, the continuity of which, as a place of habitation, obviously stretched back to the last century, we sat before the fire and reminisced. There was reassurance in the personality of my hostess: shrewd, cheerful, intimidated neither by age nor loneliness, neither accepting entirely nor rejecting entirely the modern world that pressed at the door, holding quietly, with neither apology nor heroics, to values now generally in contemptuous discard. To meet her here and talk with her was like unexpectedly meeting someone from home in the wilds of Siberia; only these were the wilds of time, not of place. It was clearly this older New Englandish Wisconsin, not the one around us outside, to which I belonged.

My program, as a visitor to the college, began the day after my arrival. I had protested, in advance, that I could not deliver lectures to the classes in Russian and American history they wanted me to attend. I could only sit in on them as a visitor and take part, perhaps, in the discussion. All to no avail. At the Russian history class that first morning, there they all were: regular students, other students, faculty members, and townspeople, seated expectantly before me, with that maddening, complacent, irresponsible expectancy which always makes me feel they are saying: "Get up and talk. We want to see what you look like when you are talking." There was nothing for it. Then, and in the American history class the following morning (where there were well over a hundred), I had to declaim, impromptu, for the full academic hour to a curtain of curious, respectful, but impassive faces, scattering my little seeds and leaving them to their fate on this unknown soil.

Lunch was eaten, in company with some students, in the great modern cafeteria where the whole student body of some eight hundred takes its meals. It was my first good chance to look at the students. They gave the impression of being more relaxed, less troubled, less involved, than those at Princeton. The faces were open, pleasant ones, but with curiously little written on them at all. The girls, as always, seemed more mature personally than the men, superior to them, too, socially and in style: more cosmopolitan, less provincial, more a part of the age, in general more like modern women in Vienna or Milan or wherever else you like than the men of similar age in those places. The girls took, it seemed to me, a larger view of the competitive sphere in which they considered their lives to evolve—the reflection of an awareness, perhaps, of the relative uniformity in women's problems everywhere. The men were good-natured young louts, immersed in their world of records and athletics and fraternities and summer jobs, mildly curious about the great wide world beyond, but less closely keyed to it than the women. It is the woman who is truly international.

Observing the greater relaxation of the atmosphere and faces in this heterosexual common room, I thought of the recent demand of the Princeton college editors for coeducation at Princeton. Plainly, it would be easier, softer, more comfortable, with women around. Life would be more agreeably homogenized, less harshly stratified into the components of term and vacation, of study and recreation, of indulgence and abstention. But would the intellect benefit? The intellect, after all, was a lazy, sluggish faculty. Its growth occurred only under discipline and discomfort. It had to be scourged into the unfolding of its powers. This was why the great environments for the flowering of the spirit had been not the sunlit gardens of California or Florida, but rather the dark, cold rainy ones—the ones that involved deprivation, personal discomfort, loneliness, and boredom. Coeducation produced, no doubt, better-adjusted people; but was there not a certain conflict between this ease of life and the training of the mind.

In the evening, in the bareboned gymnasium, with its shiny floors, its overhanging basketball boards, and its faint smell of sweaty tennis shoes, I delivered my formal lecture—to an audience of several hundred. (I spoke, on that occasion, about America's major international involvements of the past century, pointing out the inadvertence by which we had backed into them, our tendency to make moral crusades out of them once we became involved, and the irony of the relationship between these lofty objectives and the actual political consequences of our involvement. "It is," I said, "simply not in character for such a country as ours to try . . . to produce great changes in the lives of other people, to bring economic development and prosperity to everyone, and to assure to everyone complete peace and security under law. This is true whether the effort be made . . . by force and coercion or by sweetness and light.") I came away, as usual, disliking what I had said, feeling that I had hacked my way through the delivery of it like a droning snow-plough, unable to gauge the effect, wishing I had never undertaken the effort. Afterward, rather mercifully, there were drinks at a professor's house.

A blizzard had set in during the evening. When we left the professor's house, around ten o'clock, the wind was howling and the snow was drifting heavily in the streets.

Back in the guest flat, I darkened the rooms and sat by the

window, watching the storm and the night scene: the drifted campus, white and deserted now under the streetlights; the black bare tree trunks, swaying slightly as they reached up past the window and disappeared into the gloom above; and everywhere the clouds of blowing snow—the blessed snow that everyone professes, these days, so to dislike—sweeping, drifting, cleansing, covering everything, mercifully and impartially, with its shroud of momentary purity. Staring thus out into the night, I was suddenly struck with a surge of feeling for my long-dead, honored father: this shy and lonely man, this misplaced aesthete, struggling to bestow the imprint of true spiritual distinction and elegance on the stuffy, claustrophobic existence of the house on Cambridge Avenue; a man whom almost no one understood and whom I myself came to understand properly only after he was gone; a man whom I must have hurt a thousand times in my boyhood, by inattention, by callousness, by that exaggerated shyness and fear of demonstrativeness which is a form of cowardice and a congenital weakness of the family. I thought of his one-time presence in this place; of our respective lonelinesses; of our diffident, fumbling, helpless affection for each other, disrupted—always and everywhere—by the chatter and irrelevance of daily life; of the chasms of time and death that now separated us.

I wondered, suddenly, whether we were not, at that moment, very close. He must surely have stood, on just such a night, at one of these windows, in his shabby farm-boy clothes, and looked out at the storm, must have been conscious, as I was now, of the land falling away from the hill into the darkness on every side and of the great snowbound countryside beyond; and his wonder of what lay further afield in the night could scarcely have been greater, for all his youth, than the questioning I now felt, for all my wanderings and experience. Were these chasms of time and death real ones? Was there not a unity and a fellowship in the sensing, the living of this moment? Was there not a tapping of his hands

(à la *Wuthering Heights*) in the dry crackling of the snow
against the window?

And so the silly dialogue formed itself and rattled away in
my mind through the unslept hours, like the notes of some
idiotic song that goes, unwanted, through your head.

"Father, father. Have I done right to come all this way to
make myself close to you through the scenes of your youth?
Or was this an act of maudlin sentimentality? There is so
much I could have given you, and didn't. Does this help?"

"Soft, soft, my son. You should know better than to pro-
voke these mysteries. The moment is indeed the same. This
is the same snowfall. The ninety intervening summers are as
nothing. Beyond that, it is not given to you to know. Do what
your deeper nature tells you to do. Give it, if you can, a break,
in the face of all the dust and rubbish of life. And meanwhile,
take comfort in the beauty of the storm and the night; see the
strength and indifference of the snow for all it falls upon;
sense its lesson. And if you feel a nearness, then know that it
is true. Your own sense of time and space is of no consequence. For the sort of nearness you long for there is no
theater, anywhere or at any time, other than in the individual
soul."

In the morning the snow had stopped and there was brilliant sunshine. Escaping momentarily from my hosts, who
had exhibited unfeigned horror at the idea that I should walk
anywhere alone, I took an early-morning walk through the
sparkling whiteness of the residential streets, drawing suspicious glances from housewives shoveling the family car out of
the garage.

Later in the day there was a final reception and dinner in a
restaurant called the Republican House. It was only a few
paces from the little structure that is ticketed as the birthplace
of the Republican Party. From this proximity and from its
name, presumably, the restaurant drew trade, combining
(like the Princeton barbers with their pictures of past college

football teams) the pretension of an institutional allegiance with a desire to make money. Signed photographs of celebrated Republican figures decorated the walls. The collection had, I was told, included one of the late Joe McCarthy, but the students had a habit of stealing it, and the proprietors, commercial instincts prevailing as usual over the political ones, had finally decided to leave the place vacant. Even without McCarthy, I had a sense that I was breaking bread there under the scrutiny of baleful, unbenevolent eyes—eyes not directly hostile, but imperious, contemptuous, and intolerant of all my weak-kneed philosophizing and theorizing. The faces in the photographs evidently thought so, too, for the food disagreed with me. I spent another, and final, sleepless night: no father this time, only the Republican Party glaring huffily and unkindly, in the bright moonlight, through the window.

I flew back the next day, in and out of the airports that all looked alike, unseeing, uncaring, surfeited with the fatigues of travel and of memory. And by late afternoon I was able to resign myself gratefully to the consuming triviality of what is now, in the immediate sense at least, home.

The diaries contain a number of accounts of cruises, in our own boat, in Scandinavian waters. The following are excerpts from the accounts of three such cruises, conducted in the summer of 1968.

JUNE 24, 1968
RANDESUND–KRISTIANSAND

It rained again all night, the water dripping patiently and evenly into the rain barrel outside our window. In the morning, after breakfast, just as we were preparing to leave for the train, there was a squall and a heavy shower. After that the weather turned fair. At 1 P.M., after various errands in town, we entrained—the four of us: Annelise and I, Wendy, and a nephew—in one of those second-class cars with semiseparate compartments, each with a little table between and facing wooden seats. I sat opposite a couple of lovers, wearing identical Norwegian sweaters, who cooed and whispered and snuggled like a pair of turtledoves over the long hours, he with a pleased, relaxed young face, she still very young-girlish in figure but with a hawk nose and a mouth turned sharply down at the ends, bespeaking the uncertain, secretive, and somewhat calculating mature woman who lay, latent, inside. (I find in myself, as one of the manifestations of increasing age, a tendency to try to discern in young people the features of the budding adult.)

The remaining members of our family sat across the aisle.

The young people of our party read and played cards, hour after hour, while the lovely Norwegian countryside, fresh with the bloom of spring, swept past the windows, and I marveled once more at the uncuriousness of people of that age when they travel. Was I that way, I wonder? Probably. It is almost a form of shyness, the repulsion of the external, the leading of an inner life.

Annelise and I stayed at the hotel, the two young people at the B.'s. We all had a lovely dinner there. Then Annelise and I walked back to the hotel. It had been warm, inland, on the train, and on the station platforms, but here the evening was clear and a cold north wind was blowing. The quiet provincial town had that clean, windswept, and deserted aspect, at once lovely and trying to the soul (because desolate, tight-lipped and forbidding) that lies over so much of human habitation in this northern country—an aspect that makes one (me, at least) conscious of the fact that for every inviting, relaxed, sunny day there are about forty-nine cold ones with wind and rain.

JUNE 25, 1968

Found the *Nagawicka,* beautifully painted, lying at the yard's dock, next to a fine old Colin-Archer gaff-rigged ketch. Spent most of the afternoon tidying up. A number of loose ends remained to be tended to. The battery was dead. The topping lift was missing, and a few minor objects. New gaskets were needed in the head and in the bilge pump. Some of these problems were solved in the course of the day, others not. Meanwhile, fair weather held, but it blew a half a gale from the southwest, pressing us against the fenders and rather locking us in. We installed ourselves on board, but with some difficulty: no electricity and the nearest drinking water a third of a mile away.

JUNE 26, 1968

Battery taken out for a day's charging. The wind continued
to blow the same half-gale from the southwest. Annelise and
I made an expedition by bus to Tønsberg, some twelve miles
away. The heavens, while generally stern and unfriendly,
were merciful to us on this occasion: while we were on the
bus, going to town, it poured; it then forbore sufficiently to
permit us to do our errands; then, while we sat in a *konditori*
and ate our sandwiches and drank our coffee, the heavens
opened again, relenting once more just soon enough for us to
catch the return bus.

This trip to town was a mildly painful one, full of sadness
and contrary feelings. I am not oblivious to the Norwegian
virtues. If I really had my pick of places to live in, I would
probably choose Norway. *But* (and all these buts were visible
in Tønsberg today) the climate is harsh; nature is spare and
grudging; and everyone is as busy and determined as he can
be to promote the most rapid possible destruction of the
beauty and peace of the country and of the inner harmony of
its life through the reckless, unlimited cultivation of the internal combustion engine. If, some twenty to thirty years ago,
the Norwegian government had come to the solemn conclusion that in the shortest possible time every Norwegian town
and village must be exploded, disintegrated, and rebuilt to
worse standards; that every small white traditional Norwegian house—the house that fits so magnificently into this
landscape—must lose its function and be replaced with some
sort of a concrete block; that the air as well as the coastal
waters must be polluted with maximum speed; that Norwegian youth must lose its modesty, its respect for its elders, and
its love of nature, and learn to see its own identity only in its
association with the motorbike and the automobile; that railway and maritime transport must be deprived of their function in favor of the motor vehicle and the investment in them
written off as rapidly as possible—and if this had been its

decision, it could not and would not have acted otherwise than as it has. It is difficult to believe that what is happening in this country could happen otherwise than on the basis of a decision that there must not be a single one of the evils of American life, excepting only the racial problem, that is not to be appropriated into the life of the Norwegian people—and this with greatest urgency.

JUNE 28, 1968

On our return to Sandøsund, we made fast alongside another fine Colin-Archer, the same size as ours, and newly built. Sandøsund was a cozy little port, with the pilot vessels from the central Oslofjord lying at the granite breakwater, and the shops, the little square for the bus stop, and the fish market, all ranged along the dock. Toward evening, youth—youth international of 1968—youth in the abstract, complete with blue jeans and streaming shirttails, all looking as ragged, dirty, and repulsive as they could contrive to look—gathered on the little square next to the two yachts, and sat down in groups on the cobbles, where they remained, doing nothing in particular, until after midnight. Except for one character with a motorbike rigged for sound like a machine-gun, who advanced his claim to respect and admiration by gunning the contraption mercilessly and then charging wildly up and down the wharf, they were not really obnoxious. There was only one drunk, and if any of the others were doped up, they were at least quiet about it, and inoffensive.

It occurred to me, as I tried to overcome my distaste for these people, that after all, they existed; they had to be somewhere; you couldn't just hide them or turn them off like a TV set; and since this was so, there could have been worse places for them to be, and worse things they could have been doing. But one longed to see them full of life and gaiety, interested in nature and capable of enjoying it, conscious of their own potential beauty as youth and concerned to cultivate it, instead of in this gray, shabby, subdued state. Why, then, this desperate and defeated state of behavior? A reaction to the older generation, they would say. But it was not their parents, surely, who compelled them to dress in rags and to sit all Friday evening on the dusty cobbles of the little wharfside square. The parents who provided them with motorbikes and outboards and the money for hashish were surely not going to deny them the means for healthier and more rewarding forms of recreation. Home, with its TV set and its socially isolated, lonely, satiated parents, might be unexciting. But there were other ways of passing time, even outside the home. There *were* libraries. And there was the great outdoors, and not just the quayside at Sandøsund.

SUNDAY, JUNE 30, 1968

We got off at the usual time (about midmorning). Between us and the sea there was, initially, the lovely long island of Jom-fruland, fertile and inviting, with its green meadows and dark evergreen forest, like nothing else in Norway. When we reached the open sea, we moved out about a mile to get a heading and then set sail and tacked laboriously all the way to Sildeodden, where we entered Nordfjord and moved up the sound to Risør. There, in the quiet of an early Sunday afternoon, we found a place to take on water. We then set out again for another short sea passage of some five miles. It was rough this time, the wind dead ahead, and the coast foul, so we had to keep well out to sea. I used the motor, holding it down to three to four knots in order to ride the oncoming seas instead of slamming into them. By late afternoon we reached Lyngørfjord, and ran into the side cove of Dypvåg, where, after searching in vain for a suitable anchorage, we made fast at a dock. It was the dock where the island vacationers leave their cars when they are on the islands and keep their motorboats when they are on the mainland. At the end of it is a little summer general store, and there is much coming and going.

In the evening Annelise and I walked up the road a few hundred yards to see the old Dypvåg church. It is a perfectly lovely building, much like the New England church: white with dark trim, partially medieval, partly eighteenth-century in origin. It lies in part, unfortunately, facing the hillside instead of away from it, but is nevertheless a thing of beauty. The door was locked, but on our return, we met the parson, sweatered like any other Norwegian, recognizable nevertheless by the thick black trousers and squarish, clerical shoes. He was inspecting his potato patch. All the land around, including the narrow but fertile valley below us, belonged, he said, to the church, and had once constituted a part of the parson's living. In those days the parson had had servants and could operate the farm. Now all that was gone. Even the neighboring farmers were gone. They had sold their land, or exploited it only as woodland. In general, everyone lived by the summer-visitor trade. In winter the region was deserted. There had been greater changes here within his lifetime, he said, than in all the preceding thousand years.

JULY 1, 1968

Good weather once more.

Before making our departure Annelise and I went up the hill again to see the interior of the church, which, we were told, would now be open. It was, and we were not disappointed. It had been beautifully restored some years ago to its eighteenth-century state. The prevailing motif was that of a primitive baroque, so naive that it did not spoil the artlessness and simplicity of the building as a whole. Representations of pilasters and of a great drapery behind the altar were painted directly on the crude hewn logs of the wall. The place was light, airy, and sunny, like New England churches at home.

These people, I thought to myself, had enough of darkness and chill. They wanted none of the cold, cryptlike, stone-slab atmosphere of the great cathedrals further south in Europe. Great warm logs, crudely squared, and large windows with the sunshine, or at least the light, streaming through them: these were what they wanted, and here they had them.

But how to explain the stern monotheism of these northern climes? No saints adorned these walls. Even Christ was scarcely in evidence. There was, to be sure, a cluster of angels at the center of the ceiling, curling their figures against the very Norwegian clouds of the painted sky; in a bank of wood carving over one of the rafters, there were four Grecian ladies depicting the virtues of the then-reigning Danish king; and there were the naive representations, on the panels of the chancel, of the four evangelists, each busily writing away at his particular gospel; but this was all. No gracious intermediaries functioned here between man and his Maker. This was, as the inscriptions reiterated, "Guds Hus"—God's House— not the house of the Saviour, or the Virgin, or Saint So-and-so. Only the distant Danish king laid claim here to some sort of special intimacy with the Almighty, trying in this way, one sensed, to reinforce his authority and prestige with his pious but stubborn and recalcitrant Norwegian subjects. Was it the greater independence of these people's lives, the isolation of their forbidding northern valleys, the more critical quality of their intimacy with nature, or their earlier remoteness from the great hierarchies of Byzantium and Rome, that made the difference? Whatever it was, the world of their faith clearly had the same stark austerity and simplicity as the natural world they inhabited.

The purpose of this expedition was to take the NAGAWICKA *over to Skagen, in Denmark, and deliver her into the hands of four youths—Christopher and three of his friends—who proposed to take her across to Sweden and then proceed with her north along the Swedish coast on a cruise of a week or ten days' duration, to end at her place of winter storage in Oslofjord. My task was only to make her available to the boys at Skagen. After that, her fate would depend on them—and theirs on her.*

The next day, Sunday, there was a southerly breeze, and we sailed the whole thirty-some miles back to Skagen, with the genoa winged out to port, profiting now from the strong northerly set of the current. We arrived there at three o'clock, just in time to make the connection with Christopher's friends, who had been casually instructed by Christopher, weeks before, to look for us there that day.

It was Sunday afternoon. The port lay hot and dead in the long, even northern sunshine. The water, covered with an oily yellow-green scum from the fish factories, stunk worse than before. Everyone felt tired and listless. The other boys, I felt, wondered why they had come. Wearily, the rest of us packed our belongings, sought out a taxi, and took our departure, promising to return at dinnertime so that Annelise could cook dinner for the boys. We went to a hotel, where we had ordered rooms through a travel bureau; and there then followed one of those low moments—moments of failure, adversity, and frustration—that seem to accompany every journey. The hotel proved to be miles out of town, on the seashore. The room was cramped and hot, and stunk from a clogged washbowl. The one thing we most wanted, after days on the boat, was a bath; but the bathroom, separated from us by endless stairways, was seemingly permanently occupied. Annelise had lost her glasses, I my traveler's checks. There was insufficient money. The passports, by my negligence, had been left behind in Norway.

At eight in the evening, still exhausted, we drove back to the harbor. The boys, unable to stand the stench in the inner port, had moved to the outer harbor and made fast to the inner side of the long cement breakwater. We had to abandon the taxi and traverse a wide expanse of sand even to get to the base of the breakwater. As we did this, we could see them across the slip, in the distance: four slim, lanky figures lounging at the top of the breakwater, nothing near them but the long expanse of gleaming concrete and the boat, very small and slender, down below. They looked, against this pitiless, barren background, like something out of a surrealist painting; and I was suddenly seized with a great pang of love and concern for these young creatures: so helpless, so vulnerable, so endangered despite all their changed voices, their incipient whiskers, and their great protective show of callous amusement over life—vulnerable and endangered not so much by the sea to which I was now entrusting them in my little boat, and not so much by the built-in tragic nature of the individual human predicament which men had always had to face, but rather by the enormity of what the human community was now doing to itself, with its overpopulation, its precipitate urbanization, its feverish hyperintensity of communication, its destruction of the natural environment, and its cultivation of weapons too terrible for the wisdom and strength of any that might command their custody and use. In the midst of all this these boys would have to live. With all of this they would have to contend.

We traveled back to Kristiansand the following evening on the ferry from Hirtshals. There was first some twenty-five miles of taxi ride across the flat Jutland countryside between the fields of barley and oats. Then the waiting room for the new great automobile ferry—the main connection now, between the Continent and the south of Norway. There, in the far-too-small, stuffy waiting room, we passengers, clutching our belongings, were herded together like sheep; and there, like sheep, we patiently waited until we were released from that particular pen and permitted to file, through fenced lanes, up the metal staircase and onto the high decks of the ferry. And we deserved the treatment, I thought, because we were, like almost all modern travelers, a motley lot: mussed and dopey from long driving in automobiles, most of us clad in worn, smelly sport clothes, some, particularly the young, with hardly any clothes at all.

Gone are the days when it was possible to travel with a certain elegance. In travel as elsewhere, the insistence on equality—on the leveling-out of standards—leads not to everyone's living well but rather to no one's living well, so that good taste and comfort, once available to the rich, or to anyone who could—and cared to—make the necessary sacrifice, are now available to no one at all.

With these thoughts in mind I stood on the stern of the great thundering ferry, watched the Danish coast recede, and let myself be hypnotized by the sight of the vast boiling wake the ferry left behind her, wide as a boulevard and stretching out across the miles. In the middle of the Skagerrak we passed a great fleet of some sixty to eighty large Soviet trawlers, all herded together under the watchful eyes of their secret police admirals, lest one or the other of them have contact—just think!—with a foreign port or a foreign vessel. There they lay, scowling at our capitalistic ferry and any other foreign vessels that might pass by, and taking advantage of their international rights to divest the central Skagerrak of whatever fish it might once have contained.

From our high decks, the Oksøy lighthouse, at the entrance to Kristiansand Fjord, became visible before we had fairly covered half the passage; and nearly an hour before we arrived, the lights of Kristiansand appeared, stretching in a broad band across the dark horizon, gleaming with that meretricious allure, suggestive of crowds, festivity, and excitement, that is common to the lights of all empty, barren, sleeping cities seen from a distance at sea.

On the third of three visits to Africa, in the years 1967–70, I visited, among other places, South-West Africa (and particularly the northernmost province of Ovamboland) and Lesotho. Here: excerpts from my accounts of those visits. (Tsumeb is the major mining center in the north-central part of South-West Africa, the mines being then under American ownership.)

Shortly after 8 A.M. Mr. M. and I were already flying northward, over the parched veld, in a Piper four-passenger plane like the ones they use for air taxis at home. We reached Tsumeb about 10:45 and spent the hours until 4:15 P.M. (except for a lunch period at the hotel) going through the great copper-lead-zinc mine and the compound that houses the 3,000 black bachelors who work there—for the most part on twelve-month contracts. (The pay is somewhat better than Angola, and much better than in the black African countries.)

Then we set out, in late afternoon, on the long drive (140 miles) to the present administrative center of Ovamboland—Ondangwa. The road, very well surfaced, ran straight as an arrow across the flat, dry, empty countryside. For at least 130 miles there was not a building to be seen on either side, not even a filling station, with the exception of the customs house at the Ovamboland border, and almost no people. Once or twice, we passed parties of horses and mules or donkeys being trekked northward by one or two Africans. At one point, where the road touched the eastern end of the Etosha game park, we could see large herds of elephant grazing in the distance; and once, shortly thereafter, we came upon a group of four or five enormous ostriches, who went trotting away into the bush with their curiously soft and springy gait, flouncing their feathery skirts in a way that was both ridiculous and slightly suggestive—like clowning chorus girls. As we approached Ondangwa, the dry bush gave way to relatively well-watered terrain, sandy and with palm trees, and there were many more signs of habitation: numerous herds of cattle and goats and even some small boys standing by the roadside with bows and arrows for sale—also women, similarly, with baskets.

We had the fiery African sunset almost before us as we approached Ondangwa, and it was dusk when we pulled into the European compound there. We went directly to the residence of the chief director for Ovamboland, Mr. Duprey, where we were received and put up for the night. The evening was passed pleasantly in the company of these kindly, humorous people, who think they are doing the right thing, ask only for time to produce the results, fail to perceive the painful personal aspects of their own harsh, schematic policies, and are offended, as though one had said something tactless and insulting, if one points to the obvious inadequacy and unreality of these policies as a solution to the problems of industrial labor, and indeed of the status of nonwhites generally, in South Africa proper.

APRIL 30, 1970
LESOTHO

Slept well. Cold at night, but bright sunshine in the morning. After breakfast I sat at one of the dining-room tables and wrote up yesterday's diary, as a little boy looked over my shoulder.

The morning was taken with a drive to the university—the University of Lesotho, Botswana, and Swaziland, some twenty miles distant. The road crossed fearfully eroded, largely treeless, and obviously greatly overgrazed country, highlands with the remains of eroded hills protruding here and there above the surface, a countryside not without a certain pale, calm beauty, but pathetic in its ravaged, depleted character. The university made upon me, like so many things in Africa, a sad, incomplete, unsuccessful impression; and I couldn't help but think, as we strolled around its rather empty premises (the students were away), how unfortunate the white man had been, in all his undertakings for Africa, how false and misconceived had been his effort to Westernize the African—even in religion; how much better it would have been if all of them—missionary, educator, merchant, adventurer, medical man, journalist, and administrator alike—had stayed home and ministered to their own kind. All of it—all that the white man did and created for the black man—the schools and hospitals and churches and whatnot: they were all, as the Russians put it, *nye to* (not, that is, what they were intended to be, or what they should have been). I have learned simply to dislike the spectacle of the white man resident in the African milieux—to dislike his pretensions and to resent his presence.

Before returning home we visited a pass from which we had a lovely view over great dim reaches of countryside, and I reflected once again on the quiet, dry vastness of this southern African countryside—its endless expanses of rock and dry grass and forbidding, uninviting country. Why anyone should have wanted to trek across it and to establish himself in it in the first place, I could not understand.

There follow two pieces about Leningrad, widely separated in time of writing. The first is composed of the initial passages from my first book on the early history of Soviet-American relations, RUSSIA LEAVES THE WAR, *published in 1956 by the Princeton University Press. The second was the account of the impressions of walks in that city in 1973.*

PROLOGUE

> *Shine out in all your beauty,*
> *City of Peter, and stand*
> *Unshakeable as Russia herself.*
> *And may the untamed elements*
> *Make their peace with you.*
>
> — *ALEXANDER PUSHKIN,*
> THE BRONZE HORSEMAN

The city of Sankt Petersburgh—St. Petersburg, Petrograd, Leningrad, call it what you will—is one of the strangest, loveliest, most terrible, and most dramatic of the world's great urban centers. The high northern latitude, the extreme slant of the sun's rays, the flatness of the terrain, the frequent breaking of the landscape by wide, shimmering expanses of water: all these combine to accent the horizontal at the expense of the vertical and to create everywhere the sense of immense space, distance, and power. The heaven is vast, the skyline remote and extended. Cleaving the city down the center, the cold waters of the Neva move silently and swiftly, like a slab of smooth gray metal, past the granite embankments and the ponderous palaces, bringing with them the tang of the lonely wastes of forests and swamp from which they have emerged. At every hand one feels the proximity of the great wilderness of the Russian north—silent, somber, infinitely patient.

Over this community there pass, in endless rhythm, the characteristic seasons of the north: the long winters of snow and darkness; the protracted in-between seasons of gray skies, slush, and a pervasive dampness; the white nights of the summer solstice, with their unbelievable, eerie poetry; and finally the brief, pathetic summers, suggestive rather than explicit, drawing to a close almost before they have begun, passionately cherished by the inhabitants for their very rareness and brevity.

In such a city the attention of man is forced inward upon himself and his own kind. Human relationships attain a strange vividness and intensity, with a touch of premonition. Under such a sky, fingers of fate seem to reach in from a great distance, like the beams of the sun, to find and shape the lives and affairs of individuals; events have a tendency to move with dramatic precision to denouements which no one devised but which everyone recognizes after the fact as inevitable and somehow faintly familiar.

The city is, and always has been, a tragic city, artificially created at great cost in human suffering, geographically misplaced, yet endowed with a haunting beauty, as though an ironic deity had meant to provide some redemption for all the cruelties and all the mistakes. For two hundred years it remained the center of a far-flung apparatus of bureaucratic power. But it was not destined to stand indefinitely, as

Pushkin had hoped, against the forces of nature and the hand of change. In the twentieth century it was to endure trials and sufferings second to none in the annals of urban experience, and to lose its preeminence among the cities of Russia.

The following are excerpts from the piece entitled "Reflections," published in THE NEW YORKER *in 1974 (issue for April 29), recording some of my impressions when revisiting Leningrad some months before.*

STREETS ONCE REALLY SEEN OR SEEN IN DREAMS

The train, on this early-autumn morning, is leaving behind it the wastes of the Karelian Isthmus, where a young second growth of birch and evergreen now covers the scars of recent warfare, and is moving onto the wide, flat reaches of the northern Leningrad suburbs. The land lies under a milky mist—the characteristic good-weather mist of the northern European autumn. The foliage—every leaf— glistens with moisture; in some places the tops of the evergreens are concealed. Soon the mist will wear off, and the far, slanting sunshine, still palpable and enjoyable if it is the right time of day and you get out of the wind, will break through.

The suburban stations begin to flick by: long, narrow wooden platforms crowded with waiting commuters who witness impassively, with a cultivated indifference, the passage of our privileged, thinly populated sleeping car. The scenes multiply in variety. Here, on the road below us, a smartly uniformed officer emerges from the door of a long, low residential building and hurries off toward the station, briefcase in hand, armed, obviously, for the bureaucratic day. There, at the barrier, the ubiquitous Soviet construction truck, muddy and battered, workers of both sexes huddled in the back, waits for our train to pass. Now there is another commuter, a civilian this time, also hurrying to the station, and he is accompanied by a child, who clings to his hand and talks eagerly to him as they go.

On the horizon, a forest of construction cranes marks one more of the multitudinous undertakings of a regime that has always preferred to build rather than to maintain. Stretching to this remote horizon are great avenues of cement apartment blocks, rising, gray and heavy, from the mud of the construction sites. One senses the proximity, beyond the horizon, of the sea—in this instance the end of the Gulf of Finland at the Neva delta—and for a few moments the mind of one traveler, at least, becomes lost, as it is repeatedly to do over the course of these coming days, in flights of memory and association. The flight this time is to the curious island town of Kronstadt that lies in the middle of the bay, with its old naval base and its great cathedral and its gloomy history. I think particularly, for some reason, of the scene of its evacuation at the close of the unsuccessful Kronstadt Uprising of 1921: members of the sailor garrison, revolting now against the Soviet authority they had once assisted to power, trying desperately to fight their way across the ice to the northern shore—the villa-lined shore that must, come to think of it, lie right there, beyond the construction cranes and the distant tree line. This city—this region—has always had for me an inexhaustible historical eloquence—beautiful, terrible, and tragic. I feel the spell descending upon me before we are fairly in its precincts.

Here at last is the Finland Station: the same old tracks and platforms, but a new station building, modern and handsome—one of the better things, in fact, that I have seen Soviet architects do. At one side of the large open-air foyer that divides the station proper from the platform gates, there stands, in honored dignity, on a little track of its own, the locomotive that pulled Lenin's train into the station on that memorable night in April 1917: a fine piece of Edwardian machinery, looking somehow surprised but pleased as well to find itself, after all the years of mundane labor, thus preserved and honored, and all for the performance of a task that must have seemed at the time like many another.

But now I am whisked away by kind friends, over streets familiar yet unfamiliar. Whether they are streets once really seen, or seen in dreams, or merely imagined from reading about them, I cannot distinguish. Here on the Liteini (the former Alexandrovski) Bridge, the whole breathtaking panorama of the Neva and its magnificent banks opens up again in all its calm, quiet vastness. And soon we are in the streets of the central city, where associations tumble in in such profusion that they form a meaningless roar and numb the mind.

I wander almost aimlessly about, this first morning, in the old Admiralty Quarter, somewhat drunk, as it seems to me, with the past. I find myself following the banks of the Moika Canal: past the Summer Garden and the Field of Mars, toward Palace Square. These streets, despite, or perhaps because of, the intimidating profusion of great palaces that frown down on them, seem strangely empty, neglected, almost deserted. One is tempted to suspect that this emptiness is some sort of punishment inflicted upon them by the Soviet authorities, resentful of their onetime glamour; but then one recalls that precisely this same observation—about their emptiness—was made by travelers who visited the city a good hundred years ago.

At the Pevcheski Most, the old Singers' Bridge (because the Court Singing School once occupied one of the buildings that look down upon it), I find myself facing the windows of the eastern end of the enormous crescent-shaped structure that frames the southern side of the square before the Winter Palace and once housed (and this with ease) the General Staff offices, those of the two great Ministries of Finance and Foreign Affairs, the palatial residential apartment of the foreign minister, and even the home of his senior assistant. What confronts me now is the Foreign Office end. Behind those windows, it occurs to me, such men as Nesselrode and Gorchakov and Giers must once have lived, given their ponderous diplomatic receptions, edited their elegant diplomatic notes—normally in French—and sparred poisonously with the foreign ambassadors. I would like to go in and see the rooms where all this took place, but this part of the building seems now to be used as some sort of clinic, and I am afraid of bewildering the medical personnel, or bringing them into embarrassment, if I simply appear and try to explain so curious a purpose.

Instead, I wander into the courtyard of a building on the Moika, the old Volkonski Palace, where, in a modest apartment overlooking the canal, the poet Pushkin died, in February 1837, from the wounds incurred in his duel with a wretched hanger-on of the diplomatic colony. For a full century the place was used as a regular apartment, occupied by a long succession of ordinary tenants (and at one time by a police office). Despite a plaque on the outer wall, for many of the tenants those tragic hours in 1837 can have been little more than a vague legend. But the Soviet authorities, greatly to their credit, have now reclaimed and restored the apartment—restored it with that peculiar and impressive love which Russians devote to such things when they address themselves to them at all—and today one can see it all, stocked partly with original items from the Pushkin ménage of the time, partly with others of the period, the rooms arranged as they were at the moment of the poet's death, still indicated by the hands of the stopped clock. In a brilliant inspiration of the curator's art, there have been pinned to the old entrance door, still visible from the staircase by which one ascends to the apartment, two scrawled chits, the second of them sad and despairing, that friends of the dying man actually pinned to the door at the time to inform the crowd outside of the progress of the poet's agony.

A little flock of Soviet visitors has assembled here to go through the apartment. Fading as best I can into this human landscape, I go with them. The guide is a wary-looking young man who has learned his lines (not too well) by heart, mumbles them in a hurried, evasive monotone, and obviously could not be less interested in the people who stand before him. But nothing could diminish, for anyone who cares about Russian literature, the mute expressiveness of the scene. Here, surrounded by all these bits of genuine Pushkiniana, one feels that one can see the frail, tortured frame of the writer—the man without whom the Russian language as we have known it would be unthinkable—stretched out on the leather *couchette* beside the partition of bookcases: the strong, calm face with the high forehead, the curly sideburns, the slightly African features, as they appear in the death mask.

"I have erected to myself," Pushkin once wrote, "a monument not fashioned by the hand." Well, so he did; even a foreigner knows it and understands it, and I emerge onto the sunlit embankment of the canal scarcely less shaken, it seems to me, than must have been some of those who stood there, waiting for the end, on that epochal winter afternoon.

The return to my quarters is made by bus. The stop is on the former Morskaya, or Sea Street, which is now called Ulitsa Gertsena. (How much more natural and attractive were some of the old tsarist street names than the self-consciously political ones that have replaced them.) As one stands there waiting for the bus, one finds oneself confronted, across the street, by the high facade of what was once the famous Imperial Yacht Club: the swankest and most exclusive of the Petersburg establishments of this sort, the haunt of grand dukes, Cabinet ministers, diplomats, and other dignitaries, most of whom had never been nearer to a yacht than the premises of the club itself. There is nothing remarkable today about this building. Its facade looks little different from that of any of the other four-story row houses of that section of town. The place now houses (one suspects an ironic smile on the lips of the Soviet official who committed it to this use) some sort of state administration for internal waterways.

Theoretically, and from the social standpoint, this is no doubt a better use. But one sighs a bit, looking up at this once so formidable and exclusive facade, to think of the meals once eaten, the wines once drunk in the rooms behind it, not to mention the service, which must have been incomparable. And one finds oneself asking the question (a blasphemous one indeed in these surroundings) whether it did not actually add something of color and variety to the city for the people of that day to know that here, in these premises, there was being prepared, even if they didn't eat it, some of the finest food eaten anywhere in northern Europe, that here things were being done elegantly, impressively, to the connoisseur's taste. Is there, in other words, not a certain reassurance, a certain twinge of hope, to be derived from the reflection that some-one, at least, in the place you inhabit, even it it is not you, lives well, from the knowledge that to live well is at least theoreti-cally a possibility?

The bus lurches exuberantly down the wide reaches of the Nevski Prospekt, its standing passengers protected from the dangers of unsteadiness by the density of their collective mass. (No one has enough room to fall.) I sneak glances of avid curiosity out the windows to every side, insofar as the heads of fellow passengers permit. The lanes of wooden-block pave-ment, on which in earlier days the horse-drawn vehicles moved so silently and comfortably along this thoroughfare, have made way now for those vast expanses of unbroken asphalt which Soviet city planners seem to favor. But the street is still very much the main street. Thick, antlike streams of pedestrians choke its sidewalks. The city fathers seem to have recently made a serious effort to restore some-thing of the traditional variety and elegance of the storefronts that line it. But only within limits is the effort successful, and I finish my bus trip pondering the reasons for this failure.

The route from the bus to my lodgings takes me through a long side street in the eastern section—one that was never exactly fashionable but was at one time a habitat of the

semiaffluent bourgeoisie and intelligentsia. It is a street like
many others: treeless, cheerless, stretching cavernously along
between rows of heavy, high facades. These are now fading
and peeling. Formidable as have been the achievements of the
city fathers in restoring buildings after the deterioration occasioned by revolution, civil war, five-year plans, and finally
war and blockade, there have been limits to what they could
do. But on one side of the street, I notice, along the sidewalk
at intervals of some forty yards, someone has placed square
boxes of nasturtiums. They must have been faithfully wa-
tered, for they appear to be thriving. Not only that, but on
one of the buildings lining the street, next to a police station,
there is a hopeful, almost wistful, sign: "This house is compet-
ing with others for supremacy in the maintenance of exemplary good order and a high level of culture in everyday life."

There is always something moving in these attempts to
achieve by collective social effort something of the tidiness
and freshness and smartness that are often, not always,
achieved elsewhere by individual initiative. One is conscious
of a theoretical superiority of motive here; of course, it should
be possible for people collectively to do for the benefit of all
what in the West is done, as a rule, for the benefit of the
individual proprietor, either for his material gain (in the case
of commercial establishments) or for the sake of his social
prestige with his neighbors, or sometimes even for the grati-
fication of his own sense of good taste. And yet, as everyone
can see, it never quite works that way. Things never look
quite the same. Can it be that the imperfections of man are
such that the development of individual taste—or, if you will,
selfish taste, even class taste—must come first, until habits are
formed, expectations inculcated, and aversions bred against
what is not tasteful at all? Still, one feels, as one walks through
the side street, the impulse to cheer the flower boxes and the
ambitious sign, and to wish the inhabitants of this particular
house well in their competition for supremacy in the maintenance of an exemplary good order. May the effort not just

flag, as so many similar efforts have done in Soviet Russia, from discouragement, from indifference, or from the transfer elsewhere of some enterprising Party secretary.

Leaving aside the canalized channels of the estuary, there must be twenty miles of artificial canals in just the main portion of this city, south of the Neva. They are all legacies from the original design of Peter the Great. He had actually envisaged far more of them. They add, of course, to the picturesqueness and the uniqueness of the city; it would not, in fact, be the same city without them. Yet, comparing them with canals elsewhere, one cannot say that they are entirely successful. Their granite-faced sides are too high, too steep, too forbidding. They lack the intimate quaysides of Amsterdam, the lower embankments of the Seine. They are not enlivened by any floating traffic. The odd oarsman—the chap who has hired a skiff at the Summer Garden to take his girl for a cruise and ventures out into the turnings of the Moika or the Fontanka—looks forlorn, seen from the bridges or the embankments: so far down there, between the steep, frowning sides, with no place to hold on to, few places to land. One has the feeling that if he fell overboard there would be, as in some great cistern, no place to swim ashore to.

The pleasantest of these canals, it seems to me, is the Fontanka. It has the air (I can, of course, be wrong on this) of being a bit wider and less sluggish than the others. One of the best places to see it from, surely, is the old Bridge of St. Simeon, halfway between the Nevski Prospekt and the Summer Garden. Here, looking to the north, the eye follows the embankments to the gardens of the Engineers' Palace, where, when the building was young, the unfortunate Emperor Paul was strangled one night by his amiable courtiers, and where, for decades since, generations of students have struggled to expiate that untoward event by their bouts with slide rule and drawing board. The view to the south, reaching to the fine facade and canalside garden of the erstwhile Sheremetyev Palace, is no less pleasing. Off to the west is the old building of the Circus—one of the few notable relics of the high period of nineteenth-century Petersburg architecture that still serve the purpose for which they were built. All this is eighteenth- and nineteenth-century Petersburg at its best.

But most agreeable, on a fine September morning, is a tiny square, lying at the eastern end of the bridge, that looks as though it might have been inadvertently created by the destruction of a building there during the war. A single birch tree rises from it; there are also bushes and a few benches. The sun strikes into it in the morning and at midday, and the tall surrounding structures protect it from the northerly winds. There, obviously, people like to sit in the warmer hours of the day: older people, for the most part, some of them, no doubt, people who experienced the siege and famine and are now content to enjoy whatever peace life can offer. On the paths before them the children play (for in Russia baby-sitting and baby-walking are the great occupations of the elderly), and pigeons strut about.

I watch this unselfconscious little company of bench-sitters, basking, gossiping, and feeding the pigeons, and wonder what it is that makes the scene so welcome. It occurs to me that here is something one misses elsewhere in this spacious but severely ordered city, something we might call the pleasingly unstructured, unexpected, and unintended. The little park breaks symmetry in this most symmetrical of urban designs, and the effort is startlingly agreeable. How long, one wonders, will it take the city planners, here as elsewhere, to realize that what people really want in an urban community is not—or, at least, not entirely—great ordered vistas and tidy geometrical configurations, but variety and intimacy: the crooked street, the sudden turning, the niche in which nothing is straight, the place, the house, the room that is like no other place or house or room. This is not *all* they want: in Leningrad, of all places, no one would wish to dispense with the magnificent squares and parks and "prospekts" with which a bygone dynasty endowed the place. But one does long at times for some of the genial disorder of Rome or London, or even that of prerevolutionary Moscow, which the fathers of that city are now working so hard to destroy. While both have their place, the search for grandeur is obviously the enemy of coziness, presumably because it attempts to remove man from the reassuring disorder of nature, in which he once had his habitat, and in the incalculability of which he was accustomed, over millions of years, to look for his security.

It is another morning, and another part of the town. From the sidewalk on the south side of the Nevski Prospekt one can step directly into the inner-entrance court of what is now a Pioneer (scouting) center but was formerly the Anichkov Palace, a gilded prison in which, from time to time, members of the imperial family, including the unfortunate Nicholas and Alexandra, resided. The building stood in closest proximity to the great crowded street and had to be guarded accordingly.

Plainly, if you are to be guarded at all, it makes little difference whether the guarding is for the purpose of keeping you in or keeping others out, or both. The effect is much the same. After the 1860s in particular, the tsars, like most rulers who hold many others prisoner, were in effect prisoners themselves, as their successor Stalin was to be. Not for them the freedom of obscurity and anonymity. Not for them the priceless privilege of walking down a street—any street—observing and yet unobserved. The physical appointments of the prisons in which they were confined were, of course, comfortable by comparison with those of their victims (though not always as comfortable as people suppose); but the warm sociability and camaraderie that went so far to make life tolerable in the ordinary Russian prison were not for them, nor was the solace of considering oneself the victim of somebody else's injustice. The sentences *they* were serving had been passed upon them by the accident of birth, an accident for which, much as they might have wished it had not occurred, they could expect no sympathy from others, only envy and resentment. All of which goes to suggest that the general unhappiness of Russian society in the nineteenth century was not a condition inflicted by happy bad people on unhappy good ones, as the Marxist-revolutionary myth would have it, but a common predicament, embracing them all. The role each was to enact in the common scenario was determined, as a rule, not by his virtue or the lack of it but by that unfathomable selection which decrees that each of us shall be the child of *his* particular parents and no others. The happiness of the role, or its unhappiness, was not necessarily a function of the inherited station in life.

Not far from the Anichkov Palace, on the same side of the Nevski, there opens up the pleasant little park before the old Alexandrinski Theater (now the State Academic Theater for Drama, commemorating A. S. Pushkin). The hour, on this occasion, is early. The paths of the park are still clean. The patient, kerchiefed elderly women who—year in, year out, century in, century out—do this sort of thing in Russia have swept them carefully with their twig brooms this very morning, and the patterns cut by the wide, curved swaths of the twigs are still pleasantly visible in the damp sand. The imperious figure of Catherine the Great, sweeping forward, scepter in hand, after the fashion of sculptured monarchs, still presides over the park from its lofty perch. Having had the good fortune to rule in an age when Russia had neither an industrial proletariat nor a modern revolutionary movement for her to oppress, she survived the dangerous period of the 1920s and 1930s, when she might well have been torn down; and she is probably set, if the gasoline fumes do not get her, for at least another century.

Beneath her, on a circular stone bench that surrounds her pedestal some halfway up, still sit the legendary figures of her political and personal entourage, people bearing the great names of eighteenth-century Russia: Derzhavin, Rumiantsev, Suvorov, Potemkin, et cetera. Beautifully costumed, vigorous and animated in posture, but slightly self-conscious, precariously perched and exposed as they are up there, with the pigeon dirt streaking down their elegant coiffures, they look like people on a dais trying to appear casual despite the numbers of eyes trained upon them.

The Alexandrinski Theater appears unchanged. The original quadriga is still there, the horses rearing and straining and pulling in different directions, after the fashion of quadriga horses everywhere who know their business. Beneath them, on the triangular face of the portico, the two reclining Graces, delineated in white bas-relief against the yellow background so characteristic of Petersburg architecture, stretch out their wreaths, in sisterly communion, to the lyre that now stands between them (replacing, apparently, the imperial double eagle of tsarist times).

The theater is just now undergoing what the Russians call a *bolshoi remont*. Scaffoldings have crept up two of its sides. A placard at ground level permits one to suspect that this is by way of preparation for the forthcoming appearance here of the Arena Stage, from Washington, which is to play *Our Town*. I recall that it was from this theater that the unhappy Anton Chekhov fled after the grotesque, incredible flop of the first performance of his *Seagull*, in October 1896—fled, heartsick and embittered, to wander despairingly until two in the morning among the crowds on the Nevski, avoiding his friends and vowing that he would never write another play. *The Seagull* was, of course, far from being his best play, and remorse over its imperfections was probably never wholly to leave him. But it had in it gropings toward the great plays that were to follow—plays that would in some respects lay the very foundations of the modern stage—and I find myself wondering, as I leave the theater behind me, whether if Chekhov had not made that initial effort and endured that agony there would ever have been an *Our Town* for the Arena Stage to play.

No more than the present Leningrad was the erstwhile

Petersburg a city made up exclusively of scenes of light and
space and hopeful aspiration. It had its gray, gloomy, oppressive thoroughfares, plenty of them: long, straight streets, nar-
rower than the great "prospekts," lined with unbroken rows
of oppressive, ponderous apartment houses in the Wilhel-
minian-Berlin style (*Mietskasernen,* the Germans would have
called them)—unrelieved monotony, hostile, even menacing,
to the human spirit. I am approaching such streets now, as I
move westward from the Alexandrinski Theater toward the
onetime Hay Market and the area around it. Gogol knew
them, as did Dostoyevski. They are the streets in which the
latter's Raskolnikov wandered in dreamlike misery in the
aftermath of his crime. They are the opposite poles to all the
beauty and magnificence that lie so near them; and the sinis-
terness of the one is no less accentuated by the high northern
latitude than is the beauty of the other. It would behoove the
architects in far-northern cities to bear in mind that all the
effects of their handiwork, beautiful or ugly, hopeful or dis-
couraging, are destined to be lengthened, like the shadows, in
a world where the sun, if visible at all, is always at a somewhat
lower angle than elsewhere. Even the normally indefatigable
author of the 1914 Baedeker recoiled, lost his enthusiasm, and
retreated when he encountered such districts. The inner
parts of Vasili Island, he recorded, "offer no attractions to the
stranger."

Yet somehow, even in the dichotomy of darkness and light
which marks this city, there seems to be some hidden intent
and meaning and unity—the intimation of some veiled design, wider, deeper, and more mysterious than just the crude
naval and political ambitions of the ruthless giant—part boy,
part tyrant, part genius—who conceived it all and laid it out.
Some higher hand, knowing full well what it was doing, was
at work here, arranging these bodies of water, these islands,
these gardens and squares, these sectors of gloom and menace.
The poetry of significance itself eludes one; one gropes vainly
for it in memory and imagination, as for something once

dreamed which was all clear and coherent in the dream but cannot now be quite recovered—and yet one knows it was there.

An afternoon walk takes me to the eastern end of the southern Neva Embankment—to the point where the long line of palaces (thirty or forty of them) stretching east from the Hermitage ends and gives way to less glamorous habitation. The embankment is basking now in the declining sunshine of an autumn afternoon. The facades of the palaces, facing north as they do, and thus normally deprived of the sun (the inhabitants, for all the grandeur of the premises, often complained about this), are given a brief hour of warm illumination. Near the old Alexandrovski Bridge, fishermen are lined up, leaning across the granite balustrade, poles extended to clear the slope of the stone facing beneath them, brothers all, for the moment, in this most ancient and peaceable of human pastimes. Before them terns, presumably out after the same tiny fish, wheel and dive over the cold gray-green waters. Across the river, at the entrance to the interisland channel known as the Bolshaya Nevka, can be discerned the old-fashioned outlines of the celebrated cruiser *Aurora*, now a museum piece—a vessel that achieved greater fame by merely firing blanks as a signal for the fighting to begin on the evening of November 7, 1917, than most warships have achieved with even the greatest output of live ammunition. Like so many other objects in this city, the vessel has entered now into what we might call the mythology of history, and has meaning not for what it actually did but for what it is popularly conceived to have done.

Behind the fishermen, in the street that runs along the quay, there is little traffic. People are walking dogs; and just beyond the bridge, before what was once the French embassy, two of the latter are having a mock battle, like dogs anywhere—like capitalist dogs, in fact. Ten or twenty years ago one would not have seen dogs at all.

On the way home I pass the prerevolutionary American

embassy, on the former Furshtatskaya. The building has now been greatly spruced up, and a new central entrance has been added. It bears a placard describing it in some such terms as "Office for the Registration of Documents Attesting to Personal Status." It is, in other words, the marriage bureau; and the authorities, still concerned to compete with the Church in the solemnization of an event of personal life that people feel an unquenchable need to solemnize, has spruced it up and endowed it with a sort of wedding-cake elegance that it did not have even in the years of its diplomatic function. Here behind those windows, in the harrowing months of 1917, Ambassador David Francis, former mayor of St. Louis and governor of Missouri, smoked his cigars, pursued his French lessons with a lady of German name, and feuded tensely with his more polished career aides, who suspected the lady of the wrong political connections and harbored dark misgivings as to the consequences of this association. Now in 1973, on this cool autumn evening, a row of special taxis, vehicles provided expressly for this purpose by the thoughtful city fathers and distinguished by linked rings affixed to their roofs, waits at the curb. In the first of them, attired in traditional long white dress and veil, sits the bride, excited and triumphant; next to her is the groom, in dark suit, ruffled shirt, and no necktie, looking unhappy and self-conscious; around them, after the fashion of weddings everywhere, a little crowd of passersby has stopped to gape, to admire, to criticize.

Next door to the marriage bureau is a similar institution for the registration of births—the intended surrogate for baptism. Here again there is a little party of participants, but this time they are standing on the sidewalk—the entire family group: grandparents, relatives, father, and, above all, of course, the young wife, bearing the baby on a lace-covered cushion and exhibiting it to be oohed and ahed at by all comers. The half-light of evening is on this little scene; there is a wonderful unselfconsciousness about it, and vividness as in a Renaissance painting. One is aware, standing here among the small band of rubberneckers, that one is witnessing the irrepressible insistence of ordinary people on living as people have always lived, hoping as people have always hoped, affirming a species of faith in the continuity of personal life, a faith that has nothing to do with reason and nothing to do with political doctrines but triumphs, in the end, over both.

After long and patient climbing of the circular stairs, I stand, this last morning, on the walk that surrounds the high dome of St. Isaac's Cathedral. A light rain is falling. The roofs of the city are beneath us. From somewhere in the forest of masonry behind us, the canned voice of the official guide-propagandist booms out, informing us that the density of the housing visible to the west of us was the result of the greed of the capitalist developers—true, no doubt, but scarcely the whole story. In the north one sees old Petersburg at its finest and proudest: the Admiralty, the Winter Palace, the Alexander Garden. It could be said, I suppose, that capitalists built them, too.

The Marquis de Custine described Petersburg, in all its grandeur, as a monument to the future. The past, he thought, had certainly not deserved it, nor did the present. What we are seeing now is *his* future, and it cannot live up to the grandeur either. No human society could. One has to concede to the authors of the Revolution that the pomp, the pretense, the implicit claims of this city exceeded every possible dimension of mortal man. No one, least of all poor Nicholas II or the eighteen-odd grand dukes who surrounded him, could possibly have done justice to it. This inadequacy applied not just to the architecture and decor but to the whole structure of institutional grandeur at the pinnacle of which the monarch stood: the court, the bureaucracy, the guard regiments, even the hierarchy of the state-controlled and bureaucratized Church. Any mere men, plagued like other mortals by their fears, their passions, their jealousies, and their infirmities, must have usually looked absurd, uncomfortable against a stage setting that so dwarfed them. No one could be wholly oblivious of this anomaly—this hopeless gap between pretense and reality. It invited ridicule and contempt. It produced, with time, a physical isolation of the privileged classes which contributed, in the end, to their undoing.

Well, one may say, the revolutionaries were right: these people were claiming too much, striking poses not justified by their real quality, living in unmerited luxury; they deserved their misery; good riddance to them.

Yes, but . . . this was not just Russia's problem. It was a problem that existed wherever dynasties surrounded themselves with the trappings of grandeur. It existed all over Western Europe, too. It was an unvarying feature of the dynastic age. And was it all so useless? These buildings, this symbolism, these titles and uniforms and decorations—all this pomp—was this ever supposed to be the reality? Was anyone ever really supposed to be fooled by it? Was it not, rather, the dream, the vision, the ideal of man as he might conceivably be—of man ennobled, inspirited, in command of himself, risen above himself? And without this theater, without this never-ending ritualistic enactment of that which did not yet exist but which you liked to hope might someday do so, without this testimonial to one's faith in man's future, what would there have been of art and architecture, of design and decoration, of good taste, of imagination and inspiration, in old Europe?

I went out, just yesterday, to see the magnificently restored suburban palace of Pavlovsk. (The Russians can pride themselves here on what is certainly one of the finest works of restoration, if not the finest, of all time.) There is no better illustration of the dilemma of royal grandeur. No man could really *live* in this structure, in the sense of using every room, sitting in every chair, noticing every stroke of decoration, enjoying every touch of elegance and dignity. Any mere human frame was bound to rattle around in it. Yet without it where would have been the model of decorative brilliance and good taste for hundreds of other buildings? Where, in fact, would architecture all over Europe have been without the great royal establishments that set the tone? Was it not desirable, in other words, that some people, albeit ordinary, inadequate people—people who after each performance bathed sweaty feet, said unfitting things, and misbehaved in all sorts of silly ways, like anyone else—was it not desirable that they should act the parts, rather than that these should not be acted at all, if only in order that the settings might have an excuse for existence and might continue to remind people of what men *could* be, or could be imagined as being? It was by just such visions, surely, that men lived through the low moments of history, surviving what would otherwise have been unadulterated squalor, hopeless and intolerable.

It is with such rumination, over questions to which there is not and will never be a wholly satisfactory answer, that I make my clattering way down the metal steps of the circular staircase and out onto the great square before the church, where the rain sifts down, the pavement glistens, and the eye wanders from the old German embassy, where the mob threw the furniture out the window when war broke out in 1914, to the Blue Bridge and the noble outlines of the Marie Palace beyond.

It seems to me, on the basis of these few days of exposure, that a real and significant change—or at least the beginnings of one—has come over Leningrad in these past few years. It is not just that here, after so many vicissitudes and against the still-enduring background of an ideologically militant system, something like normal life is again breaking through: that people fish, dogs play, pigeons are fed, and the great events of personal life—birth, marriage, and death—are again celebrated by the real sacraments or by their imitations. Contemporary Leningrad, beyond that, is rediscovering its own past and, above all, its own enduring bond with that past. It is like a person who has suffered years of amnesia after an accident (the accident being in this case the Revolution) and now begins gradually to recover his memory and to become aware of the life that was lived before and of his own connection with it. Together with Leningrad's awakening come the beginnings of a revival of the erstwhile quality of the place as a world city. Ten foreign consulates have now been opened here, there having been none since the purges of the 1930s. Foreign visitors have multiplied, and not all of them are tourists. Foreign students are again in residence. There are the beginnings of a foreign colony. Slowly and laboriously, with creaks and groans, the place is resuming the continuity with the city of the past and the communication with the outside world that made it once one of the world's great cities, capable of giving as well as receiving in its relationship to the world without.

The problem of the relationship of the regime to the cultural and intellectual dissidents, here as elsewhere in Russia, has obviously not been solved. Was it ever solved, in fact, in Russia—except briefly in the period of the last three tsars, against whom, as though by way of punishment for their relative liberalism, the intelligentsia then rebelled? This failure is no laughing matter. People elsewhere plainly cannot be other than concerned about it. But one wonders, looking at this city, whether beneath the surface other changes, slow, less visible, more elemental, are not also in progress—processes of growth and adaptation more important and more hopeful than all the current mistakes and timidities of policy that make the headlines in the Western press.

It is my last day here. To complete this visit, there is the customary, almost obligatory, visit to the Piskarevskoye Cemetery on the northern edge of the city, where the victims of the siege of the city in the Second World War, some 800,000 of them, are buried. It is unquestionably impressive: the long rows of grass-grown mounds, the solemn music, the combined sense of hush and horror and sadness which lies over the place. Everyone feels here that he is in the presence of tragedy beyond the capacity of imagination. Even the one ambiguous and slightly threatening line of Olga Berggolt's otherwise beautiful lament, inscribed on the wall at the end of the cemetery ("Be aware . . . that no one is forgotten, and nothing is forgotten"), cannot ruin the impression that here in these mounds is a silent reproach that goes beyond the passions of the war itself and applies to the weakness and follies of mankind as a whole, so that attempts to relate it to the wickedness of one political regime or the virtues of another appear only as trivial manifestations of poor taste.

The return journey to Finland is again by train. Once again the young birch forests of Karelia flash past the windows of the car. I find them, as always, strangely moving, these young birch trees of the North. Fresh, tender, sometimes trembling, full of youth and enthusiasm, they stand as a defiance to the rigors of the climate, as an affirmation of faith in the ability of life to survive hard winters and wars and revolutions, and even individual death. It occurs to me that many of them grow, here in Karelia, on spots where young men fell in the Winter War and now lie buried. In this sense, the young forest strikes me as no less eloquent a memorial to the dead than the cemetery at Piskarev, and I am tempted to say that never does the birch appear more virginal, more beautiful, more appealing than when it draws its strength from the remains of some boy—be he Russian or Finnish—who gave up on this spot the privilege of leading a life through, like the rest of us, in all its satisfactions and disappointments.

I accepted, in 1976, an invitation to join a cruise ship scheduled to visit the Black Sea in the autumn of that year and to lecture to the other passengers, mostly patrons of the Metropolitan Museum of Art in New York, on the Soviet ports to be visited. Weather was bad throughout; some of the visits even had to be canceled. Here, however, are brief glimpses of Yalta, Sochi, Tiflis (to which an inland excursion was made), and finally, Mount Athos, Greece, where, lacking a harbor, the ship lay offshore and the male passengers paid the briefest of visits to this ancient ghost town.

OCTOBER 22, 1976
YALTA

Our stay, in late afternoon and evening, was short. A cloudy, heavy day. Buses were waiting for us in a roped-off area on the dock. We lost no time in boarding them. A stocky girl guide, who gave her name (rather unoriginally) as Tamara, belted out over the radio the usual singularly unconvincing and boring boasts about the achievements of Soviet power, replete with statistics on the number of "holiday-makers" accommodated by Yalta and its vicinity. As the bus climbed up the hills at the edge of the town, one got only indistinct glimpses of well-tended parks, of an almost dry, stone-enclosed river bed, and of the walls of houses. Soon we were above the town. The clouds now closed in on us. Nothing was visible. There was only the voice of the guide—the characteristic Russian woman's voice, high but not shrill, telling us how many "holiday-makers" were accommodated by each of the invisible places we were passing.

Our first point of call was the great palace at Livadia, where we were to see the "Museum of the Crimean Conference." The fine gardens had been well tended and preserved (if Russian Communists, one reflects, had only cared as much about people as they do about plants), and it was a pleasure to walk through a part of them, despite the cold and the dampness. But the visit to the "museum" consisted only of a shuffling group-walk. It went first through the vestibule, with its ghastly painting of all those well-remembered characters associated with the conference (including a Chip Bohlen who, I thought, looked more like me; I wondered whether they had confused us). Then came the celebrated ballroom, with the large table where the negotiations had taken place still standing in the middle of it. Then there was the now empty wing where the failing FDR had slept.

The guide's patter, and the surrounding placards, still reflected the official Soviet view of that futile and fumbling gathering known as "Yalta"—the hearty reassuring vision of European and world affairs being soundly reconstructed by three great statesmen under the wise and benevolent leadership of Stalin and Molotov. But I knew all that I wanted to know about the Yalta Conference; and while the guide droned on, my mind kept returning to the image of the coming-out ball, in May 1913, of the eldest daughter of the last tsar, the Grand Duchess Olga, in this same palace. I could see it all in retrospect: the great French windows thrown open to the view of the sea; the smell of the roses and the perfumes; the brilliance of the candles and the uniforms, the many jewels, and the flowers in the doomed girl's hair, put up for the first time in honor of the occasion. (Five years later she would be shot, with the rest of the family, in the cellar of the Ipat'evsk house in Yekaterinburg [now Sverdlovsk], in the Urals.)

Back into the buses, and up into the clouds once again. What can be seen of the roadside from this misty high road is less beautiful than what lies below. The journey—longer, this time—took us to Alupka, the fantastic palace, English-designed and English-built, of Count Mikhail Semonovich Vorontsov, the all-powerful governor-general for all of southern Russia in the time of Nicholas I. To me this was historically interesting; for while most of the furnishings had been removed at the time of the Revolution by members of the family (the Polish Branickis) of Vorontsov's wife, a few items remained, including interesting busts of Vorontsov himself and his beautiful lady (whom Pushkin so unwisely admired, thus exacerbating his celebrated conflict with Vorontsov). In the great dining room (the structure has 150 rooms) there were two large paintings on each side of the fireplace; but whether these were the original ones referred to by Churchill in his memoirs (he was housed there during the Crimean Conference), or, if not, what had happened to them, I could not tell, nor was the guide any wiser. But on the steps before the building leading down to the sea, there were still the famous Italian lions, replicas of those that grace the tomb of Pope Clement XII in Rome, the one at the bottom still sleeping the most charming, peaceful, and innocent sleep that any sculptured animal ever enjoyed. He had slept it through storms and tumults, through wars and revolutions, through German occupation, through liberation, through transformation of the palace—first into a rest home, then into a museum. Might he continue to sleep it, I thought to myself, until a new era of lightness, graciousness, and fantasy breaks over this beautiful but tragically afflicted peninsula!

On the way back to the ship the bus descended the narrow street where Chekhov's house still stands. We were able to glimpse, in the gathering dusk and through the dripping foliage, only a roof and, briefly, a wet stucco facade. But I was grateful for the memory of the visit I had paid to that house so many years ago, when Chekhov's devoted sister, Marya

Pavlovna, had taken me through the house herself and talked to me about her brother's life.

Back at the port, there was a rather uninspiring walk along the rain-swept promenade, with its drenched gardens and its agitational posters. Then back to the ship, and out, once more, into the nocturnal blackness of the sea called Black.

OCTOBER 23, 1976
SOCHI

It is late afternoon as we approach Sochi. I cut short my briefing for the passengers so that they can go on deck and watch the approach.

Dreamlike, there rise in the distance the snowcapped peaks of the Caucasus. (It is nice that we can see them; for this, though we don't now know it, is to be our only and last glimpse of them.)

A white launch comes out with the pilot. Its surly helmsman bangs the ship's side so angrily that he knocks his own fender off and nearly causes the pilot to share its fate. Looking toward the port, we can see, to my surprise, a fleet of small sailboats disappearing rapidly behind the breakwater, as though alarmed at our approach.

As we move into the little port, we pass a patrol boat, with a gun, lying offshore, protecting it, no doubt, against those numerous enemies by which the Party-police establishment sees the Soviet Union surrounded. And at the entrance channel through the breakwater there is a tower where an armed guard makes sure that none of those enemies, having eluded the vigilance of the patrol vessel, slips through—as we are now doing—into the little port.

The boat once docked, we go for a walk. It is dark now. There is a maritime station, Stalinist-style, with a tall spire, à la Petersburg Admirality. Before it, across the quay, lies a fine white Soviet passenger vessel: the *Ukraina.* Below it, on the quay itself, there lie, now mounted on wheeled cradles, the little sailboats we saw hurrying in from the sea a few moments before, and near them is a van bearing the legend, in English, "Soviet Olympic Sailing Team." Hydrofoils of the coastal lines come and go at one dock. What appears to be a freight vessel, moored stern-to at another dock, is disgorging, for some reason, a dense mass of passengers. There seems, in short, to be everything you could expect in this little port—except spontaneity.

The town has changed beyond recognition. There is a large and fine park, just behind the Maritime Station, replete with kiosks of all sorts, a movie theater *(Around the World in Eighty Days)*, and a restaurant. Through this park the crowds course; and there is the familiar Soviet smell of perfume and makhorka. Along one side of it, there is heavy traffic, with many buses, for this is now the center of a metropolitan region. From a restaurant across the street, rock-and-roll booms out; a wedding party is evidently in progress.

OCTOBER 24, 1976
TIFLIS

Back (from Yerevan) to Tiflis, in the rainy blackness, to our lofty hotel, where we have barely time to freshen up before boarding the buses once more. We go, this time, to a Georgian restaurant, in a cellar. The din, as usual, is fearful. The food, though served only at interminable intervals, is not bad. Male Georgian dancers—lithe, small men with broad shoulders and spider-waists, dressed in black and full of the usual martial fire and arrogance—dance with a ferocious, explosive agility around the one serenely gliding lady, who seems unimpressed with all this animalistic passion, and not in the least afraid. I, however, have enough of this after an hour or so, and I walk back to the hotel, alone, in the rain, under the tall, dripping trees, pushing against the rough-faced crowds that still surge, night and rain notwithstanding, along this ancient, battered thoroughfare.

All night the rain drips off the hotel balconies; and somewhere, at intervals during the night, a woman's voice can be heard, as though over some distant loudspeaker, giving something resembling orders to some invisible horde of submissive followers—or are they travelers?—or workers?—or prisoners?

Who knows?—Russia.

OCTOBER 30, 1976
MOUNT ATHOS

On Saturday, the thirtieth, there was a brief call at Mount Athos. The weather, as it has been throughout this journey, was overcast. Low clouds hung over the scene; we never saw the famous mountain. A number of us males were taken ashore in an overcrowded cutter, our abandoned ladies (for Mount Athos is exclusively a male community) hurling obscenities at us from the deck of the ship. We were led up a path to see the Greek monastery, Vatopedi, one of the few still nominally operating in this ancient monastic city. A weird, eerie sight it was, too; this great and beautiful ghost town, where eight hundred monks had once lived, and where there were now only twenty, of whom we saw two. I tried to picture what life must now be like in this strange, almost wholly deserted place: the claustrophobia, the emotional abnormality, the getting-on-each-other's-nerves, the gossip, the snooping, the intrigues; the monstrous stillness of the nights in the deserted buildings and courtyards; the tense awareness of the slightest strange sound; the furtive nocturnal doings— God knows what.

Air passage, New York to Kristiansand, Norway.

He sat, full of misery, and feeling very sorry for himself (for he so detests flying), in the departure lounge at Kennedy Airport, awaiting the departure of the night flight for Bergen. Canned music merged so confusedly with the chatter of the fellow travelers and the screams of the children that it was impossible to tell what tune it was. Out to the west, visible through the window curtains, were the rays of a vague setting sun, diffused by the airport smog.

The check-in girl had said that the plane was booked full. He heard this with a shudder, for he knew what it meant: at least three hundred human bodies, many of them heavy, lumpy, and unpleasant, jammed in upon one another in the long metal cigar; then the dragging, laborious takeoff, the heavy plane crowding the point of no return before finally heaving itself, with its crushing load of fuel, luggage, provisions, movie-projection machines, New York newspapers, and God knows what else, sullenly off the runway, to roar then upward over the mud flats of southern Long Island. Then there would be the long, cramped night, the plane hurtling along through a medium men were never meant to exist in—a medium short of both heat and oxygen. There would be only a couple of hours of darkness. Around midnight, somewhere south of the Greenland Sea, the early dawn of the Arctic spring would begin to gleam through the chinks of the curtains, and a glance outside would show that the sun was already tinting the vast billowly floor of cloud cover, thousands of feet below. Around 1:30 A.M., New York time, the stewardesses would turn the lights on in the plane; and the sleep-drugged passengers, still bilious from a dinner consumed only three hours earlier, would be offered hot towels and breakfast.

An hour or so later there would be the long descent through the cloud cover. Glimpses would open up of the islands and leads of the Norwegian coast, the surf breaking and foaming on the outer skerries, the surface of the inner leads corrugated by the morning breeze. The same breeze, sharp and tangy from its passage across the great northern ocean, would tear at the garments of the passengers as they descended from the plane. And then, mussed, unslept, and uneasy from the overearly breakfast, one would sit through the morning hours on the upholstered benches of the transit lounge, fighting sleep, eyeing one's companions with that malevolence reserved for fellow passengers one does not know, until the plane for Kristiansand would be called out and one would struggle, with all one's bundles, into another and smaller metal cigar. What a way to travel! Not travel at all, he reflected, but anti-travel: every pleasure and benefit of real travel sacrificed to the passion for speed.

He thought, as he sat there in the Bergen departure lounge, that he could even pursue the journey further in his imagination. There would be the arrival at the little Kristiansand airport, with the view of the wide fjord off the end of the runway. Then the drive out to the archipelago through rocks and woods, with glimpses of coves and bays below. Finally, the arrival at the cottage on the seaward side of the small peninsula. Here, one had arrived so many times over the past thirty years that one could picture the whole experience almost photographically: the few steps up the path from the parking place; the view of the little lawn-between-the-rocks behind the cottage, where the fruit trees would be in bloom and the leaves would just be coming out on the other trees; and then, as one walked up to the terrace before the house, there would be the breathtaking, ever-exciting view of the wide sound, bounded first by wooded islands, then widening to the barren outer skerries, and finally, framed by two lighthouses a mile apart, the open sea itself, endless-reaching, disappearing into the far horizon—no limits here, no confinement, no pettiness, no claustrophobia.

So, in imagination, he conceived it; and so, roughly speaking, it all was.

In early July 1977, Annelise and I, in company with two good friends, who were also co-owners of the NORTHWIND *our new sailing vessel, set out from Copenhagen to cruise around the south coast of Sweden, with a stop at the Danish island of Bornholm, to Stockholm, where the boat would be left over the coming winter.*

Here: excerpts of the account of this cruise, in which Annelise and I participated only as far as the port of Kalmar on the east coast of Sweden.

JULY 1, 1977

Left Kristiansand in early morning on the ferry for Denmark. A gray and rainy Skagerrak, the ship rolling in the wind and swell from the southwest; the passengers, to the extent not seasick, dozing in the airplane seats of the salon, disturbed only by the crying children, the rumbling of the engines, and the strains of the music to the *Zhivago* movie drifting in, indistinctly, from somewhere in the ceiling. Outside: a gray, empty sea, flicked by a force-5 breeze and spittings of rain; the usual occasional fishing smack; a small and not too hopeful company of seagulls; now and then a shearwater. The passengers: Europeans all, mostly German motor tourists; a number of young couples, blue-jeaned and, on the male side, bearded, well-enough behaved; occupants, all of them, of the intellectual and spiritual vacuum which the

European welfare state produces; comfortable enough now, in a sort of proletarian way, with their little cubicles of flats, their TV, and their puddle-jumpers, but the victims of a deeper sort of drugging than just the atmosphere of the Ska-gerrak ferry, and with time running out on all they know: the petty affluence, the social security, the liberal supplies of en-ergy, and above all, the international peace. A curious, empty interlude, this, before the new, terrible, and possibly final storm.

JULY 3, 1977
COPENHAGEN

During the night the wind finally abated. Lying awake around midnight, I could tell it was abating by timing, in my own consciousness, the frequency of the gusts. We rose, there-fore, at 3 A.M. and got under way by 3:40. The heavens, mean-time, had clouded. The serried ranks of yachts, given respite from the scourging northwester, now lay quiet and asleep. The great sound was enveloped in the misty grayness of dawn. With the breeze behind us, we, carrying only a jib, drifted down the marked channel, past a Copenhagen still sleeping tightly in the Sabbath dawn, past the oil refineries, past the airport, where one of the night planes from New York was coming in and another was testing its engines at the end of the runway, and you could smell the exhaust fumes far out to sea. Then we changed course and made passage, in an hour or so, across the sound to the lines of buoys leading to the short Falsterbo Canal. This we transited, and from it we emerged into the Baltic Sea.

Our destination for that day, after leaving Bornholm, was a tiny emergency harbor carved out of solid rock in the midst of a cluster of barren and uninhabited skerries some twelve miles out at sea, off the southern coast of Sweden.

The sea was now running fast and high, and dead against us. The *Northwind* was more comfortable, as always, under sail alone; and had it been for the wind alone, she would have handled nicely. But the high-running sea set us back, particularly on the port tack, where we seemed to make no heading at all. We all began to wonder whether we would ever reach our destination by daylight, or whether we would have to sail all night—a dismal prospect, not because of any great attendant danger, but because we would all, by that time, be cold and hungry and, above all, exhausted. No normal life seemed to be possible below. I was able to go down and rest, once or twice, throwing myself in my damp clothes on one of the bunks and trying to brace myself against the motion; but that was the limit of my capacity. B., with a heroism not second to that of her husband, contrived twice during the day to go below and make soup, which she then brought up, with crackers, to the cockpit. Beyond this there was not much anyone could do in the direction of comfort.

Twice during the day, the second time in the afternoon, when we might have been some twenty miles off our destination, we sighted the young German couple in whose company we had left in the morning, sailing beautifully each time, once so close that we could exchange waves. Then they disappeared, on a westward tack, and we saw no more of them.

D., in midafternoon, went below and tackled the direction finder, an undertaking which I viewed with wonder and admiration because swinging its little hand-held compass about in a heaving and swaying cabin is one of the few things guaranteed to make me seasick. But he stuck to his guns; and by dint of persistent bouts with this apparatus, punctuated by periods of dozing off while sitting bolt upright with the head-phones still on, he finally got the signal from our lighthouse destination and was able to give us bearings on it for the remainder of the day.

We must, meanwhile, have made better heading against the wind than I thought we were making, for about 6 P.M., when D. and I were both below, there came a cry of triumph from the female part of the ship's company, still in the cockpit; and sure enough, there on the dim, dark horizon, over the mael-strom of breaking crests, was a tiny needle-like finger which could be no other than our lighthouse—Utklippan. It was a discovery, I felt, which we owed exclusively to D. for his tireless work with the direction finder.

It was seven o'clock and some fifteen hours out of Born-holm when, amid the final flurry of anxious commands, warn-ing cries, injunctions, and disagreements with which tired people often enter a strange and poorly marked haven in heavy weather, we moved through the reefs into the relatively sheltered lagoon behind the lighthouse, and then, seconds later, passed through the gate leading into the wholly shel-tered inner basin, marveling that water could become, in so short a time, so still, and the boat so steady.

This inner basin was a fine but small rectangular expanse, blasted out of solid rock, lined with excellent granite quays supplied with heavy mooring rings. It was designed as a har-bor of refuge, and this it was indeed. It had been cut into the northernmost of two skerries, separated from each other by an east-west passage, enterable from both sides. On the south-ernmost skerry, accessible from our northern one only by passage in a small boat, was the lighthouse. This was automat-ically operated from shore, but the former lighthouse keeper's house was now occupied by a fisherman-caretaker, who chugged over to the basin once or twice a day to remove the trash bags the Swedish government had kindly provided, and to collect the daily ten-crown fee from the visiting yachtsmen.

On our northern skerry there were no buildings other than

a lone outhouse, situated at some distance from the little harbor, and the remains of two granite fishermen's huts. Once installed in the inner basin, with a storm raging outside, one was, in other words, secure but effectively isolated, unless one wished to take a dinghy and hazard the passage over to the other skerry, where one's social world might be enhanced, if you will, by the presence of the fishermen, but diminished by the loss of that of the other yachtsmen.

There were some thirteen other yachts in the basin, all sheltering from the storm; but we were too tired to take much notice, and soon gratefully fell into our bunks.

THURSDAY, JULY 7, 1977
UTKLIPPAN

During the night the wind, which we had hoped would decline, continued to build up. There could be no prospect of going on. It was clear that we were here for at least another twenty-four hours (it proved to be more like three days), effectively marooned.

MONDAY, JULY 11, 1977

This morning, for the first time in a week, the wind had died and the sea was still. We could, at long last, have done some shopping in Bergkvara; but Kalmar, some twenty-five sea miles farther up the coast, was a larger town with more to offer; so off we went, on engine, over the strangely calm sea, into the narrow part of the strait, watching the coast of the long outlying island, Öland, come nearer, seeing in the distance the great bridge recently built to span the strait (to the great detriment, no doubt, of the quality of life in Öland), and letting the noble outlines of Kalmar Castle grow on the horizon. Finally, shortly before noon, we felt our way (not without the usual disagreements about buoys and sticks) into the large and busy commercial port of Kalmar.

In the afternoon, after a splurge of shopping and lunch ashore, we went to visit the castle. It was near the port, separated from it only by an intensely beautiful park. (How well the Swedes do things when they want to!)

It is easy to romanticize these ancient structures. It is harder to picture what the construction of them, and life within them, really meant to the people of the time—what it must have required in the way of drudgery on the part of both man and beast to fashion, to bring together, and to erect this vast assemblage of heavy stone, tens of thousands of tons of it, and this in the days before the use of combustion as a source of power—what life, even the life of royal personages, must have been like in this extensive but confined place, with its walls and moats: what claustrophobia, what frictions and intrigues, what cruelties in the deep, round dungeon underlying one of the towers. All this strains even the imagination of the professional historian; and for most of the vaguely interested tourists, shuffling from room to room under the droning voice of the indifferent young Swedish guide, it must have been wholly invisible across the intervening ages.

Four glimpses of life on the south coast of Norway in the 1970s. The first is of Utvaar, a small island off the coast, normally uninhabited.

Utvaar was deserted. The nine little fisherman's shacks were not boarded up but were evidently devoid of inhabitants. So we had the place initially quite to ourselves. But soon after we arrived, a fisherman in a large motor-dory came in, deposited some gear at the veranda of the first cottage, and disappeared again.

We made fast to the rocks on the southern side of the cove. Four sheep, one with a collar bell, appeared over the rocky hill, descended a bit, inspected us for a time with their fixed, solemn stares, then resumed their meandering among the rocks.

In the evening another fisherman chugged in, bearing in his dory a middle-aged woman and a dog. These he deposited on the dock before one of the shacks, after which he, too, departed, not to be seen again.

The woman opened the cottage, fussed around with something—probably a well—under one of the bushes, tied the dog, then sat motionless in the doorway. But for us and the sheep she would have been totally alone in this rocky little archipelago. We thought at first she was the fisherman's wife, and this his home, but later concluded that she was a summer visitor.

Darkness fell. With no sounds in our ears but the bell of the sheep, the crying of the gulls, and the slapping of the inevitable unruly halyard, we turned in and went to sleep.

JULY 2, 1976
SKOTTEVIK, A TINY COASTAL PORT

Wakened by the sound of the slow-chugging, ailing diesel of a fishing boat, somewhere across the island, I came up on deck in early morning to see how we were lying; for the bow, when we lay to for the night, was within inches of the rock. Then I sat in the cockpit, drinking in the lovely morning scene. On a nearby skerry the gulls were quarreling and screaming. An oyster catcher, taking off from a low-lying rock, circled the bay at high speed with his fast wing beat and bulletlike flight, skimming the water and missing the rocky shores only by a matter of feet, then settled down nearby. The white fishing smack, whose engine I had heard, its nocturnal labors now evidently completed, came swinging around the promontory at high speed, the quiet bay resounding to the roar of its diesel as it entered the cove, and lay to at the dock by the store. Its arrival caused the owner and inhabitant of one of two small sailboats, which had been lying improperly at the dock, to rouse himself hastily and move his little craft out of the way. After a short interval three men, now attired in city clothes, emerged from the fishing smack. They were joined on the dock by the man from the sailboat and a large, happy police dog who ran for sticks. There was long palaver, with much laughing, until finally one of the fishermen disappeared up the road and shortly reappeared in a very shiny and elegant automobile, in which they all then departed, leaving the sailboat operator to continue to throw sticks for the ecstatic dog.

JUNE 25, 1977
ST. JOHN'S EVE

Night before last—the night before St. John's Day, the short-est night of the year—no complete night at all, in fact—we went out to the summer home of friends, in the islands, for the traditional celebration. We were ten to fifteen people. First, there were drinks on the dock. Then we moved up to the little lawn by the house for grilled frankfurters and ham-burgers. The house, a veritable gem of an old Sørlands house, stands down in a hollow, protected on all sides by rising rocks from the winds above; for the island is near the open sea and relatively exposed. The frankfurters consumed, we moved inside for coffee and brandy, crowding the cozy little living room, with its raftered ceiling and its prints of old sailing ships. Then back to the dock for the lighting of the great traditional fire, long-prepared, wigwamlike, near the water's edge. Two other fires were burning elsewhere on the shores of the little sound. There was a great coming and going of motorboats. Songs were sung by the fire. Then back home by motorboat, through the narrow passages of Skippergaten, into the wider leads behind it, where the unceasing glow of the northern sky shone across the water and a dim quarter-moon competed feebly with it from the other side.

It was nearly midnight when we got back to our cottage. I suddenly remembered the small bonfire I had myself pre-pared, down on a big rock just offshore, before I knew that we were invited elsewhere. So I went down, climbed out there, and lit it. It blazed brightly and vigorously, casting its flickering rays across the adjoining rocks. Before we went to bed, the dawn now approaching, a motorboatload of young people, drifting past, took note of my fire, brought their boat up, climbed to the top of the rock, and sat around the fire in the fading magic of the northern night singing, while the armada of motorboats, returning to town, chugged past, far-ther out on the sound.

The long days have come to this part of the world. At seven
in the morning I sat on the bench outside the front door, in
the sun, clad only in pajamas, and was comfortable in the
early sunshine. The sea lay still, below me. The day's fresh
breeze—the good-weather breeze from the southwest that
reaches its maximum in the late afternoon—had not yet set
in. The usual two blackbirds appeared on the lawn, inspecting it for early-morning worms or insects, waddling about
and pecking into the grass with their bright yellow beaks.
The old hooded crow appeared, wheeling over the treetops on
his round of matutinal inspection. A great black-backed gull,
flying steadily and purposefully on some mysterious mission
of his own, traversed the horizon. A small trawler, coming in
from the night's work at sea, hurried along the landward side
of Oksøy, the lighthouse island, on its way back to the fishing
port on Flekkerøy—one of the few of its kind still left around
here. (For what young man wants to accept, these days, the
hardships of deep-sea fishing—the cold wet clothes, the endless rolling and pitching, the hauling of the heavy nets in the
night, the jelly-fish burns, the lack of regular sleep—when
he could be earning fantastic wages on the oil rigs, or in industry, protected by the union, doing only a minimum of
work, and defying with relative impunity the authority of the
foreman?)

The NORTHWIND *having been in Stockholm over the winter of
1977–78, my wife and I, together with her brother, Einar, went
to Stockholm in June 1978 to pick up the boat and bring her back
to Kristiansand—a journey of some seven hundred miles. In
view of our ages, we subsequently always referred to this passage
as "the geriatric cruise."*

*There follow excerpts from the diary account of this cruise,
which included a stop in Oslo en route to Stockholm, then the
passage to Visby on the Swedish island of Gotland, and thence,
around the southern coast of Sweden and north, through the
Kattegat and the Skagerrak, to Kristiansand.*

JUNE 1978

Annelise and I went to Stockholm by train. The afternoon train ground its way around the innumerable
curves between Kristiansand and Heddalsvatner, climbed
over the hills to the east of that long narrow arm of the sea,
then gained speed and hurried down the slopes to Drammen.
It deposited us in Oslo on an unnaturally warm, tired Monday evening. We taxied uptown to call on Annelise's cousin
S. and his wife A. They are old, now. S., in his eighties, is long
retired. They can no longer entertain as they once did. But
they gave us a drink. We sat in the familiar lovely living room,
with its Munchs and other fine paintings, and exchanged

family gossip. The house, where we have stayed so many times, had remained the same: the epitome of the haute-bourgeois comfort and good taste of the early years of this century—not overly luxurious nor ostentatious, but spacious and harmonious.

This house represents a form of life rejected and sacrificed by the present age—sacrificed, one supposes, to the ideal of the welfare state, to the prevailing egalitarianism, to the frantic urbanization that has depopulated the Norwegian countryside and brought fully a third of the population of the country to huddle together, often on pensions or various other forms of public support, in the Oslo area. The sacrifice of an attractive and gracious form of living on the part of a few is rationalized by the same arguments about better conditions for the many that has led to all these great and depressing urban accumulations, in Europe and elsewhere; but it is not the real reason for them. The sacrifice was not even necessary in order to make them possible—not even economically necessary. I strongly doubt that the frugal and modest existence led by A. and S. in this house cost the Norwegian economy any more than that led by the average Norwegian pensioner or labor union member of the present age, with his little box of an apartment, his abundant gadgetry, his charter trips to Majorca, and his extensive dependence on subsidies from the public purse. No, the sacrifice is the expression of the politics of envy—one of the meanest and least creditable of political impulses—plus the compulsions of the recent technological age, with their overevaluation of mechanical devices and their underevaluation of human resources.

It was for me, in any case, both reassuring and alarming to sit once again in such premises: reassuring to see that they still existed at all, alarming to realize that they were an anachronism, soon to be in some way or other remorselessly eradicated. The ideal of the welfare state, I fear, European or American, is not that more people should live really well, but that no one should.

The sleeping-car train for Stockholm left late at night, so

when we left A. and S.'s, we whiled away the long, bright summer evening by dining in the railway station restaurant. The restaurant was on the second floor. The warm weather (*heat*, to Scandinavia) was still on; the windows were flung open; the breeze tossed the curtains. Below us, on a little square by the harbor, we could see a few people sitting at outdoor tables by a kiosk-café. Men who looked as though they had come off ships coursed the empty streets, and one had the impression that they were vaguely on the prowl, with small chances of success, after women. Next to us in the restaurant a tipsy old fellow, once a sailor, was entertaining two silent younger men with tales of his drinking ability and the inadequacy of his pension.

The train was late starting. It was impossible to find out from which track it would depart. So we hung around for an hour, with our small mountain of sacks, in the train shed, before it finally appeared. Then it took off, northward, into the late far-northern twilight, to round the northern shores of the great Lake Vänern, and to roar through the night across the fields and forests of central Sweden.

THE FOLLOWING DAY
STOCKHOLM

The warm weather, at that point, was still holding. In Stockholm, throughout the evening, I was being made conscious of touches in the scene—in the light sky; in the ponderous Germanic apartment building that housed W.'s office downtown; in the milling-about of the crowds on the paths of the Tivoli, making the most of the brief northern summer; in the vegetation; in the coolness of the night breezes—touches that reminded me that I was separated only by a relatively small body of water from Riga and Reval and the scenes of my youth. And I was prodded from inside with jabs of nostalgia which no one else could ever understand—nostalgia for that bleak Baltic landscape, for its long dark winters and for the wonder of its brief fleeting summers, for the mystery of the white nights, the sense of proximity of something intensely beautiful and marvelous, the thirst for it, and the awareness that it was not to be.

The next day went, once more, with the stowing of gear, the stocking of supplies, and the accomplishment of the last minor repairs. By evening we all felt that we were as nearly ready as we were ever likely to be; so we said our good-byes to the friendly yard owner (having paid him, I may say, no small sum of money) and took our departure.

It was late in the day. There could be no question of going any great distance. So we drifted along in leisurely fashion through the islands to the old fortress-port of Vaxholm, where we made fast for the night. A quayside festival was in progress, with music and dancing. A small fleet of old coal-burning passenger steamers, of the type once used for communication in the archipelago, had brought excursionists out from Stockholm for the occasion. I was overwhelmed with nostalgia by the sight of their tall smokestacks, the familiar smell of coal smoke, and the deep voice of their whistles, each blast preceded by the emergence of a plume of steam from the top of the stack. The fiesta was brought to a halt in late evening, by a sudden thunderstorm, after which the little fleet of steamers took off again, with its human loads. As the steamers left the harbor, one after the other, I was surprised by the graceful silence of their movement (which I, at any rate, had forgotten), and I realized how much had been sacrificed in the change to the brutal, noisy, and vibrating diesels.

SOME DAYS LATER
GOTLAND

So, having taken our departure for the island of Gotland from Savösund at 4 A.M., we powered southward until early afternoon. Then, a faint breeze having come up from the northwest, we sailed—or rather drifted—south for some further hours and entered the port of Visby at 7 P.M., finding a berth among the usual accumulation of Swedish, German, Danish, and Finnish yachts just inside the harbor entrance. We had covered seventy-five nautical miles that day from our departure at Savösund.

Soon after our arrival at Visby, but before darkness had even fallen, a gale began to come up from the north. By morning it was blowing strong, with heavy rain, and it was now unseasonably cold. There could be for us, under these conditions, no question of departure (no one, in fact, sailed from Visby that day), so we rented a car and drove out into the interior, to see something of the island. And an extraordinary place we found it to be—flat, rather sandy, but plainly very fertile, almost totally devoid of villages, but replete with two forms of improvement: rich, prosperous individual farms with fine buildings (barns and residences) not inferior to ours in Pennsylvania; and an amazing number (over eighty) of beautiful, surprisingly large, well-preserved, late-medieval churches, many of them, judging from the ones we saw, at least partially of Romanesque inspiration, though often with later Gothic features. Two things were obvious: first, that there had been, here, no large landowning nobility and none of the feudal breakdown of society common to the European continent, and, secondly, that this was an island relatively little ravaged, at least in its interior, by war.

We visited one old farmstead that had been made into a museum. Deep grass, wet with the persistent rain, surrounded the buildings. Inside, they had been fixed up in the old style. We were shown around by a cheerful little woman, as diminutive as the people who once lived in those little rooms and had slept, half sitting up, in these tiny curtained beds, set into recesses against the walls. A part of the house had been rebuilt and used, in the nineteenth century, by some intellectual; and these spacious, simple rooms, with their bleached pine floors and their view out over the fields, reminded me of Tolstoy's home at Yasnaya Polyana.

While I knew that such a one as I might eventually die of loneliness and boredom in this rural setting of a tight little island, I could not help reflecting that just so, in just such a simple room, without electricity and heated only by wood stoves, is the way I would have liked to live. Compared to that, the present age, with all its noise, its overpopulation, and its mad wastage of energy, strikes me as a nightmare.

AGAIN, SOME DAYS LATER

A further short day's sailing, which involved rounding the southeastern cape of Sweden, took us (with some long tacking and careful navigation) to the fine old Hanseatic port of Ystad, which we had visited last year in company with the Strauses (but only for one warm late Sunday afternoon). Walking about it again on this occasion, I was impressed to recognize the curious ways of memory: how soon it begins to draw a veil over such small experiences as last year's visit to Ystad—how seemingly fortuitous and arbitrary are the things one remembers, how dreamlike and absurd the half-memories, how inexplicable the blank spots. Scene after scene, in this reencounter with Ystad, stirred memories that I did not know I had. Here, of course, was the bus station. (Why "of course"?) Oh yes—I once stood here, on the square before it, did I not, looking for a taxi? And I had had some business on a neighboring street. Where could it have been? Oh yes, of course, it was at some sort of telegraph office. What was I doing there? I had left my wallet on the counter there; and I had to rush anxiously back for it, hurrying and sweating because I was holding up the departure of the whole company. And here, to be sure, is the beautiful but seemingly boarded-up theater with the little park and the lovely flowers in front of it, where I saw, that other time, old people sitting on the benches in the evening sunshine, and rather envied them, and speculated about what life would be like if I could acquire one of the fine old cottages in the nearby streets of the old town and settle down here and sit, like the others, on those benches and let the world go by. Comfortable, I dare say, and visually gratifying, but lonely and isolated, devoid of stimulus, and wholly unacceptable to my good wife.

A further long day's passage, made mostly on engine because of a slack breeze, brought us to Copenhagen, or, to be more precise, to the great yacht harbor of Skovshoved, north of the city proper. Here there was a two-day stop. Daughter Wendy, fresh from Tehran and full of wonder over this unaccustomed sea-level world of rich damp air and tidy good order, joined us on the first of those days. Mail was received, full, to be sure, of bad news: neighborhood property problems in Princeton; further attacks on myself and my allegedly wrongheaded views, into which chorus Solzhenitsyn had now entered; misuse of my name by the Moscow correspondent of the *New York Times,* attributing to me a statement of the Committee on East-West Accord which I had never even seen, much less signed. Abruptly yanked back in this manner from the harsh but simple realities of the sea to the unpleasant ones of professional life, I wandered disconsolately about in the great marina, with its forest of indifferent masts. But by evening the trivia of cruising, particularly as a skipper and navigator of sorts, had again enveloped me, and the annoyances of life ashore, about which for the moment one could do so little, faded from consciousness. This, I suppose, is the therapeutic quality of cruising in small sailing craft.

There was much argument over when we should take our departure from Skagen the following day for the passage over the Skagerrak. B., cheerfully optimistic as always, was sure we could make it in the course of a day, and wanted to take off at 3 A.M., as we did last time. I, remembering the difficulties of approach to the Norwegian coast in the evening, with the lingering sunshine blinding the sight of the shore, preferred to come in upon it at night, when one could pick up the coastal lighthouses. I won, to the extent of postponing departure until about 7 A.M.

The weather report being inaccurately favorable, we left at the appointed hour, looking forward to a leisurely day's sail across a relatively placid Skagerrak. In this, once again, we were to be grievously disappointed. We faced the hardest day I had ever had at sea in this boat. Scarcely had we rounded the long reef in which the Skagen peninsula finds its end when the wind came up strong, directly from the west, supporting the powerful easterly current that runs off the north coast of Jutland. The best we were able to make against it, for the first couple of hours, was almost straight north. Then, as we got out of the current, our course leveled out, but it was clear that we could not possibly make Kristiansand on a single tack. We continued on the port tack, as high on the wind as we could bring her, hoping for some sort of a change in wind direction. The wind, however, remained steady out of the west, and also increased steadily in intensity throughout the day. By afternoon the boat was laboring, and it was clear that under an unreefed mainsail and the largest of our regular three staysails, we were carrying too much canvas. But I was again reluctant to let B. go forward in what was now a heavy sea, and we both hoped that toward evening the wind would subside, as it so often does. This, alas, it not only failed to do; it continued to increase throughout the afternoon and well into the evening. By midafternoon a heavy sea was running. We were heading it with good speed, but the lee rail was under water much of the time, and the spray over the cockpit was incessant. By late afternoon it was blowing a small gale, and the boat was clawing her way across the foaming crests of the high seas.

For us, elderly landlubbers that we were, it was now impossible to do anything useful in the cabin. Annelise, though not actively seasick, had reached the limit of her capacities and lay helpless in the lee bunk of the main cabin. Things that had resided decently in their respective racks for six years, under all sorts of weather, now began to fly out and sail off to other parts of the cabin. At one time the entire contents of the bookcase, breaking through the two slats that held them, tore loose, soared through the air, cleared the table, and landed in a great heap on the floor on the opposite side of the cabin, below Annelise's bunk, where, I may say, they continued to lie undisturbed through the rest of the passage, none of us being up to the task of trying to restore them to their normal resting place. B. and I relieved each other hourly at the helm, each of us perching high on the windward rail to be able to see the oncoming seas and allow for them. Wendy was marvelous, retaining at all times her puckish sense of humor, sometimes sleeping, head on knees, in the little watch-seat by the companionway, but always cheerfully volunteering to descend into the dancing, tilting cabin and do such small things as had to be done. Annelise, fortunately, had prepared soup and sandwiches at midday; after that, the preparation of food was beyond the resources of any of us.

This was the heaviest sailing I had seen in the *Northwind*. She took it magnificently, standing hard on the wind, making amazingly rapid forward progress, rising well to the oncoming seas. There was no danger, at any time, to her; the only danger was that of our own possible exhaustion. I was troubled by my inability to establish our position. I had never been able to make the direction finder serve me in these last two or three seasons. It was hard enough to climb, monkey-like, below and look through streaming glasses at the chart, bracing one's self with one dripping leg against the bulkhead of the galley. To have tinkered, then, with the wretched direction finder, swinging its compass around in the air as one had to do, would have exceeded the resistance of even my stomach.

At 7:30 P.M. B. and I agreed that the jib had to come down, so he, strapped of course to the guardrails, crept forward and performed this trying task. Reefing the mainsail presented, for us, too much of a problem, so we proceeded on a full mainsail, running the engine lightly to take off the drag of the propeller and making a scarcely diminished speed. This helped a bit, but it was still a lively ride, the boat climbing up the huge seas, surmounting each of them with a great growling and roaring of their crests under her stern, then charging and slamming down into the trough again, only to meet the next one the same way.

In the early evening hours, the wind, while undiminished in intensity, became slightly more favorable to us than it had been throughout the day. But we remained on the same tack, at the same angle to the wind, and I was now able to estimate a landfall somewhere off the island of Tromøy, just east of the port of Arendal. The log now showed nearly eighty miles, all into the wind, since our departure. I had calculated a landfall at some time between seven and nine in the evening. But visibility had now somewhat deteriorated; and it was no earlier than nine-thirty when I, dodging the sheets of spray and peering over the top of the spray hood in the intervals between them, convinced myself that I had really seen the first faint, faint shadow of something other than the sea horizon off the starboard. For another hour, as the darkness gathered, it seemed to remain little more than a shadow. But around ten-thirty there was the welcome flash of a light. At first, it was too irregular to be counted, but soon the intervals became more regular. Unable to use a watch in the cockpit, I first timed it by beating out estimated seconds with my hand against the cabin top. Instructed by previous bitter experience, I had written down on a piece of paper before starting the characteristics of every lighthouse along some seventy miles of the Norwegian coast; and I had it in the pocket of my foul-weather jacket. I thought I recognized this particular one; but just to be sure, I had Wendy measure it against the cabin clock, I shouting down to her the moments of its appearance and disappearance. It was indeed the Torungen light, off Arendal, sixteen to seventeen miles away, to be sure, blinking faithfully every twenty seconds. I knew now where we were and where we could make an entrance into the islands, and I was immensely relieved, for I was not sure whether I could have stood the effort throughout the further hours of the night. There would then have been nothing for it but to take down sails, creep into the cabin, leave the boat to herself, and try to put things together again on another day.

The light, at the west end of Tromøy, was exactly where, according to my dead reckoning, it should have been. We did not even need to change course to come in upon it. This last, however, took a long time. It was midnight before we put in past the light to the relatively sheltered water beyond and struck the mainsail. And it was nearly one in the morning when we reached the inner harbor at Arendal. The little town was, of course, by this time fast asleep. The reflections of the streetlights gleamed peacefully over the water. The northern sky was still slightly pale with the long Arctic daylight. The silhouette of the church steeple presided over the empty streets and crowned the lovely, sleeping scene.

Drenched, cold, and for the first time in my life seriously exhausted, I jumped off onto the quay and made fast the bow line, but then I discovered I could not stand up on dry land and had to lean for a time against a pile of packing crates until I could recover my strength and equilibrium.

On checking the chart the next day, I established the fact that the *Northwind* had made 107 sea miles on a single tack, as high into the wind as she could be driven, at an average speed for the whole sixteen hours of some 6.8 knots, and this against heavy sea. The credit was all hers. We had done no more than to hold her to it.

JULY 20, 1979
KRISTIANSAND

The day dawned gray and cool. The cold, strong northwest wind that had been blowing for days was still blowing. A few raindrops were falling.

283

It was a bad day. I was not myself. So, remembering the devil's advice somewhere in *Faust* that when the demons get into you the best thing is to go out and take a spade and dig, I sacrificed my usual morning of books and correspondence, went out, finished breaking up the partially rotten but still incredibly tough old oaken well covers that were replaced two years ago, extracted the still effective screws, made firewood out of some of the parts, burned the others (taking care to shake the ants out, lest I make myself the perpetrator of another of mankind's most cruel and unforgivable forms of executions), then cut down the big dead evergreen near the path over to M.'s place, pinching a finger and scraping an arm in the process.

The lowest moment of the day came when I was taking the remains of dinner down to the rock for the birds. Making my way down, on the fine stone steps I once built, it seemed to me that I had never felt more lonely, more hopeless, and more helpless. Yet at the same time, I was reproaching myself for my weakness and saying to myself, You are a rag of a man. But I continued on my mission. The lone seagull who inhabits the promontory of rock just to the north saw me, took to the air, and uttered a little cry of excitement as he soared over the swill. But the old sentinel crow, who usually gets frightened away by the aggressive gulls, beat him to it this time, got a piece of the food, swallowed it as he took off, and flew away with a caw of triumph (That to you!) for the gulls.

At sea the northwest wind, which had risen to the force of a small gale in the afternoon, was still blowing hard and persistently under the cold, long-reaching rays of the evening sun, which had now momentarily appeared, tinting the rocky slopes of the islands across the sound, but leaving them cold, mute, and unyielding.

Seeing a daughter and son-in-law off at the Kristiansand airport.

The sky was cloudless, with brilliant summer sunshine. The persistent west wind had gone around to the south, carrying the lively chop into our bay, and the sea, all blue and spray-white, was gay and laughing. But it was still cold in the wind.

On the small enclosed area behind the airport building, where you look out onto the field, the wind did not reach you, and the sun was pleasantly hot. There were masses of children there, waving good-bye to someone in a Braatens plane. In the next enclosure there was a whole family saying good-bye to Norwegians and talking American (self-consciously and a bit too loudly, I thought) after the fashion of Scandinavian-Americans.

There, in the open-air enclosure, among all the children, we said good-bye to Wendy and Claude. I made the usual observation about not knowing when I would ever see them again, and wanted to add "Perhaps never," but I didn't.

We watched the preparations for departure of the plane: the progress of the last stragglers across the apron; the signals between the man outside with the earphones and the captain, invisible in his cockpit; then the starting of the engines, the wheeling around, the high-whining movement off the apron, and the disappearance down the long runway.

While approaching Dvergsnes on the way home, we could see the exhaust streak of the plane high over the sea, marked, at its head, by the almost invisible midget of the plane itself. And what an inexorable midget it was, I reflected, bearing away our youngest child, the survivor of so many fearful trials of adolescence, the repository of so much originality and so much lurking charm—bearing her not only away from us, but away from our generation, even away from the memories of home and childhood, into another life, another time, a world as remote from us, and as final in its quality as a barrier against return, as the sky into which she was now disappearing. Such are the partings of parents from children, in a world that is moving too fast for anyone's good.

Lecture at the Air Force Academy, Colorado Springs.

FEBRUARY 12, 1977

Was surprised to find both Colorado Springs and the Air Force Academy not *in* the mountains (which rise suddenly, like a great escarpment, out of the vast plain) but near the foot of them. On the one side, the great, arid prairie—flat, treeless and monotonous; on the other, the wall of rugged, rocky (literally) mountains, tree-covered on their lower slopes, cut with valleys and the other scars of erosion, and not very impressive to the view because the plain out of which they so suddenly rise is already so high (7,000 feet). The area has been suffering from a serious drought, so neither the plain nor the mountains were snow-covered. It was below freezing at night, but warmed up to nearly fifty degrees under a clear, thin, unblinking sunshine—the mercilessness of which in summer I could well imagine.

As one approached the foot of the mountains from the east, the prairie—gray brown, empty, and sterile—became undulating; and here, across the low, sweeping rises, habitation was scattered: the trashy, impermanent habitation of the American West—trailer camps, condominiums, commercial enterprises—but all strewn about, with wide expanses of useless, barren prairie between them; and everywhere, of course, the roads: these four-lane arteries of dark asphalt so dear to the modern American heart, stretching endlessly across the emptiness, with traffic signals where they cross in the middle of nowhere. And everywhere, the scurrying beetles of cars, whirring drearily along, turning distance into time. Strange people, these Americans: they seek out such places as these, I suspect, not really to live but to await death, justifying themselves by the fact that the sun shines and that life is easy—a sort of trancelike unreal state of existence, drugged by the sedatives of advertising, TV, and the wheel of the automobile—all enjoyments vicarious.

The Air Force Academy is a stark and forbidding place:—a cluster of severely rectangular steel-and-glass buildings, situated on a windswept tableland, miles from anywhere, near the foot of the mountains—with nothing around it, no place to go, no other human habitation, it seemed, within miles, but with a view out onto the great plain that would stretch all the way to the Appalachians. A less comfortable place for an educational establishment would be hard to imagine, and one wonders why they chose it, unless it be that there is endless room around it for airports.

Commencement at a large American university.

Sunday morning in a wretched motel, waiting for the commencement ceremonies. The motel barricaded like a fortress against the fresh air and sunshine of the spring morning. Not a window open. Everything locked up tight, the air conditioners roaring incessantly. Unventilated corridors, smelling of stale tobacco. An overcrowded cafeteria, with sloppy service. And through the sealed-up windows, a scene of asphalted desolation such as only the American developer, given his head, can produce: an enormous Ford dealer's headquarters, lying amid its parking lots like an island in a sea; warehouses; factory chimneys; tall buildings in the distance; a bank, empty, still, and similarly barricaded by vast empty parking lots; sloping sides of turnpike elevations; but not a tree, not a pedestrian, not a sign of actual life except, here and there, a moving car, its occupant likewise walled off against nature in his own tiny, lonely, air-conditioned world. Not a touch of community; not a touch of sociability. Only the endless whirring and roaring of the air conditioners, the wild wasting of energy, the ubiquitous television set, the massive bundle of advertising pulp that masquerades under the name of a Sunday newspaper. All unnatural; all experience vicarious; all activity passive and uncreative. And this wasteland extending, like a desert, miles and miles in every direction. A fine end-of-the-world we have created in the American city.

Later. The commencement is over. Matters of memory, now, are the chance introductions in the robing room; the smell of the gymnasium (right out of St. John's Military Academy [1917–21] and Princeton [1921–25]); the hot, sun-baked stadium; the yelling, whistling students; the dreadful list of doctoral dissertation topics in the program ("A Comparison of the Academic Achievement of Sophomores Living in University Residence Halls with That of Sophomores Living Off-campus in Selected State Universities"); the inevitable appeal to come and teach ("We hoped we could get you here"); the empty student faces.

And yet, and yet: the vitality of these places; the truly superior faculty; the magnificent library; the unflagging belief in the country; also, the many people who have read my books and speak kindly to me about them. Truly, this country whipsaws you.

On a cold winter day in 1979, Annelise and I received news that one of the three daughters of the farmer at our Pennsylvania farm, Shelley by name, having accepted an invitation to drive home from a nearby town with some other young people, had been killed in a tragic motor accident. We immediately left for the farm.

We drove out Thursday afternoon. It was a cold winter day but with bright sunshine. There had been a fresh snowfall during the night, and the fields lay quiet, now, under their fresh white blanket. The tire tracks were deep in the snow as we drove in the lane, and the farm, lying there as usual in its wintry state, with the rays of the setting sun sweeping across the gleaming fields, never looked more beautiful. All was so normal, so reassuring, that it was hard to realize what the place now was, that it was now our stricken farm—stricken by tragedy—stricken as it had never been stricken before in our time.

We went right over to the farmhouse to see the mother. She was seated on the sofa, a plaid over her knees, drawn with grief. She said: "I'm better today, but G. (the husband)—he's worse. See what you can do for him." I went out to the barn. He was there, crouching among his cows, still sobbing and distracted. With him was a sister of the dead child. I asked

George whether there was anything I could do. They had tried to phone him today, he said, from the insurance company. Perhaps we would see to this; perhaps we could help.

The sister, herself still very young, but now, at this moment, the strength of the family, talked to me, there in the barn, intently and almost breathlessly. The radio was blaring away. Between that and my deafness, I could hardly understand a word she was saying. But I was aware of what strength lay in that young face, turned up to mine.

There was not much more that I could do. I went back to our house and built a fire.

In the evening a heavyset blondish man, an uncle of the children, came to the door and said: "Most of the other ones is leavin'; if youse would like to come over now, you should come." The children were all sitting quietly around the kitchen table. The mother was still on the sofa. Annelise and Joan went and sat with her, one on one side, the other on the other, each holding a hand. The father took me out onto the porch and talked to me. We were all impressed with the dignity of the children and the depth of their devotion. Then we went home, hoping that exhaustion would finally overcome the parents.

The following day was like yesterday—cold and windy, but with brilliant sunshine gleaming everywhere on the fresh snow.

We left almost an hour early for the funeral. People were already in the church and standing in line to greet the family. The latter were seated on chairs, in a row, in a room at the back of the church. The father had the youngest child on his knee.

We moved into the nave of the church. The service began. The organ played. There was still much sobbing. The high-school classmates of the dead girl filed in and were seated in a sort of box near the altar. The young pastor, the same who had had the terrible duty of breaking the news to the parents in the middle of the night, conducted the service and spoke very nicely and perceptively about Shelley, whom he had taught in Sunday School and confirmed. "Oh God, Our Help in Ages Past" was sung.

The service over, we all walked, in the bright sunshine, over the dry crisp snow, to the village cemetery. The undertakers had erected a small canvas shelter over the grave and had placed some chairs, with rugs, for the family. Some sixty or seventy of us stood around while the graveside service was read, with "ashes to ashes" and the Lord's Prayer. The family were then invited to leave first. Before doing so, the mother bent down, picked a red rose off the wreath, and laid it on the casket. Then we all trudged back over the snowy field to the village.

During the service the cold northwest wind had subsided, as though out of respect for what we were doing; but as we walked back, it freshened again; and small streams of dry snow, swept along by the wind, were already drifting across the path under our feet.

The farmhouse, afterward, was packed with people. The dining-room table was laden with food, much of it what other people had brought in. There was conversation. Everyone, now surfeited with emotion, felt, for the moment, a bit better. But all were aware that the deepest bite of grief, dull but unrelenting, was yet to come.

I had been reflecting, during the day, on how completely Shelley was a child of this farm. It was the only place she had ever lived, the only home she had ever known. She was as much a part of it as the barn or the stream that lies at the end of the meadow, or the oak tree in the middle of the circle. It was *her* farm. It would never be quite the same without her.

On October 1, 1980, I delivered the principal address at the Second World Congress for Soviet and East European Studies, held in Garmisch, Germany.

It was on this occasion that I made my plea to the nuclear powers to abandon the whole wretched preoccupation with nuclear weaponry:

"For the love of God, of your children, and of the civilization to which you belong, cease this madness. You have a duty not just to the generation of the present—you have a duty to civilization's past, which you threaten to render meaningless, and to its future, which you threaten to render nonexistent. You are mortal men. You are capable of error. You have no right to hold in your hands—there is no one wise or strong enough to hold in his hands—destructive powers sufficient to put an end to civilized life on a great portion of our planet. No one should wish to hold such powers. Thrust them from you. The risks you might thereby assume are not greater—could not be greater—than those which you are now incurring for all of us."

worked all morning in the hotel on my speech. The office of the congress kindly consented to retype four pages of it for me; and I went over in midafternoon to pick it up. Since it was not ready, and I had no other place to wait, and my legs were failing me, I went out and sat for some time in the faint, failing afternoon sunshine, on a bench in the little square before the Kongresshalle. A number of older people were sitting on the other benches, their backs to the bushes that separated them from the busy street.

There I sat, and I thought to myself, Tonight I deliver what I sincerely hope and trust is the last of many, many speeches. There was the usual wondering whether what I had to say was of any suitability and effectiveness at all, together with the fatalistic awareness that whatever it was, it could not now be changed. But I also fell to wondering what I could and would do if I really abandoned this crazy life of mine— stopped, that is, all this lecturing and telephoning and corresponding and traveling—whether I would ever be able to bring it to the point where I could sit, like these other old people, peacefully on a bench in the park in the faint late-afternoon sunshine without having before me the pressure of delivering a speech, or some other sort of pressure, and whether any good would come of it—any useful reflection, or indeed anything other than physical and intellectual decay— if I did.

Well, however that may be, the evening came. There was dinner, with my principal hosts, at some hotel. At five minutes to eight I had to remind these peacefully eating hosts that the address was scheduled for 8 P.M. We rushed over to the Kongresshalle. Hugh Seton-Watson gave some excellent introductory remarks—a real contribution in themselves—better in a way, I thought, than anything I had to say. Then, before some 1,300 people, I went through my address, fumbling with the language only once, and then not badly, and even managing to withstand a piercing scream from a woman somewhere in the audience just as I was getting into the most eloquent passage. (The scream, I was later glad to learn, had no connection with the lecture.) My performance was followed by a reasonably cordial and polite applause, but one which left me as uncertain of the suitability (not the truth) of what I had had to say as I had been before saying it.

In October 1980, invited to visit China and to meet with schol-
ars and officials there, I set off, accompanied by my wife, on
what was to be my first journey around the world.

The first stop, after leaving Europe, was at Delhi, where we
spent a day or two as a guest at the residence of the American
ambassador, Robert Goheen.

OCTOBER 6, 1980
ARRIVAL AT DELHI

The Delhi airport between 2 and 5 A.M. is something to be seen. All the great international night planes between Europe and the Far East arrive and depart at that time, because Delhi is the half-way spot, useful both for refueling and for the traffic generated there. The airport is therefore normally in a state of pandemonium in those hours, and so it was now: a great crowd, shouting, screaming and milling about in the main airport hall (one could not call it a lounge); eight hundred pieces of incoming baggage being shuffled around in massive confusion. For two and a quarter hours Annelise and I sat, or lay, dead tired, in a barren little VIP room provided, mercifully, with three sofas, while our two newfound friends fought the dreary nocturnal battle of finding our luggage, which they finally did. At 4:30 A.M. our baggage cart was being pushed relentlessly through the milling and shouting crowds, and soon we emerged onto the loading space before the building, where there were more crowds: turbans, costumes of every conceivable sort; bronzed, striking faces; the chaos multiplied, this time, by a grand traffic jam. The embassy limousine, after much backing, filling, honking, and screaming, finally extracted itself from this maelstrom. We drove, then, down wide dark boulevards to the embassy. The shapes of free-roaming cows could be seen, filing silently along the roadside. At one point there was a glimpse of a human figure, seated and making mysterious gestures, in the grass of an adjacent park. At 5 A.M. we turned in at the embassy residence, to be greeted, to my mortification, by Margaret G., whose night's sleep we must greatly have disturbed.

Excerpts from the account of a day's excursion to Agra, India.

OCTOBER 7, 1980

Because our driver encounters unexpected obstacles and loses his way, we are a long time driving in this unspoiled, semiurban, provincial India before attaining our first objective. And what a sight it is—mile after mile of it—rather uneven blacktopped roads, stretching to the horizon through densely inhabited areas and literally teeming with life and movement of every sort: people, pedestrians of every age and costume; veritable clouds of cyclists; bicycle rickshaws, also by the thousands, some of them unbelievably overloaded; the same for donkey carts; trucks and buses, battered and dirty, but with garish decorations on their fronts wherever there are places to put them; animals—stray dogs, pigs, goats, not to mention the ubiquitous cows, sometimes attended by people, more often wandering about by themselves, under the feet of the pedestrians and the wheels of the vehicles; oh yes, and the oxcarts, pulled by lumbering pairs of these great ungainly beasts, the driver squatting on the massive yoke between their respective necks.

Through this teeming, confused, and never-ending throng of human and animal creatures we, together with the trucks and buses, are obliged to push and thread our way with incessant blowing of the horn and an endless series of near misses, many so incredible that one could only assume the influence of some benign unseen hand, defying all the laws of probability. To either side, across the dusty earthen shoulders of the road, there are lines of small open-faced commercial and handicraft enterprises of every conceivable sort, some so tiny that they are installed on the platforms of two-wheeled carts, some deploying their activities in the open: people cooking, tinkering, cutting hair, selling what you will, right on the open ground, under the feet of the thronging passersby, human and animal.

It is an unforgettable sight: this seemingly endless flow of humans, beasts, and vehicles, bordered by the equally endless rows of servicing establishments. Yet no great sign, anywhere, of unhappiness. There is poverty, of course; but all is sociable, intelligible, and workable, in a small way. Life is not all that complicated. One can usually help one's self, either with one's hands or one's legs, or with the beast's legs. One is, for the most part, not at the mercy of great unseen forces, mechanical and technological.

After a half hour or so of horn-honking and pushing around in this turgid stream, we reached our first objective of the day: the surviving residence of one of the Mogul emperors in a place known as Fatehpur. It is well described in a host of guidebooks and tourist circulars: a complex of buildings and courtyards, all in heavy stone, laid out in severe rectangular patterns, the open spaces all stone-paved. We took (were obliged to take) a bearded guide who had a remarkable facility for speaking what appeared, by faint resemblances, to be English, but spoken in such a way that not a sentence could be understood. The complex was impressive in its scale, simplicity, and cleanliness of form, and in its quality as a reflection of the enormous output of back-breaking labor that obviously went into it—itself the product of a ferocious oriental despotism. For the thousands upon thousands of great stone slabs and columns out of which the whole was composed were massive, and the cutting and moving of them must have been, in the technology of that day, an immense task.

Having completed our tour (which involved fighting off at every turn the importunities of scavengers trying to sell us things or to get tips for minor alleged services), we repaired to a very fancy new Sheraton hotel, incongruously planted in the midst of all this Indian squalor. After lunch, while the ladies inspected the extensive trinket shops in the hotel lobby, I went outside and, standing under the canopy of the entrance drive, contemplated at close range two bored and unhappy beasts kept there to give exotic rides to the tourists: one a motionless camel with a baleful and supercilious look, a misanthrope if I ever saw one, under whose great shaggy feet a small boy kept dashing pailfuls of water to cool them; the other an elephant, attended by another boy, no less bored than his charge, who sat in a box high up on its back, leaning over from time to time to flick the animal's ear with a stick in order to make it keep to its appointed place.

Passing up the opportunity to get ourselves photographed (for a princely sum) riding on one of these unfortunate creatures, we went on to see the Taj Mahal. I had seen, of course, a thousand pictures of it, but I was not disappointed with the reality. Larger and grander in real life than in the photographs, as most such objects are, it was impressive not just by its beauty of line and shape but also by its magnificently landscaped setting. The meticulous intricacy of the stonework, the great chiseled screens and the elaborate inlays with metals and with other kinds of stone, repeated thousands and thousands of times—all this I found more depressing than impressive, for it struck me as little else than a form of ostentation, reflecting once again the exactions placed by a cruel tyrant on great masses of enslaved handicraft workers. And I could not see that all this laborious detail added greatly to the true glory of the ensemble, which lay in the work of the architect and landscape designer.

There was, after this, some time to be whiled away before the departure of our plane back to Delhi. This time we spent parked beneath a tree along the street outside the Taj Mahal, consuming quantities of bottled soft drinks (one dare not drink much else in such places) and watching the bicycle rickshaw coolies, lean and emaciated, perforce dismounted from their seats and pedals, pushing by hand up the slope of the road their heavy and complacent human loads, on whose sensibilities the straining of these pathetically spindly shanks made no impression.

This, my first and only visit to China, arranged and scheduled by the Chinese authorities, was conducted with the help and kindly attention of a highly intelligent and efficient but reserved Chinese companion, and included, in addition to the officially scheduled academic exchanges and courtesy visits, only brief excursions to the most common tourist objectives in Shanghai, Sian, and Peking. The nearest thing to an exception was an overnight stand in Hangchou, from which was derived this sole glimpse of the China I had hoped to see.

Awoke in early morning to hear a new set of sounds, audible because the incessant honking of horns that was to fill the air for the rest of the day had not yet begun. The sounds came from across the lake and were very pleasant: strange cries, perhaps from wild fowl, perhaps from humans; something that sounded like a gong or a church bell; and then, from time to time, the whistle of a genuine old-fashioned steam locomotive (such being still in use here). Got up, looked out over the lake, and was so struck with the sight that I even woke my wife to make her look, too, and was not even scolded for it. For the day was just dawning; the mists were rising from the lake, revealing the dark, jagged shapes of the islands and peninsulas, with the shadows of higher hills in the distance; and the whole scene was so unbelievably Chinese, in the sense of its resemblance to the scenes from Chinese paintings, that one was quite startled. One does not expect places these days really to look like what they are supposed to look like.

Russia, again, as a guest of their Institute for the USA and Canada.

We went last night to the Bolshoi (by kindness of Arbatov's institute; otherwise, we would have never gotten tickets) to see a performance of the *Romeo and Juliet* ballet, with Prokofiev's marvelous music. It was, generally, a closed performance, given for a particular group of people (we never learned who they were—presumably the staff of some institute or bureaucratic entity in the provinces). The whole thing was too long and repetitious, with inordinately prolonged sessions of agonizing and writhing on the part of the unfortunate Romeo, who was even obliged to go through these contortions alone while they changed scenes behind the curtain. The dancing was good. Many of the scenes were striking. The music was its own haunting self. But there was, from the standpoint of the dancers, almost no audience. A duller, less understanding, less responsive crowd, I have seldom seen. The fact is that the regime has, in one way or another, destroyed or driven away the sophisticated public whose perception and enthusiasm once made any ballet performance at the Bolshoi an exciting event.

The Bolshoi remains, as its name indicates, one of the world's great theaters. The effort, the discipline, the training of the corps de ballet, the musical standard, the attention to detail—all this remains at a high level. But one must ask how long all this can be maintained in this species of cultural vacuum, the best dancers (the male ones, at any rate) running away the first chance they get, the remainder compelled to dance before dead, uncomprehending audiences. What a price this culture pays for the regime's fear and hatred of spontaneity!

Today, it occurs to me, is the seventy-seventh anniversary of the death of my mother, the woman without whose sacrifice and agony I would not have existed. I try to picture her to myself: beautiful (as I know from her photographs) but provincial. I can more easily imagine her voice: the slow midwestern drawl I can recall from her sister, Aunty Ven.

Once, a few years ago, I dreamed that I saw my mother. I knew it was she. She stood, motionless and silent, before me. She could not speak; the barrier between the dead and living made it impossible. I understood that it must be so, but never doubted the reality of the image.

Accompanied by an American tourist-friend (here referred to as Stephanie) and by a kind gentleman from the American consulate general in Leningrad, we paid a visit to the famous Summer Palace of Peter the Great, known as Peterhof. In addition to having another glance at this place, which I had seen many years before, I was interested in finding, if possible, whatever remained of a well-known monastery-retreat known in tsarist times as the Troitsko-Sergievskaya-Pustyn', where a notable Russian statesman (Nicholas Giers), whose career I had treated extensively in one of my historical works, had been buried.

APRIL 24, 1981
LENINGRAD

It was a very cold day, unusually cold for this time of the year: the temperature down in the twenties, with a cutting northwest breeze, and from time to time dense, blinding snow flurries. To the east of the city, beyond the famous Putilov works, there arose vast areas of new standardized apartment-house construction—thousands of persons in reasonable roominess, if not always in the highest comfort. (This goes on in other large areas adjacent to the city as well. Yet I was told that about 30 percent of Leningrad's inhabitants still live in communal apartments. This caused me to reflect on Khrushchev's penetrating observation that it made no difference how much housing they built in the great Soviet cities: more immigrants would always come to the city and fill it up to the maximum density of human endurance.)

In any case, on we drove, passing the innumerable dump trucks characteristic of Soviet construction areas, bumping over the occasional thank-you-ma'ams in the wavy pavement, the wide lakes of construction mud sliding past the windows on either side.

Peterhof (I refuse to call it Petrodvoretsk) was not at its best on this windy bitter-cold day. The fountains were stilled. The gardens and trees lay in soggy, sullen patience, waiting for the spring. The wind blew—fresh, damp, and penetrating—from the Gulf of Finland. A small expanse of the gulf could itself be seen, sometimes blue, sometimes cold grayish, through the opening at the foot of the small canal leading from the terraces and fountains down to the sea. Above us, dark gray clouds, laden with snow, swept across the sky, punctuated by brief intervals of blue sky and flashes of sunshine.

The interior of the palace was packed with groups of tourists, shuffling along in their cloth overshoes between the roped-off places. One could hear the voices of the guides, droning away at them in a half a dozen languages. Our own guide was a slim, attractive young woman with arresting pale blue eyes and clothes that had the musty smell of those that are kept over a winter in overcrowded apartments. She talked to us, for Stephanie's sake (although Stephanie never listened) in a studied French; and she had obviously done her homework with much conscientiousness.

As for the palace, most of it had been well restored. It did not have the magnificence of the restored Pavlovsk; but it was, after all, a summer palace, and an early one as Russian palaces go. It was therefore simpler from the very beginning.

I was most interested in the portraits of the various Russian monarchs, beginning with Peter the Great and running over the century following his reign:

+ The young Peter himself: tall, active, extroverted, full of venture and enthusiasm, and immensely ruthless in the pursuit of both.

♦ Peter's morganatic wife-mistress Catherine, a power-ful, buxom, dark-haired woman, with all the robust strength of her earthy village origin.

♦ The Empress Anne, granddaughter of Peter's unfortu-nate half-brother Ivan, a portly, sensual, and rather smug woman.

♦ The Empress Elizaveta Petrovna, Peter's daughter, huge, maternal, and imperious in her billowing bustles and skirts, warm-hearted but choleric, much beloved of her Russian subjects.

♦ Near her, in several places: Catherine II, Elizaveta's daughter-in-law, who had first appeared at the Russian court as the miserable young bride of Anne's weak and emotionally unstable son, Peter III, but now, in these paintings, was very much the monarch, Catherine the Great, a woman whose face reflected experience, intel-ligence, sharp skepticism, and wariness but not un-kindness: in short, a woman no longer young, a real ruler, fully aware of her power, not to be lightly im-posed upon.

♦ Her son, Paul, this diminutive, abnormal son of an even more abnormal father: the strange, unbeautiful face—the wide lips, the small, rather fierce eyes; a disfa-vored figure, to be sure, but, in his own shrill drill-masterish way, also a ruler.

♦ And finally, her grandson, Tsar Alexander I—tall, handsome, blondish, well-fed; ambivalence written all over the clean-shaven and strangely unexpressive face—the first bit of physically presentable male roy-alty in nearly a hundred years, but as perplexing a phenomenon to the painter and to other contemporar-ies as he has been to posterity.

After the visit to the palace we went on to see the so-called "cottage," a relatively modest summer house, standing in the woods about a half a mile from the palace, but, once again, with an opening among the trees through which one had a glimpse of the sea. Built in the mid-nineteenth century (in the last years, I believe, of Nicholas I), this was the place where, on their visits to Peterhof, the Emperor Alexander III and his Danish wife, Dagmar, preferred to stay, enjoying the privacy and the family intimacy the place permitted. It had a very early-Victorian air about it. I could picture them best having tea in the little pavilion in the garden, or seated, with all their children, relatives, and hangers-on, at the long dining-room table with the beautiful imperial tableware—doomed people, all of them, but wholly unaware, I am sure, of the measure of tragedy that hovered over them.

Then—the drive back. We looked, along the way, for the Troitsko-Sergievskaya-Pustyn'—once a monastery complex of sorts, consisting of one large building designed by Rastrelli in 1797, and behind it a great enclosed space with four large churches; and, then, adjacent to it what was presumably a cemetery, for it was there, according to the old Baedeker, that a number of eminent personalities were buried. The first thing we saw as we searched for this place was a small cemetery, called by the name of Sergievo, at some distance off the road. I splashed over to it on foot but could make nothing of it, it being fearfully crowded with graves, inundated with mud. Whether it was the one I was looking for, I never learned. Then we went on and discovered, not far off, the old main building (or what appeared to be that), and with what, again, appeared to be a church of some sort behind it. But it was protected from the road by a formidable fence and gate, and our Soviet chauffeur, who appeared to know more about it than he had previously confessed, assured us that it was now some sort of a training establishment for the police and hence wholly unapproachable.

Poor Nikolai Karlovich Giers: the finest Russian statesman of the final decades of tsarist power, and next to Bismarck the finest European statesman of his time, a man who did all in his power to keep Russia from embarking on the course that was to take it to disaster in the twentieth century: his grave now desecrated, his foreign office and residence turned into an anonymous hospital, his memory destroyed by the gendarmes of another age—by those beady-eyed fanatics whose intellectual horizons never rise above inculcated hatred, suspicion, and xenophobia! Oh well, what are graveyards, buildings, premises? Eventually, they all fall prey to the agencies of destruction, human or natural. But the natural agencies can't help it. The human ones, if they cared anything for their own civilization, could.

In the late 1970s and early 1980s, historical research (for two volumes of European diplomatic history) required occasional protracted spells of work in European archives—primarily those of Paris and Vienna. Here: a touch of what this meant in terms of daily life.

Our life here is relatively quiet, especially in the evenings. This small hotel occupies one small wing of the Schwarzenberg Palace. The great drawing rooms of the palace are rented out, as occasion presents itself, for all sorts of private purposes: parties, exhibits, whatnot.

Our windows look out on the park of the palace, quiet now in its wintry sleep, the water in the pool of the fountain sometimes partly frozen, the statues covered with square plastic hangings, the tennis courts empty and damp, the lawns neat but brown—everything waiting. A young black dog is let out there every morning. Sometimes he has companions; and with these he plays happily when they will join him. When we first arrived, seagulls—for some strange reason—wheeled over a section of the park (*so* far inland!). They have now left, but their place has been taken by some birds from the south, northward bound, unidentifiable at this distance. Otherwise, the park lies deserted.

I make my way to the Archives every weekday morning by

means of the D tram, which stops right before the palace. Back of me as I wait for it, below the fenced parking place of the palace, is the Soviet war memorial: a semicircular colonnade, with the tributory legend spelled across it in large golden Cyrillic letters. In the middle, at the axis of the semicircle, there rises a high thin column, surmounted with the symbolic heroic figure (and not a bad one) of the Soviet soldier of World War II. It is, I fear, no place of reverence today—a fatality, no doubt, to the behavior of the Soviet troops in 1945 (the rapes, the plundering, the executions, and other excesses) and to the political brutalities perpetrated upon so much of the rest of central and eastern Europe. The Viennese make fun of it, referring to the figure on the top, for some reason, as the *Erbsenkönig* (the pea king). I, alone, perhaps, in this city of nearly two million, view it with sadness, sympathy, and respect, seeing in the millions of Russian youngsters who laid down their lives in that war a tragedy rising above all the political emotions of that time—a tragedy no smaller than that of any of the young men who fought on the other side. May those who sent all these men to their death, on whatever side, someday be compelled to account for their action to the God who had caused these victims to come into this world, at one time, as sweet innocent children, needful of love, and normally surrounded by it, only to leave it, unfulfilled, in circumstances of such pain, bewilderment, and misery.

The streetcar D turns at the end of the Schwarzenbergplatz and pursues its way up the Ringstrasse, past the Opera, past the great buildings of the Hofburg on one side and those of the museums on the other, past the Greek classical parliament building, to the Burg theater, resplendent now in its restored neo-Renaissance glory. Here I get off and make my way along the side of the park to the Bundeskanzeramt (the Federal Chancery), where, through a rear entrance opposite the Minoriten Church, one enters the Archives. One fills out the daily form and mounts the old stone staircase, between the full-length white statue of Maria Theresa, very impressive in her smart dress with the narrow waist and full skirt, and the equally white bust of Franz Josef, halfway up the staircase. Then, into the dusty but wonderful old documents—these colorful and poignant memorials of the realities of a bygone day brought to you, after a decent and respectful interval, by a silent elderly retainer who himself has the look of an archival personality of the eighteenth century, so that you find yourself wondering, in this ambiance of the past, whether he, too, like so many of the documents, has not mysteriously survived from that earlier day.

The official personality was, as it seems, always the enemy of the personal one, so that the years as ambassador to Belgrade (1961–63) were devoid of such observations of the local scene as would fit into these pages. But these Belgrade years left warm friendships, and returns to that city in later years were vivid experiences, replete with memories.

Today, with Saleh (the embassy chauffeur of earlier years) driving, we were taken out, as Maria A.'s guests, to the restaurant on the road to Avala where several years ago we had spent the memorable and hilarious evening with the J.'s. On the way we stopped first to see the beautiful new park just across the Sava, where that great river joins the Danube. Then we went on to the similar place at Topcider. The weather was magnificent: the first fine warm spring day. Everywhere people were out enjoying the advent of spring: children playing, people strolling and sitting on benches, balls being kicked around, lovers caressing—all magnificently informal, natural, unselfconscious. This obviously is one of the rare happy times Serbia has known.

At the restaurant there was a similar milling-around of people. I was recognized, embraced, and kissed by the major domo. We sat outside on the terrace, in the sun. Next to us we discovered, to our surprise, a whole company of American officers—this year's members of the National War College, as it turned out, on a tour of Europe. These insisted that I, as an erstwhile (in fact the first) "deputy for foreign affairs" at that institution, be photographed together with them (something that would, I am sure, have been greeted with stupefaction by the present secretary of defense had he known of it). Plum brandy was brought, and marvelous freshly baked bread, as fine as any that could be found anywhere in the world. There followed wine from the grapes of the premises, and course after course of Serbian meats.

A young boy, detaching himself from a large family party at a nearby table, came over and interrogated us sternly, in his schoolboy English, on our provenance and status, running back repeatedly to report the results to the whole family.

The sun shone benevolently. To both sides of us the land fell off, and there was a wide view—on one side off to the lovely hills of Shumadiya, on the other, out onto the great plains of the valley of the Sava. It was a good moment.

But finally, the sky clouded gently over. A cool breeze came up from the plain. I was again kissed and embraced, in recognition of the solemnity of departure. Drugged with all this food and kindness, and slightly shamed because we had not succeeded in preventing our Serbian hostess from paying the bill, we were driven back to town.

The Pennsylvania farm, in these latter years of the 1980s, has passed into the possession of a daughter—one who loved it as I had. But it remained, in her custody, still the family center—a place where my wife and myself were always made to feel welcome, where the main bedroom was always vacated for our use, and where, whenever this proved convenient, members of the family could gather. A spacious, generous, and hospitable place, that farm, always ready to to accept into its relaxed and restorative arms whomsoever loved and understood it.

APRIL 10, 1982

Here we are, at the farm, over Easter. As we drove out yesterday afternoon, it was snowing, wetly and uncertainly, all the way from Princeton. Here at the farm all was slushy snow and mud. But it cleared off for the night, as it so often does in this curious little area, and today the strong mid-April sunshine is beating down, thirsty for its spring work, so long delayed by the late and inclement winter.

I strolled around this morning after breakfast, to see what had survived, and what had succumbed to the hard winter. My little chestnut tree, transported hither so many years ago as a small self-planted seedling extracted from our lawn in Princeton, has since survived a host of vicissitudes—from being nibbled across the fence by the horses to being crowded out by locust shoots. But it has finally established itself with real authority and promises to become a proud, defiant, healthy tree. The old locust next to it (which it was supposed to replace someday) appears to have finally died. Its removal should now give full breathing space to the chestnut. The old plum tree by the wooden fence seems also to be on its last legs. But such is the nature of the farm. Except for the trees, life here, for plant and for animal, is a short cycle consisting of birth, exuberant youth, rough treatment at the hands of man and nature—and early death.

Later in 1982 there was a reunion of myself and my four siblings, who had not (so far as any of us could remember) come together in any one place for at least sixty years.

OCTOBER 17, 1982

The weather was of autumn's loveliest; a bit windy and chilly but mostly sunny; small white clouds scurrying across a pale blue sky; the fields, their heavy crops now for the most part harvested, lying, peaceful and relaxed, under the gentle autumn sunshine; the blackbirds swarming; the foliage turning; the corncribs filled to overflowing; the mountains of baled hay and straw reaching to the highest rafters of the great barn; the spiny husks of the chestnut fruits lying thick in the grass before the house; the farmer cutting silage corn from the field along the lane and blowing it up, with much roaring of tractor engines, into the tops of the silos.

For us five children it was a momentous occasion. The uncertain lines of fate and experience that had taken their departure so many years from the oddly positioned, partially dark, and not always happy home on Cambridge Avenue in Milwaukee had divided us widely and over many years from one another. Yet even at the end of this division we were not strangers. The community of childhood proved stronger in the end than all the intervening ups and downs of life. Memories were kindly and without rancor. Mutual sympathy—for all that life had done to us, the good and the bad—was felt but left unspoken. In none of us was there any self-pity; nor was there much of the melancholy of old age. And the reunion was made richer and more reassuring by the presence of the others: spouses, children, grandchildren. Without their youth and strength the occasion would have lost much of its happiness.

NOVEMBER 25, 1982

I got up in the dawn, leaving all the others still deep in sleep, and went out to stroll around. The wind had died. Sky and air were crystal-clear, the long rays of the rising sun falling, in great shafts of brilliance, across the bare, frosted fields. Over the pond, still unfrozen, the mists were rising. The cattle, having been left out over the cold night, had now assembled at the feeding trough and were standing there, motionless and patient, still numb from the cold, waiting to be milked. The farmer and a young male relative from West Virginia were standing at the entrance by the feeding trough, passing the time of day. One cow, previously observed to be ready to calf, had failed to return from the pasture with the others. The farmer had been down to find her and had fetched her back to the barn with her newborn offspring. But the milking had not yet begun.

I was introduced to the relative. We exchanged the usual observations about the weather (in this case, a serious drought, doubly threatening because of the prospect that the fields would freeze before they had absorbed any moisture). Then I went on up the field above the house, along the new road the establishment of which we had so regretted, to where one could look out over most of the farm. The sun was slightly higher now; the shadows were shortening; the surface of the field was thawing from the stiffness of the frosty night. From the direction of the stream pasture came the muffled thuds of the shots of some Thanksgiving Day hunter, peppering away where, no doubt, he ought not to have been.

I took in the scene and then, leaning on my own old self-fashioned oaken stick, the knees complaining from the inroads of old age, the feet and I myself both leaden under the weight of unanswered and unanswerable problems, I wended my way back to the house.

Days in Florida, where Annelise and I were guests of a kind, charming, and very generous friend.

We came down here day before yesterday to spend a few days with A. E. It is a wonderful rest—nothing but reading, talking, paddling around in bare feet, walking, and snoozing. The impressions from and around this old-fashioned cottage are wholly jumbled and incoherent. There are, for example:

♦ The sea, protected here by the invisible offshore reefs—shallow, lakelike, rather dirty; no beach, just ridges of wave-washed trash at the most recent high-tide mark, and below it, great reaches of shallow opaque water, through which one gets faint glimpses of coral patches interspersed with pockets of sand.

♦ The remains of a rotted, disintegrating wooden pier just off the property of a next-door neighbor—a few isolated pilings and short surviving stretches of a sagging deck, on all of which there roost throughout the day the members of a heterogeneous colony of cormorants and terns. The cormorants have a right to the pilings, on the tops of which they stand by the hour, like brooding philosophers, devoid of all sense of time, heads to the breeze, contemplating the in one sense unchanging, in another sense always-changing, sea before them. Only when the cormorants move off do the terns occupy these prestigious perches, vacating them unprotestingly whenever the cormorants return.

♦ On a protruding reef not far beyond, the pelicans sit, in great numbers, equally motionlessly, their silhouettes appearing for some reason to rise to implausible heights above the horizon.

♦ At night the great Alligator Light—an unmanned steel skeleton tower rising some 130 feet above the reefs, three to four miles offshore, rears its profile and flashes its signal (four flashes at four-second intervals, following by a twenty-four-second general interval) through the night. Beyond it, in the daytime, one can see the small shapes of motor vessels and the tiny white specks of sails, making their way, well off the reefs, along this dangerous stretch of coast.

♦ The natural vegetation of this terrain, where uncultivated and untended, seems to be a thicket of high bushes and small trees, of what species I know not, but obviously very trashy, so that the ground along the fringes is always covered with an unattractive layer of sticks and leaves, often supplemented by little deposits of that abundant man-made trash which so many of our countrymen seem to love to consign here and there to the mercies of nature.

♦ At the inland end of A.'s property runs a small artificially created canal, along which are arrayed small residences, a number of them with docks and motorboats, a scene like a thousand others in this part—mostly new, modern, and tidy—of Florida. But when I look at them, I don't believe for a moment in their permanence. I see these properties in my mind's eye, at some time in the future: crumbling ditches, silted and swampy, the remains of the houses littering their banks, identifiable in many instances only by their foundations, the remainder—everything, in fact—fallen victim to the hurricanes, the dampness, the insects, and the ultimate collapse of civilization as we know it.

The key at this point is only two or three hundred yards wide. Along the center of it runs the highway—Highway 1—straight as an arrow, emerging from the distance, disappearing into the distance, on these final stretches of its 2,000-mile progress from the north of Maine to Key West—2,000 miles of the trashy paraphernalia of American roadside development on each of its sides—all of it alike, emphasizing by its alikeness its indifference to, indeed its contempt for, the natural setting through which it runs.

In the spring of 1984 I went to Moscow to chair a meeting of Soviet and American professors, assembled there to discuss Russian-American relations around the turn from the nineteenth to the twentieth century. The following account was written during the return trip from Russia to Norway.

JUNE 16, 1984

During none of the remaining days in Russia did I have any time to write. We are now, to my great relief, on our way back to Norway. Of these last days, all emotionally and intellectually strenuous, I can give only an impressionistic picture.

To the Mayakovski Theater, for the performance of a modern Soviet play with the implausible and wholly irrelevant title of *She, in the Absence of Love and Death.* We are met at the door by a complete stranger, a young man, well dressed and very serious, accompanied by a young woman with a large dark face and eyes. They do not identify themselves by name or function, but they have the tickets, and proceed to take us in charge. The play, to me largely unintelligible, is some sort of Soviet extreme modernism. There is in it nothing even resembling political propaganda. The dialogue, insofar as we can understand the modern Soviet jargon, is original and funny, the acting fantastically good, particularly the persistent and obviously unresolvable conflict between the nervous, unbelievably high-strung, lonely mother (either widow or

323

divorcee) and the brilliant but scarcely less emotionally over-wrought daughter: the mother screaming her reproaches in a veritable frenzy of frustration; the daughter, inured to this sort of thing as only the young can become, laughing quietly at her from the doorway and going her own way.

The play ends earlier than we thought. No car is yet there to fetch us. Helplessly, we stand, the four of us, on the corner—the corner of the erstwhile Bolshaya Nikitskaya of tsarist times (God knows what they call it today), outside the now-abandoned theater. It begins to rain. We take uncertain refuge by the wall of the building; and it seems to me that the empty street-crossing before us, gleaming wet under the streetlight, so intensely Russian and so impregnated with the past, is itself a stage setting, tearing at my silly heartstrings with its silent breath of the Russia that was—all so much more meaningful to me than the Russia that is.

A DAY AT THE TARASOVSKAYA DACHA,
STILL THE OFFICIAL EMBASSY DACHA, WITH ARTHUR AND
DONNA HARTMAN (HE NOW AMBASSADOR IN MOSCOW)

There it all is, this once rather sinister, unhappy place: still a bit dark and damp in this rainy weather; still obviously hard to administer by its normally absentee landlord—the embassy; but surrounded, now, as it didn't used to be, by numbers of other dachas of the privileged. The steep bank down to the river below us has now grown up with trees, so that the river at the bottom, once so characteristic of the Russian countryside, and the meadow on the other side (where some sort of construction seems now to be going on) are hard to see.

We take a walk along the muddy road. Then there is lunch in a little side building to the main dacha, where a wood fire is lit in the metal stove; where someone plays Dixieland jazz on the phonograph; where the lunch, taken from town, is warmed up and eaten; and where, afterward—the two ambassadors, A. and I, humbly and not unhappily wash the dishes. Times have indeed changed!

We return to town over the old Yaroslav road, now monstrously built up, and arrive just in time to get a bite of supper and to leave for Kiev.

Train to Kiev. Never saw such a long one: twenty sleeping cars—nothing else. The Moscow suburbs slip by. For miles on end the suburban potato patches line the tracks; then they are replaced by forested strips on both sides that prevent you from seeing the landscape. (These evidently were meant to serve as snow fences.) But when from time to time an opening occurs, one has, through it, glimpses of the lovely rolling country beyond—Tolstoy's country, this, with its rich dark earth, its fresh spring vegetation, its winding wagon and footpaths, its great patches of heavy forest, and its occasional humble, earth-clinging villages, of which, at a distance, only the roofs are visible.

Darkness—the late darkness of the summer solstice—finally falls. Sleep is difficult. The compartment is over the wheels. The speed is too great for the undulating roadbed. Our end of the car leaps, sways, and pounds. But eventually, there are two or three hours of sleep. When I wake up, we are already on the plains of south-central Russia. Enormous fields, left in pasture or sowed to winter wheat, stretch to the horizon. I am reminded of the first lines of Pushkin's poem *Poltava*, and fancy to see before me the "limitless fields," if not the "numberless herds" of the "great and famous" Kochubei.

There were, in the autumn of 1984, visits to friends living, respectively, in the neighboring Italian islands of Ischia and Capri, where I had never previously been.

Annelise and I walked down to the center of the village this morning to change money. Traffic, at this time of day, was permitted on the main street, so that in addition to the normal human hubbub there were cars and motorcycles trying to push their way through the crowds. This obviously involved dangers and what in other human climates would have been experienced as annoyances. But here it all seemed to be cheerfully accepted.

The bank was closed, but we, having been properly briefed by our hosts before departure, found a tiny, incredibly cramped and crowded little one-room grocery store, where the patron, after running across the street to check the rate at the window of the bank, performed the transaction for us with great good humor, and sent us on our way.

We pushed our way to the place where the street ended in a sort of promontory, from which one could look down from three sides onto the sea. A stiff wind was blowing in from the west, the heavy seas thundering and disintegrating on the rocks and seawall below us. The center of the promontory was occupied by a seventeenth-century church—la Chiesa del Soccorso—dedicated to the Virgin in her capacity as the one who aids seafarers in extremity. The church stood facing the village, its apse raised like a protection against the sea. Inside, the image of the protecting Virgin was there, above the altar—on one arm the Christ child, the other brandishing what appeared to be some sort of a club. One of her feet was planted firmly on a prostrate male figure whose identity I could only imagine, while at her side, by the other foot, stood the figure of another child, apparently a boy, whose identity I could not imagine at all.

I thought, on the way back, of the qualities of this very Italian place: the incongruous mixture of tolerance, naiveté, overcrowding, sociability, family solidarity, localism, acceptance of modernism in its most hideous forms and yet with some sort of an inner self-defense against it—life led, in short, in the small dimension, full of pettiness, no doubt, and not without its small cruelties and injustices, but borne along by the broad, wise, disillusioned charity of the Catholic Church, by the comforting familiarities of family life, and by the unvarying, reassuring support of the Christian sacraments. And I thought to myself: So long as it lasts, imperfect as it is, all this, perhaps, is not the worst of worlds, and perhaps even the best one could hope for—a messy life, full of dirt, overcrowding, confusion, and disorder, but its failings, like its possibilities, limited by the intimacy of its localistic orientation; and all of it, at least in the personal sense, intensely human. Better, in any case, than the great, highly developed, impersonal modern societies, with their lordly ambitions, their nuclear weapons, and their vast, technologically advanced abuse of the natural environment.

"Little" is of course not always beautiful—that is an exaggeration. It is also not wildly hopeful. But it is also not monstrously destructive. And it at least allows for those occasional wonderful outbursts of the human capacity for creating beauty, such as the Renaissance itself, that accounted for so much of the beauty that still surrounds us in this place. So I must not, I thought, hold this littleness in disrespect.

It was four o'clock before we backed into the dock at the port on the northern side of Capri. The weather was cool, damp, and threatening, with occasional smatterings of rain. There was a long walk behind a porter to the funicular that takes you up to the town. At the top: another porter, who pushed his cart with the luggage through several hundred yards of a narrow pedestrian passage to the small modern hotel where our island hosts had reserved for us a very nice room.

The clouds had been gathering all day for a serious deterioration of the weather. The storm soon began, with thunder and lightning, before we even went out for a restaurant dinner. In the wake of the thunderstorm came a wild wind, with heavy rain. It continued all night, rising to a crescendo in the early hours of the morning, the gusts striking the side of the building with dull thunderous blows, so heavy that I thought it must be of hurricane strength. I was filled with respect for the proverbial violence of the sudden gales of the Mediterranean, and with a new understanding for what it must have been like to have been caught in such nocturnal tempests in classical times—in the vessels of that day.

The cold wind howled all day from some quarter difficult to identify from any particular point on this confusing island, and there continued to be periodic squalls and showers. In the afternoon we went up to Anacapri, to the home of our hosts. L., grandly indifferent to rain and cold, took us around the narrow passages and paths and streets of that (in contrast to Capri) automobile-ridden town. We walked up to see Axel Munthe's "villa" on the cliff, overlooking the northern side of the island. The gardens, and the semi-open stone chambers of the building, with all their antiquities, were indeed beautiful in their museumlike way; but as the damp cold wind swept through the premises, bringing occasional splashes of rain, I could conceive, I thought, of no place less cozy to live in—all just frigid, drafty, stone beauty, enlivened with glimpses of a gray storm-tossed sea hundreds of feet below.

We dined in an almost empty restaurant near our hosts' house. While we ate, there was another thunderstorm, the rain itself sounding like thunder outside the windows. Then we took the bus back across the hillsides to Capri. The driver gunned his bus and charged down the narrow roads and streets as though he were angry over something. When we sped along the cliffs on the northern side of the islands, you could still see the lightning over the Sorrento peninsula; but to the north the sky was clear, and the lights of Naples and the adjacent coastline gleamed invitingly, presaging better weather for tomorrow and concealing, as do so often the lights of New York City, all the sordidness and ugliness that lay behind them.

When we got home, I was, despite my two shirts and a jacket, chilled and tired, my mind filled with nothing but confusing impressions of walls, walls, many walls, gates, cold damp vegetation-choked gardens, and wet narrow roads without sidewalks where you had to jump from side to side to keep from being run down by the indifferent drivers.

Farewell to Paris.

This evening was, I am confident, the last I shall ever spend in Paris. Annelise and I treated ourselves to a final farewell dinner at Chez Marius. It was a cold night. We were grateful for the winter clothes we had taken along.

After dinner we rode back to where we were staying, on the familiar No. 63 bus, which we caught on the Boulevard St. Germain. It was driven by a young black girl, who, to our surprise, welcomed us aboard with a cheerful smile, her white teeth gleaming from the semidarkness of her driver's cabin. She drove with wild abandon, like a racing driver and a very good one, whisking the empty vehicle past the bus stops without so much as a sideward glance, contemptuously running all the red lights at the end of the bridge over the Seine.

Below us, to the right as we crossed that bridge, was a myriad of bright illuminations at the quay where the *bateaux mouches* lie, lighting the sky and obviously meant to suggest to the bewildered and indecisive tourists great and exciting activity. Actually, the quay was quite empty, and all this radiance was wasted—on the cold river, on the empty dock, on the gangplanks where the last of the charwomen were leaving the boats and heading homeward, to rest, like the tired, garish boats themselves, for the work of another day.

Well, the bus went roaring on up the Avenue Président Wilson, past the Gallieri Palace where in 1886 the Orleanist pretender gave his tremendous party (that last great flicker of royal display); past the Trocadéro where only this afternoon crowds of young people had for some reason gathered on the terrace overlooking the river valley and away to the Eiffel Tower beyond—and so, up the Avenue Henri Martin, between the darkened apartment houses and the dense rows of shiny parked cars on the center strip. We got off at the end of the line, where the boulevard ends. We were the last to get off; and as we left the empty bus by the back door, we heard the voice of the black girl at the other end of it calling "Bon soir" to us as we ourselves disappeared into the darkness. I heard, in this final word of farewell, or so I thought, a species of challenge, if you will—a heartrending but heartwarming challenge—a small gesture of defiance to the indifference of this great, cold, beautiful, and unfeeling city, upon whose vast and self-centered vitality our occasional presence over these recent years has made not the slightest perceptible dent, but which will always remain an irreplaceable element in our own vision of the world.

A day cruising on the west coast of Norway.

The day began once more, in Farsund, with drenching, steady rain. Weather predictions were again in all respects horrible: no end to the rain in sight; something close to a small gale forecast for the afternoon; but winds now generally favorable. In view of this last we decided to sail anyway for Kirkehavn, on the island of Hydra. This was a small harbor I had tried unsuccessfully to enter on one occasion many years before, only to be frustrated in that intention by a combination of circumstances. Now, I thought, I would correct the omission.

At 4 P.M. we entered the inner harbor at Kirkehavn. This we found to be a little fishing harbor, nestled down among great rocky hills and dominated by a large white wooden church, so poised on a knoll that it could be seen from far out at sea (this giving rise, presumably, to the name of the place: "the church harbor"). The docks ranked with Norway's dirtiest and most disreputable (which is saying quite a lot), but the site proved to be one of great natural beauty. The little bay was surrounded by a few nice houses. Altogether, the place, with its two little retail establishments, made an impression of a languid, if disorderly, tranquillity.

In the late evening, as darkness fell, a working fishing boat came in from sea and lay to at the fish dock unloading plastic containers full of shrimp boiled on the way in and now

332

packed in ice. The brilliant deck lights of the boat gave the place the aspect of a stage, and numbers of spectators assembled in the shadows to watch the process of unloading. The two young deckhands, great powerful fellows, still in their rubber pants and boots, were working the winches, slinging the heavy containers up to the deck and onto the belt, then sluicing the hatch down, lowering the heavy hatch covers, and putting the gear to rights—all with impressive strength and speed. They were, one felt, proud of what everyone knew to have been their strenuous and dangerous life at sea, and of the skills they were now so nonchalantly demonstrating. This—their dramatic arrival and the fast rhythmic work under their own sort of klieg lights, with the admiring spectators gathered around them at the dock—was obviously *their* moment, the culmination of their hours at sea, the one non-monetary compensation for all the days and nights of struggle with heavy gear on the wet decks of the swaying, pitching, rolling boats. The work completed, they at once cast off and disappeared into the obscurity and the rigors of the nocturnal North Sea. The lights went out, and Kirkehavn, content with the show, went off to bed.

In March 1987 Annelise and I, accompanied by our next-door neighbor, Mary Keating, paid a visit to Morocco, where, befriended by Mary's son, Dick Jackson, American consul general in Casablanca, we made a tourist's journey into the interior.

MARCH 23, 1987
CASABLANCA

The walk I took this afternoon led me through tree-lined streets (palms and eucalyptus), curving around the slopes of the large hill and rimmed on both sides by nothing but whitewashed walls and elegant gates, behind which one can see only portions of the equally white walls of elegant villas, drowning in great masses of foliage. Who the owners of these establishments are, I have no idea. Most of them are foreigners, presumably, though there are probably some Moroccans as well. The properties appear to be million-dollar establishments. (One of them, I was told, was built at a cost of many millions by a Saudi prince who has occupied it only one week in the several years he has owned it.) The ever-curving streets, sunlit but cool from the ocean breezes, are pleasant enough, but strangely deserted. (In this respect, as in the luxuriousness of the villas, they remind me of the wealthier parts of Lake Forest, Illinois, except that here there are beautiful broad sidewalks of small-cut stone, whereas if my memory is correct, the parts of Lake Forest I am thinking of have none at all.) My only companions on this walk seemed to be an occasional gardener tending the flowers that line even the outer sides of the handsome walls, or a chauffeur washing the master's car in the street, except that once I met a lower-class woman with an infant and a rather handsome little girl, who danced up to me most ingratiatingly and demanded, in French, a dirham, which I didn't have. The sight of these unbroken lines of walls and gates, framing the empty streets, brought home to me the Moroccan family's intense sense of privacy, with its resulting love for walls and enclosures of all kinds, assuring against prying eyes and unwelcome intruders.

MARCH 29, 1987
THE MOROCCAN COUNTRYSIDE

The rain continuing without intermission, we fell to discussing, as the afternoon wore on, what we should do with our picnic lunch. The earth was too wet to be sat upon, and the car too narrow to be eaten in. At this point our driver, Hadj, allowed as he just happened to know of a nearby place where we could turn in and eat under cover. No sooner said than done, he at once turned in on a muddy little lane and drove some thirty paces up to a small and unimpressive little cement box of a house, planted in lonely isolation in one of the great fields. There was nothing around it, so far as I could see, but an old-fashioned well with bucket and windlass just before the house, and a small drenched dog who surveyed us in a manner intended, I thought, to convey that his view of the human species was no more kindly than is the traditional Arab view of dogs. In the doorway of the house stood, with statuelike immobility, the figure of a woman in a long caftan. The driver spoke briefly to her, and she at once invited us in. Her husband, it seemed, was a farmer with some five acres of land, and who was, at the moment, not at home.

It was a three-room house, bare and unheated. Being

largely without windows, it was very dark. We removed our shoes in the little entrance hall, and were shown in to what was presumably the guest parlor of the house. This room was also devoid of furniture except for one carpet, and pillows on the carpet, leaned against the wall. The only wall decoration was what seemed to be a large sheet taken from something like a calendar, showing flowers and some kittens' faces. We seated ourselves on the carpet as gracefully as we could. Our hostess, meanwhile, lit a small propane burner on the floor of the little hallway, which evidently also served as the kitchen, warmed up some water on it, and brought this into us in a pitcher, pouring it over our hands in accordance with the Moslem ritual and offering us a towel to dry them with. We then went through with our floor-based picnic and, leaving one huge turkey leg for her as a token of our gratitude, slithered out through the mud to our car, returning the dog's dirty look as we went. Our hostess, while silent, had been sweet and kindly throughout; and I was moved by this simple example of Moslem hospitality.

MARCH 26, 1987
FEZ

Fez, one of the great centers of the Moslem faith, is a walled city, rather remotely situated, lying in a spacious hollow among barren hills. The older part of it seems to consist only of souks, compressed into a species of dense medieval beehive; the newer part (still very old) contains at least one thoroughfare wide enough to resemble a street, and is said also to contain several old and very private palaces, reputedly with beautiful gardens, but all so jealously guarded by walls and gates that the stranger scarcely knows they are there. The place contains any number of mosques. From our hotel, situated on a hillside outside the city walls and looking down upon the roofs of the city, we could see some twenty minarets rising out of the general jumble. And at fixed periods during the day, beginning at 4 A.M., the air was suddenly filled with a great chorus of the voices of the criers reciting, from the tops of the minarets (with the help of electronic amplification), the ordained prayers. It is hard to describe the audible effect of these sudden outpourings of sound: rather like a lot of village fire sirens giving their noon blasts all at once, but in this case not quite in unison, so that the wailing notes of the slowest one rang out alone over the roofs of the city.

The older, and lower, part of the walled city, seeming, as I have said, to consist exclusively of souks, was a veritable maze of tiny tunnel-like passages, running in every direction, with such little regularity that the foreigner who ventures into them unguided is almost sure to get lost. (There are said to be little boys who, perceiving the stranger's plight, offer to lead him out of the place for a sum, though sometimes leading him even deeper into the maze in hopes of increasing the value of the ultimate delivery.) These passageways are so narrow that goods can be moved through them only on the backs of the patient and ubiquitous donkey. Even then, the monstrous burdens the little beast is obliged to bear are sometimes so wide as to brush both walls as he moves through. These passages are, for the most part, not roofed over; the walls of the houses rise high above them but do not meet at the top. But the space between them is sometimes covered by a lattice of bamboo at the roof level to break whatever sunlight might otherwise have found its way in. The sides of the passages are lined throughout by tiny cavelike apertures—hundreds and hundreds of them—harboring the shops of handicraft workers or little retail establishments with their wares exhibited at the entrances. Of the various categories of the handicraft activities I can give no estimate. Metalworking and woodworking seemed to be prominent among them, but they include dozens of other things that in our country would be made by machines. In one place, for example, people were dyeing masses of silk which they twisted in great ropelike bundles of wet skeins, to be woven into cloth. In another, a master was turning out, at great speed, beautiful bowls of what I believe to have been pewter, finishing them on an electric turning lathe out of round disks of the gleaming metal—all this with the help of a small and dirty little boy whose job it was to operate the lathe, but who, I noticed, occasionally looked longingly out the opening of the cave, yearning no doubt for the freedom enjoyed by other little boys to make mischief in their own imaginative ways. Picture these examples to be multiplied at least several hundred times, and you will have some idea of the cluttered variety that goes on in the souks of Fez. The narrow passages themselves, meanwhile, are populated by the densest possible throngs of pedestrians and donkeys, all trying to push their way through from here to there, the cries of the donkey drivers, demanding clearance for their beasts, vying with the thumping violence of rock-and-roll coming from radios or stereos situated God knows where.

After a half hour of pushing and shoving in these Stygian premises, the guide mumbled to us something about our seeing the weaving of carpets, whereupon he took us, through intricate dark passages, to a large and lofty catacomb that turned out to be a particularly sophisticated tourist trap. Here we found ourselves seated on a species of raised dais, where we were served with mint tea and were treated to a rather dramatic sales talk, while flunkies unrolled before us one locally made carpet after another, several being introduced with the assurance that this particular one would "blow your mind." To the consternation of Mary Keating and myself, who wanted nothing more than to escape from this sinister dungeon, Annelise showed interest in one of these items and then kept us dangling around there the rest of the morning while she, mobilizing all her inborn bargaining powers, went to work on the eloquent salesman. At one point during this tussle, Mary and I, unable to stand the interior atmosphere, escaped to the narrow alley outside and waited there, in the jostling but colorful stream of human bodies, until Annelise, having got the man down several hundred dollars off the initial price, finally emerged somewhat grim and tight-lipped, but with the deal concluded: a nine-by-fourteen-foot item, to be given, when it arrives, to Grace for her apartment in New York.

MARCH 27, 1987

We set out around ten o'clock to drive to Marrakesh. Suffering as I normally do from a form of myopia (similar to my color blindness) that makes it sometimes difficult for me to distinguish that which is picturesque from that which is simply dirty, sordid, and depressing, I left Fez with no inordinate spasms of regret, but looking forward keenly to the 340-mile drive, first across the lower Atlas Mountains, and then along the foothills of the greater ones. I was not disappointed. It was, once more, a panorama of great beauty, variety, and interest. After some twenty miles of straight road on a flat, fertile plain, irrigated by streams from the mountains above it, we began to ascend what I took to be a crossing of the lower Atlas. We climbed, in any case, to a town, a provincial center and a skiing resort in winter, situated at an altitude of some 5,400 feet, where not only the vegetation but the buildings themselves, two-storied and with sloping roofs, more greatly resembled something in Switzerland than the surrounding Morocco. Then, after gradually descending one or two thousand feet, we drove for hours through a treeless land of jumbled rises and depressions, all descending from the mountains above us, pastureland for the most part, some of it cultivated with winter wheat, but more of it supporting great flocks of sheep and goats attended by lonely shepherds, whose biblical figures, tall and immobile, were dramatically silhouetted, on the high ridges, against the bright sky. Here and there, widely dispersed like American farmhouses, were the habitations of the sparsely scattered rural population: one-story, mud-colored masonry structures, flat-roofed and without visible outside windows, obviously enclosing some sort of a court or barnyard, nestling here and there in the more protected creases of the flowing, arid hills. And everywhere where people were moving about, one saw their inveterate companion and means of locomotion—the long-suffering donkey, his body often so encumbered by the loads he was carrying (in many instances a huge man with flowing garments on top of all the saddlebags) that only the bobbing head and the tiny, spindly legs of the beast were visible.

There was a stop for lunch in early afternoon at a species of modern motel on the fringes of a larger town where we sat by the side of a swimming pool, and there was a little buffet stand whence two surly young men, after some palaver, provided us with lamb on a spit. A large dog, perhaps recognizing in us Westerners who tended to like dogs or perhaps (more plausibly) being moved by the smell of the lamb, rather adopted us, and even at one point defended us with a ferocious sortie, when he thought he saw some other sort of an animal across the enclosure.

There were another 130 miles to be covered after this interruption. For a time the countryside was now flat, and the road was as straight as a line on the map (our driver doing 80 to 90 mph on the relatively narrow paved portion of the surface); and here the well-irrigated countryside supported vast orange groves and other fine crops. Yet not much further on there was another stretch of what seemed to be very genuine desert, like the vast Sahara that had its beginning on the other side of the adjacent mountains. At one point camels were visible in a field, as our driver had predicted they would be. (They did not seem particularly busy; there was nothing for them to eat; and I strongly suspected they were there as a tourist attraction; but I may do them and their proprietors an injustice.) But then the desert gave way again to kindlier country. Traffic increased, as did roadside habitation. Palm trees began to appear here and there around us. And finally we had the awareness of approaching our destination: the large, flourishing upland city—and voracious tourist trap—of Marrakesh. Once inside the city limits, there was a mile or two of broad streets with a lively and confused traffic of horse-drawn fiacres, motorbikes, donkeys, Mercedeses, bicycles, and intrepid pedestrians who mingled unabashed among the wheeled vehicles; and we then pulled up before our destination: the celebrated Mamounia Hotel, a luxury establishment of fantastic dimensions and appointments, unquestionably one of the world's most elaborate, costly, and presumably unprofitable hostelries; but that is a subject in itself.

MARCH 28, 1987
MARRAKESH

Despite the fact that we have spent two full days in Marrakesh, I feel that I have seen very little of it and can give no proper description of the place. This is largely because we have had a car and driver and have done no walking by ourselves. When one sits in a car in a city such as this, one is so fascinated by the endless series of unbelievably near misses in traffic—with bicyclists, pedestrians, motorcycles, carriages, donkeys, and whatnot—that one has no time to look about. But beyond that there is, contradictory as this sounds, a curious sort of sameness in even the wildest variety—a sameness that defies any ordinary descriptive powers.

MARCH 29, 1987

Our social life in Marrakesh consisted of a sole, also somewhat surrealistic, event. In the late afternoon of this our last day here, we went, all three of us, to call on an elderly Western lady—a French countess, it would seem—who, as we under-

341

stood it, lived permanently in Marrakesh in a fantastically beautiful house, who figured as the grande dame of the local foreign colony, whom one ought, of common politeness, to call upon, and to whom Mary Keating had a letter of introduction from Princeton friends. The place is a largish property on the edge of the town. It was getting dark when we arrived. As we drove up to the portico, other people—a Count and Countess Somebody—were just leaving, and being seen off by an elderly wisp of a gray-haired figure, dressed in a sweater and slacks, who turned out to be our hostess. She introduced us vaguely to these departing visitors, and then showed us in, astounding me by closing behind us with no sign of effort a huge entrance door, or gate, of great weight and magnificence, for which task I would have thought four men would normally be required.

We passed along what seemed to me to be the darkish passageway of a cloister, and were suddenly shown into a large but dimly lit drawing room with a high and richly decorated arched ceiling. Our hostess was alone. The room, silent as a tomb, had the ambiance of a horror mystery on film. A servant in Moroccan costume brought us drinks and disappeared. From behind a closed metal shutter on one side of the room came curious clicking and croaking sounds, which our hostess identified to us as those of frogs. I found my feet resting on the head of a stuffed tiger, who stared at me with a fixed and disconcertingly lifelike gaze. Our hostess then proceeded to speak, in a rapid whispered French so nearly inaudible that even my two companions, both with ears as sharp as mine are dull, could make out only a portion of what she said, and I, very little at all. What followed was a monologue that we others made, for politeness' sake, only one or two faint and unsuccessful efforts to interrupt; and it appeared to concern only her own affairs: herself, her loneliness, certain friends we did not know, her occasional travels to France, what she did with her dogs when she was gone, et cetera. She showed not the slightest interest or curiosity about any of us, and I doubt that she had any idea who we were.

We stayed the obligatory twenty-five minutes. The rapid whispered French rose and fell upon the silence of the great drawing room, sometimes trailing off into wholly uncompleted phrases. The frogs clacked and stuttered behind their iron shutter. Then, after being shown two or three other rooms of the house, including a dark dining room with a great square table in the middle, we found ourselves once again in the cloistered passageway, where the dark forms of trees in the courtyard were silhouetted against a faintly glowing night sky above them. The great heavy outer door, opened again, as though by magic, by our frail hostess, then closed silently behind us, and we found ourselves standing in the chill of evening, the stars now brilliant above us, and the rumble of the distant city traffic in our ears. We pictured our strange hostess, retiring, with God knows what thoughts and reactions, into the shadows of the deserted, brooding, and slightly sinister house. So much for the social life of Marrakesh.

I have tried here to sketch the impressions of the Moroccan scene as I experienced them, interjecting only the irrepressible minimum of my own reactions and judgments. I am quite prepared to recognize that this country, like any other long-established society, is in many respects the prisoner of its own past. It is also clear to me that, societies being (like individuals) creatures of habit, there must be definite limits to the possible speed and direction in which conditions could conceivably be changed under the most enlightened governmental hand.

This being said, I must confess that there is much that I dislike, and little that I admire, in the past that still encumbers Morocco; and while I recognize the probable necessity of the carefully limited modernization its king is permitting to take place, I can, seeing (in our own example) the direction in which it is moving, find little enthusiasm for this, too. But I am glad to recognize the force and complexity of Morocco's cultural and political inheritance, the precariousness of her geographic and political position, and the slenderness of my own qualifications for judgment. Recognizing all this, I have no criticisms to voice of its ruler, and am simply grateful that I have no share in his responsibilities.

In June 1987 I went to Moscow to chair the American delegation at a conference of Soviet and American historians, assembled there for the purpose of comparing their impressions about the course of Soviet-American relations in the crucial years 1945– 50. It was also arranged, as a courtesy from the Soviet side, that Mrs. Kennan and I might, as guests of the Soviet Academy of Sciences and its Latvian counterpart, pay a brief one-day visit to Riga, Latvia, where (as already noted) we had served some five and a half decades earlier but which we had not seen in the meantime.

The intense activity of those days did not permit the writing of any notes at the time, but some of the impressions gathered were recorded, retrospectively, just after departure.

M ost of the activities of those days in Moscow and Riga might be called semiofficial. The conference took place as scheduled, and as previous such conferences had. So did the trip to Riga. On all these occasions I was an official guest. It was like being back in diplomacy. My hosts said the right things from their side. I did the same from ours—or as near as I could come to it (I never seem to achieve it entirely). But all that, of course, was on the formal external level: orderly, structured, coherent, consisting of things that had to be done, without which neither the relations between great governments nor those between national scholarly communities could go on.

There was of course, as always, the other level: the level of inner truth. It was in essence as real as the formal level was unreal; it was unstructured, dreamlike, incomplete, its interrelationships not for us to discern, the mysteries of its emotional associations never to be revealed; but it was nonetheless there, as it always is, behind its impenetrable veil. How, then, did things proceed on *that* level? It is, as always, hard to say.

We stayed in Moscow, by the kindness of our good friends Jack and Rebecca Matlock (he having just recently taken over as the ambassador at that post), at Spaso House, that venerable building that had seen so much and was so replete with memories. Its condition—a bit worn, somewhat battered, but still performing its essential functions—seemed to me symbolic of Soviet-American relations generally at this stage of the game. The driveway up to the front door was for some reason out of use, and clearly needed repaving; one left one's car in the street and walked the rest of the way. The main entrance door, scuffed and faded, swung open day and night, as it had in the days of my own unhappy ambassadorship thirty-five years ago. The front facade of the building was, so far as frequent showers would permit, being repainted and was thus covered by scaffolding. Below it lay, in the space between the house and the iron fence along the street, a muddy, trampled, and neglected front yard. Inside, the ballroom and the grand salon were much their old impressive selves; but the rest of the building, as so often happens in the intervals between ambassadorships, had a somewhat barnlike, battered look.

We ourselves slept in the corner room on the west side. There were, in those nights, frequent showers, some with thunder and lightning; and one was aware from time to time during the night of rain pouring off the roof and banging onto the metal-covered terrace outside our windows.

Not only in this house but throughout those days in Moscow memories swarmed around me, accompanied me, distracted me, like slightly annoying companions. I was constantly obliged to remind myself that I was separated from many of the objects I remembered—the places and the persons—by a vast intervening catastrophe, the Second World War; that most of the life I had once seen and known had been destroyed in that catastrophe; that the people I was now seeing before me were in many instances not even the survivors of that catastrophe but their children or grandchildren; and that these latter were separated from the people and the scenes of my memories by a great abyss—an abyss of time rather than place—greater even than anything that had once divided me from these same scenes and people. The forces of change, in other words, were stronger than the forces of geography or even of national origin.

All this was relived, but with even greater intensity, during the day in Riga. In the face of the vividness of my own memories of the place, there was a sense of anticlimax in this present glimpse of it. For the intervening decades, and especially the catastrophe to which I just referred, had dealt rather harshly with it.

It was a windy and chilly day. In company with my Latvian hosts, kind, interested, and evidently thrilled to show their city to one who had known it so long ago, we strolled through the old Hanseatic city center, now largely a tourist attraction. The city was very crowded, its population more than doubled since the time I knew it. Most of the small amenities had naturally disappeared. The parks and public places, on the other hand, seemed much improved. The two fine old churches were still standing. One of them—St. Peter's—the one with the great three-tiered wooden tower, where our first child, daughter Grace, had been christened, was now a concert hall. Stone embankments, handsome and formal, à la Petersburg, now lined the river where the passenger ships used to dock; and the adjoining quayside had been made into a pleasant park.

Our hosts thought they had found the house, across the

river, where Annelise and I had lived through that first year or two of our married life, and to this we then proceeded. There it was, indeed, a large two-floored wooden structure, once the residence of a factory owner, built in what was at that time the compound of the factory buildings: an arrangement right out of the early period of industrialization—the kind that Marx, and Lenin as well, presumably had in mind when they pictured the capitalist. It lay close to a cobblestone street, along which the trolley car ran, and there was a little park across the street.

We all got out and looked at the house. Untended foliage had grown up around it, and it looked a bit shabby. A largish elderly woman in a black skirt emerged from around a corner of the building and peered suspiciously at us, obviously mystified and anxious about the source of our curiosity. Otherwise, things seemed much as they had been, and I had no doubt that in the little park across the street some small band ensemble still played, as one did in our day, on Saturday nights for the young apaches—played, in all probability, something even more horrible than the "Fiesta" with the endless repetition of which its predecessors used to drive us out of the house in the sultry summer of 1932.

And so—on out to the seashore, to the great wide endless stretch of sand bordering the Gulf of Riga, always referred to as "the Strand." Our mission there was to look for the little dacha where, greatly oppressed by poverty, we had lived during the summer of 1933, as the economic crisis was setting in, the government drastically cutting salaries and allowances, and the news from home was nothing less than dreadful. Accompanied again by our patient Latvian hosts, we trudged around on the narrow, foliage-enclosed streets that were in those days just sandy wagon tracks but were now paved. Here, however, the changes of a half a century had eliminated all traces, and no dacha could be found.

These researches completed, we returned to Riga to have a look, before returning to Moscow, at the small modern building that had been in those early years the American legation there, and at the great German-style apartment house on the same square where we and others of the staff had lived. The former legation, now devoid of all official dignity and used for God knows what, looked small, shabby, and pathetic; the apartment house, faded and somewhat bedraggled. It occurred to me that I was probably the only survivor of the odd cast of characters who had at that time composed the legation staff: some of them holdovers from the staff of the prerevolutionary American embassy at Petersburg; others, like myself, the first products of the post–World War I professional generation. We constituted the United States government's listening post for the Soviet Union, with which, at that time, our country had no official relations; and while we accepted and enjoyed as well as we could the amenities of the small but cosmopolitan city of Riga, our thoughts, our speculations, and our discussions late into the night all related to the great war-torn and revolution-torn country whose border lay only some two hundred miles to the east of us, with its defiantly hostile government, its still greatly suffering population, and its uncertain future—to us a spectacle of drama, horror, and inexhaustible fascination.

Thus ended our brief Rip van Winkle–like expedition into Proust's *temps perdu,* invoking upon me further reflections of the blind and helpless way in which each generation of us (as I suggested in my *Memoirs*) staggers through life: occupying briefly the little patch of apparent light between the darkness of the past we have so largely forgotten and the darkness of the future that we cannot see.

DECEMBER 9, 1987
WASHINGTON

I have been back in Washington for these past three days— not *my* Washington, of course, but let us say, the Washington that might have appeared to anyone else who had been born in 1904, who had seen something of that city in the days of his maturity, had then died at a normal age, but had been permitted, by some extraordinary indulgence of Providence, to be resurrected from the dead and to revisit this, together with other, scenes of his own brief passage across the face of history.

I, on this occasion, found the city cowering under a faint, cold December sunshine, but roaring more than ever with surface and airplane traffic; and I viewed it, resurrected as I was from the past, with a slight shudder, and an offer of thanks to Providence that I was absolved from contributing further to its active life.

Ten days ago I reiterated, in these notes, my periodic complaints about the endless series of visits I seemed to have to make, for one reason or another, outside Princeton; and I described them as "empty formality: nothing accomplished, nothing to show for it." Today's events—or one of them, at least—put those self-pitying words in their place as the overdramatization they were.

These events were both connected with the historic visit to Washington of Mikhail Sergeyevich Gorbachev. The first of them contained, to be sure, no surprises. It was a great luncheon tendered by Secretary of State and Mrs. Shultz for Gorbachev and his wife—an affair (as we used to say in the old diplomatic service) of some two hundred and fifty "plates." I shall not go into the political aspects of this affair or the speeches given by the principals; all that will take its place in the overabundant historical record, to enjoy there the privacy of a deep oblivion. I recall only that we waited an interminable time for those principals to make their appearance, and that I sat next to a lady from somewhere in the Southwest, the wife of some prominent politican, I believe, whose ignorance of my identity was as great as mine of hers, and, since neither of us was particularly interested in enlightening the other on this matter, remained that way to the end.

The afternoon appointment was another matter. It was a

reception for Gorbachev at the Soviet embassy, to which I, in company with one or two hundred other Americans, had been invited by the Russians. (How these persons were chosen by the Soviet hosts, I do not know. The press, always anxious to make a story out of it, alleged afterward that we were "the intellectuals," although I saw there a number of eminent Republicans, including a couple of former secretaries of state, who would probably resent being thus described—and in some instances, perhaps not without reason.)

The function took place at the old Russian embassy building on Sixteenth Street, right next to what was then the Racquet Club, where I sometimes went to swim on the dark winter afternoons of 1926. After penetrating the successive lines of security guards deployed for several blocks around the place, we guests had our credentials carefully but politely examined at the entrance of the building and were then taken upstairs and shown into a large and beautiful chamber, of ballroom ambiance, already densely packed with people.

Remembering my wife's admonishments not to stand uncomfortably in the background as I normally do on such occasions but to insist on meeting the guest of honor and adding my particular set of banalities to the others he was condemned to endure, I decided to make the effort. So I pushed through the crowd and eventually squeezed myself into the small circle of photographers, journalists, and other pushy guests surrounding the distinguished visitor. The latter, whom I was meeting for the first time, appeared to recognize me, and amazed me by throwing out his arms and treating me to what has now become the standard statesman's embrace. Then, still holding on to my elbows, he looked me seriously in the eye and said: "Mr. Kennan. We in our country believe that a man may be the friend of another country and remain, at the same time, a loyal and devoted citizen of his own; and that is the way we view you."

I cannot recall what I said in response to this statement. Whatever it was, it was wholly inadequate.

We soon moved to another room, filled with small tables.

Gorbachev, seated at one of these tables, delivered himself of a lengthy (too lengthy for American tastes, short by Russian standards) impromptu address. The table to which I was assigned included, as I recall it, Ken Galbraith, McGeorge Bundy, and a lady of most striking appearance, who chain-smoked Danish cigars and appeared to be rather bored with the whole performance, and of whom I was later told that I should have recognized her—as the widow of a famous rock singer.

My ears failed me badly during Gorbachev's long talk, and I amused myself by fidgeting with the earphones and trying to figure out which was harder to catch: the speaker's Russian or the plodding artificialities of the simultaneous translation. But actually, I could not concentrate on what he was saying. His words to me still rang in my ears. And as I reflected on them, the whole sixty years of my involvement with Soviet affairs (which included, at one point, being banned from Russia as an "enemy of the Soviet people") revolved before the mind's eye; and I could think of no better conclusion to this entire chapter of activity—at least none from the Soviet side—than this extraordinarily gracious and tactful statement, worthy, when you think of it, of the finest standards of royal courtesy. I reflected that if you cannot have this sort of recognition from your own government to ring down your involvement in such a relationship, it is nice to have it at least from the one-time adversary.

JUNE 10, 1988
CROTTORF, GERMANY

Here we are again, at the home of our kind and long-standing German friend, who has given us so often in the past and is now giving us again (perhaps for the last time) the hospitality of this, his ancestral home. And here is that home again, unchanged: the three cobblestoned courtyards through which one passes to reach the main residence; and then—the great, brooding palace itself; the long, quiet, elegant hallways; the beautiful dim library, hushed and reverent like a church, with all its riches; the galleries of bedrooms on the upper floors, impregnated during the nights with the mute spirits of those who once inhabited them and—as it seems to me—continue to inhabit them at least nocturnally, nursing their unfulfilled dreams and enduring only with contemptuous impatience the impermanent presence of us, the contemporary visitors, who could be expected neither to understand nor to imagine the excruciating reality of all that once went on there. Then, the view from these bedroom windows down onto the vast meadow of the game park, with its herds of peacefully grazing moufflons and deer. And finally, as the epitome of all this intimacy with the past, the strange portrait that hangs at the turning of the grand staircase and confronts you as you come down the steps: a seventeenth-century portrait to all appearances (suspected at one time, though probably wrongly, of being a Goya) from which emerges the face of a young person, ostensibly a man but it could also be a woman—an unhappy, troubled, mistrustful face—a face that has hung there so long that it seems to be living a second life in this great, so often deserted, building—in this building that seems always to be waiting, waiting in all its splendor, like the portrait itself, for God knows what. So real is the presence, so pathetic the appeal for our understanding, of this strange, bewildered, and obviously helpless person, that were the painting to disappear from its now-accustomed place, it would seem to me that its subject had suffered a second, and in this case final, death— a death shared in part, like that of any friend, by those of us who had given it, if not our understanding, then the effort of it.

Here, through all of this, the visitor is linked to a past from which the rest of western Europe is now divided, as though by some impenetrable wall, through the events of these past three centuries: the industrial revolution, the social revolution, the self-inflicted injuries of the two great European wars of this century. Through these changes in its own life—some unnecessary, some greedily courted and thoughtlessly accepted—Europe has not only cut itself off from its own past but has lost control of its own destiny; quivering as it now is under the roar of its own automobiles and airplanes; careless of the wisdom of the past; unwilling to consult—and unable to build upon—the values it once embraced; the helpless addict of its own self-indulgent habits; busily destroying its own environment, cultivating weapons that can and probably will, someday, destroy not only that environment but the humanity that lives by it.

I, the stranger, having spent half my adult life in these parts, feel this as my loss no less than that of the Europeans. Most of us Americans, after all, once had our roots here, unaware or neglectful of them as we may now be. With the forfeiture of our remembrance of them—with the inability to discern them and to preserve the tie to them—we, like the Europeans, are impoverishing ourselves. In our case, the separation is probably final and irreparable; for it is a part of the loss, what with uncontrolled and probably uncontrollable immigration and with our submission to the dictates of a similarly uncontrolled technological revolution, of the very essence of our national identity. But in the case of the Europeans (with whom at this point I must associate myself) the tragedy is greater; for their own past, however unvalued and abused, still makes itself evident here and there, mutely asserting its own values and vainly protesting, as in this old building, the continued relevance of these values to the contemporary human predicament.

Could there have been, for these Europeans, any other way to go? It seems to me that there could have. It would have had to take its departure from the deliberate abandonment of the materialism, greed, and decadence of modern society, and to have preceded to the enthronement in its place of true spiritual leadership and environmental preservation as the primary aims of civilization—to the acceptance of concern, in short, for the quality of man himself, primarily in his moral and spiritual, only secondarily in his material, incorporation, and then for the intactness and the wholesomeness of his natural surroundings. None of this, I suppose, is likely to happen. But the choice—as to whether it is or is not to happen—remains our own.

EPILOGUE

We are out at the farm for the weekend—in a strange sort of interlude, this time, between season and season, between past and future. The summer—a hard one, marked by the greatest drought in memory—is over; the autumn has not begun. The fall sowing is to begin tomorrow. Meanwhile, except at milking times when the usual sounds of activity emanate from the barn, the farm has a deserted air. The farmer's children, like our own, have grown up and gone away. The variety of domesticated animal life has declined with the change in farming. The inhabitants of the farmhouse disappear between milkings, taking advantage of the momentary lull in farm work. The elder of the two farm dogs was run down and killed by a car several days ago; the younger and smaller one, feeling himself bereaved and lonely, follows me disconsolately and halfheartedly about on my comings and goings. I do not mean much to him nor he to me, but I am, at the moment, all he has got.

So here it lies, my beautiful and once-cherished farm, mute and uncommunicative under heavy, soggy, windless skies. In earlier years, when the weather was sometimes this way, I used to think of the place as waiting—waiting, with its characteristic patience, for the more interesting, more hopeful day it knew to lie ahead. Now it seems rather to be sulking— sulking like a resentful abandoned mistress—reproaching me for my own long neglect, reproaching me for what I have permitted an uncaring, recklessly exploitative civilization to do to it in the meantime. And I find myself wondering whether it has perhaps not waited too long—to a point where hope and anticipation are no longer to be recaptured.

I might, of course, have continued to give this place what I could of my strength and devotion, as I did for a time so many years ago, instead of all the other things I have been doing in the intervening years. But it would never have been satisfied. Its demands would have absorbed the energies of a dozen such as me without ever being fully met. And I, meanwhile, like so many who had labored too long and too self-sacrificingly in rural settings, would have become narrow, tightfisted, consumed with the cloying intimacies and petty squabbles of country life, and, like others who have given too much of themselves to a single insatiable cause or a single insatiable individual, resentful of the open-ended quality of the sacrifice demanded. In the end, when these energies had been finally exhausted, Nature would have claimed her own anyway, in her usual implacable way, attacking the products of all human intrusions upon her favored uniformities, cracking foundations, rotting walls, spreading spiderwebs, over-growing lawns, meadows, and all other products of the human effort at "improvement."

So here we both are: the farm and I. We did what we could for each other, in the days when this was possible. We must now go, for better or for worse, our separate ways.

I wander, meanwhile, disconsolately around on the third floor of the house, surveying with helpless amusement the abundant flotsam and jetsam of an earlier life that have some-how become stranded in this place: the honorary degree parchments and testimonials hanging on the walls; the files of financial records from years long past; the framed newspaper cartoon showing me, left behind on foot, trying in vain to warn an indifferent Foster Dulles, ensconced on a Republican elephant, not to go into the jungle he was about to enter; shelves of old scholarly magazines having to do with Russia, once stored away with the fatuous idea that someday, when I was retired, I would sit down and read in them at leisure;

the great map of the Soviet Union mounted on four panels, for the hanging of which I always hoped I could find a suitable place in one or another of our residences but never did and never will; the old Underwood typewriter, vintage 1922, on which I wrote my first attempt at an autobiography; the files (great and voluminous) of Russian newspapers from the year 1952 which I always thought would some day be useful for a history (never written) of the strange period just preceding Stalin's death; and, along with these, boxes of older family records—photographs, faded letters from the 1850s, newspaper clippings, and attempted genealogies. From these—the abandoned shreds of an unfinished and never-to-be-finished life—mute, perishable testimonials to dreams never to find reality, destined, all of them, to be heaved out someday by some harassed descendant or new owner of these premises—from these petty and impermanent reminders of a past that could be of interest only to an antiquarian, and this, only for a day when it is questionable whether there will even be any antiquarians at all—from all of these I am now taking my leave on this dark and lifeless September day: companions, all of us, the relics and myself, in our quality as inhabitants of an uncertain interlude between a relentless, fading past and an inscrutable future—testimonials, all of us, to an insistent inner motivation which when related to the span of our own lives is called "hope," and when related to what is to come afterward becomes "faith."

It is in the company of all these reminders of an earlier life that I look back over these glimpses of the environment of that life, as assembled in this book. They, too, are flotsam and jetsam of a sort, but more useful, I would hope, perhaps even more lasting, than the clutter of personalia I have just described. They are supposed to speak for themselves. If they don't, they are not what they are intended to be. They represent, as was noted in the foreword to the volume, the interaction between a pair of changing eyes and a number of changing scenes. The scenes, as passive objects of this scrutiny, are what they are, and as such are above criticism. Vulnerable to criticism are only the eyes by which the scenes were observed and the pen that set out to describe them. And the master of those eyes and that pen would be the least qualified to assess their value.

I am startled, as I look over these items, to note the bleakness of the impressions of my own country. A reader might think that I saw in it only ugliness, vulgarity, and deterioration. I am sorry about this. Had I not had my own sort of love of the place, these imperfections on its surface would not have hit me so hard or found such abundant record in these scribblings.

I am not oblivious to the fact that the United States of 1988–89 has its glorious sides. But these seem to me to lie primarily in two areas: in the magnificence of those purely natural beauties that have not yet fallen victim to commercial development; and then in the personalities of many fellow citizens I have been privileged to know. But natural beauty alone without the human element, much as it may offer for admiration and wonder, offers nothing for interpretation and makes poor subject matter for the traveling diarist, as it does for the artist. And as for the people: yes—many have engaged my admiration, along with a considerable number who have engaged the opposite. But to depict them individually is the task of the novelist, not of the traveler—and particularly not of the traveler moving through regions where he has no personal acquaintances at all and where he sees, for the most part, only masses of small anonymous figures with whom he has no possibility of interacting. Yet it is primarily people seen in this manner that this book has purported to describe. The exceptions, such as they are, have tended to relate to individuals long since dead, and then only when the experiences of travel have evoked memories of them.

There will be allegations, I suppose, some of them reproachful, that the observations recorded in this book are those of an expatriate. I am not sure that I understand what the term means. Anyone who spent, as I did, nineteen out of the first twenty years of his active professional life in Europe would be very insensitive indeed if he were not affected by it. And to understand things beyond one's original cultural horizon is only to add them, in a sense, to what one already is. To do this does not mean that what one already is becomes discarded. Beyond which, if an American becomes "expatriated," he does so in a way which is itself an expression of his Americanism. No one who is not an American would experience expatriation, and react to it, in quite the same way.

I regard myself as indeed an expatriate—but an expatriate in time rather than in place: an expatriate from the Wisconsin of the first years of this century, not from the Wisconsin of this day. The imprints of childhood are the strongest and most enduring stamp of personality. Nothing ever fully eradicates them or replaces them. To the Wisconsin of that time I was never lost. But that Wisconsin is largely lost to me. It now scarcely exists. And I, without it, am, like many an older person, an expatriate to be sure, but an expatriate as much within my own country as outside it, as would have been the entire generation of my parents had they lived to this time. And what of it? Is that a sin?

My view of the outside world certainly had its blemishes. Whose does not? But the very blemishes are the expression of a certain species of Americanism—a lost Americanism, if you will, but one that is nonetheless genuine for its errant and homeless state. Does it make you less American to recognize as Thomas Wolfe said, that "you can't go home again"?

I view the United States of these last years of the twentieth century as essentially a tragic country, endowed with magnificent natural resources which it is rapidly wasting and exhausting, and with an intellectual and artistic intelligentsia of great talent and originality. For this intelligentsia the dominant political forces of the country have little understanding or regard. Its voice is normally silenced or outshouted by the commercial media. It is probably condemned to remain indefinitely, like the Russian intelligentsia in the nineteenth century, a helpless spectator of the disturbing course of a nation's life. If love of country includes this sort of concern for its future, then I, too, love this particular country, and am a part of it.

For the rest, what is presented in this book is offered in the hope that it will give a little greater depth to the many things of a different nature—reports, articles, speeches, books, even memoirs—I have written over the course of many years, and will help the occasional reader to test his own observations by contrast with those of another person. But another part of its purpose is to remind the readers of those earlier writings that the world around me has been seen, however usefully, by a heart as well as by a head. For whether the heart alone would suffice "as the stage for any and all adventures," as was suggested by the motto prefacing this book, the head, without it, would be a wan and feeble adventurer.

INDEX

About the Author